T

THE LA

J.M. O'Callaghan AITI

TAXATION
of TRUSTS
THE LAW IN IRELAND

J.M. O'Callaghan AITI

Republic of Ireland	Butterworth (Ireland) Ltd, 26 Upper Ormond Quay, DUBLIN 7
United Kingdom	Butterworth & Co (Publishers) Ltd, 88 Kingsway, LONDON WC2B 6AB and 4 Hill Street, EDINBURGH EH2 3JZ
Australia	Butterworths Pty Ltd, SYNDEY, MELBOURNE, BRISBANE, ADELAIDE, PERTH, CANBERRA and HOBART
Canada	Butterworths Canada, TORONTO and VANCOUVER
Malaysia	Malayan Law Journal Sdn Bhd, KUALA LUMPUR
New Zealand	Butterworths of New Zealand Ltd, WELLINGTON and AUCKLAND
Puerto Rico	Equity de Puerto Rico, Inc, HATO REY
Singapore	Malayan Law Journal Pte Ltd, SINGAPORE
USA	Butterworth Legal Publishers, Austin, Texas; Boston, Massachusetts; CLEARWATER, Florida (D & S Publishers); ORFORD, New Hampshire (Equity Publishing); ST PAUL, Minnesota; and SEATTLE, Washington

© Butterworth Ireland Ltd

A CIP Catalogue record for this book is available from the British Library.

ISBN 1 85475 616 8

Typeset in Ireland by Seton Music Graphics
Printed in Ireland by
SciPrint Ltd, Shannon Industrial Estate, Co. Clare.

Contents

Part 5 Corporation tax

Part 6 Capital gains tax

Part 7 Capital acquisitions tax

Part 8 Local taxation

Appendices

Abbreviations

Amb	Ambler's Reports, Chancery 1737-1784
AC	Law Reports, Appeal Cases, House of Lords 1890-1936
AER	All England Law Reports
AG	Attorney-General
Beav	Beavan's Reports, Rolls Court (36 Vols) 1838-1866
Bro CC	Brown's Chancery Cases 1778-1794
CA	Charities Act 1961
CAT	Capital Acquisition Tax
CGT	Capital Gains Tax
Ch	Chancery Division, Law Reports
ChD	Chancery Division, Law Reports (45 Vols) 1875-1890
ChD (NI)	Chancery Division, Northern Ireland
CIR	Commissioners of Inland Revenue
CLR	Common Law Reports (England)
Cl & Fin	Clark & Fennelly's Reports, House of Lords (12 Vols) 1831-1846
C o V	Commissioner of Valuation
Cox Eq	Cox's Equity Cases 1745-1797
Cr & Ph	Craig & Phillips Reports, Chancery 1840-1841
CT	Corporation Tax
DeG F & J	De Gex, Fisher & Jones Reports, Chancery 1859-1882
DeG J & S	De Gex, Jones & Smith Reports, Chancery 1862-1866
DIRT	Deposit Interest Retention Tax
Dr & War	Drury & Warren Reports (Ireland), Chancery 1841-1843
Drew	Drewry's Reports, Chancery 1852-1859
Eq	Equity Reports (England)
Hare	Hare's Reports, Chancery 1841-1853
HC	High Court (Irish)
HL	House of Lords
HLC	House of Lords Cases 1847-1866
ICTA	Income & Corporation Tax Act 1988 (United Kingdom)
ILRM	Irish Law Reports Monthly
ILTR	Irish Law Times Reports
IR	Irish Reports 1894
Ir Ch R	Irish Chancery Reports 1850-1866
Ir R Eq	Irish Equity Reports 1838-1850
IT	Income Tax
ITC	Irish Tax Cases

ITLR	Irish Times Law Review
ITR	Irish Tax Review
Jur (NS)	Jurist Reports, New Series 1855-1867
KB	King's Bench Division
LJ Ch	Law Journal Reports, Chancery 1831-1846
LR Ch	Chancery Law Reports
LR Eq	Equity Law Reports
LR (Ir)	Law Reports (Ireland) 1878-1893
LT	Law Times Reports 1859-1947
Madd	Maddock's Reports, Chancery 1815-1822
NI	Northern Ireland
QB	Queen's Bench Division
RC	Revenue Commissioners
SC	Supreme Court
Se C	Session Court (Scotland)
SI	Statutory Instrument
Sim	Simon's Reports, Chancery 1826-1849
Sm & G	Small & Gifford's Reports, Chancery 1852-1857
STC	Simon's Tax Cases
TA	Trustee Act 1893
TLR	Times Law Reports 1884-1952
Vern	Vernon's Reports, Chancery 1681-1719
Ves	Vesey's Reports, Chancery 1789-1817
Ves Sen	Vesey Senior's Reports, Chancery 1746-1756
WLR	Weekly Law Reports (England) 1953
WR	Weekly Reporter 1852-1906

Part 1

Basic principles

Chapter 1

Historical review

The Brehon Code

Introduction

1.01 The first known system of law in Ireland was the Brehon Code. Later the feudal and common law codes were introduced by the Normans and their successors. The doctrine of equity came into being to curb the abuses of the common law. The main benefit conferred by equity is considered to be the evolution of trusts.

Ireland was first occupied circa 6000 B.C., but after a further three thousand years it had only a population of a few thousand living mainly on the alluvial river plains. A change of climate about 1000 B.C. slowed the growth of forests and this encouraged the establishment of settled communities, which cleared land and then used it for both tillage and grazing. The only large centres of population in pre-Christian Ireland were the residences of kings. In later centuries the numerous and widespread monastic settlements became major centres of population.

Society was based on the concept of the extended family. A number of families involving common local interests was classed as a clan. The head of the clan was elected and there was no automatic right of succession by descendants. While the common ownership of land was the unifying measure it was, however, open to a freeman to build a house and claim a portion of land but there was a bar on the disposal of such property outside the extended family, measured to the fourth degree of relationship.

The pastoral nature of pre-Viking Ireland is illustrated by the absence of a coinage and the use of the cow as the main medium of exchange. Women, generally, did not enjoy a high status and a bondswoman (cumall) was considered for exchange purposes to be worth four cows. The Vikings introduced coinage and established coastal trading posts which grew to become the main cities and towns of Ireland.

The concepts and implications of the Brehon Code were not reduced to writing until the seventh and eighth centuries. The surviving tracts outline its all embracing nature extending to land ownership and rights, status and inheritance. The importance of the cow was emphasised by the Brehon Law of Status and Franchise which dealt with the duties and rights of various grades of society, distinguishing no less than six grades of cow-lord.

Inheritance

1.02 For inheritance purposes an interest in land generally descended amongst male relatives, but daughters were entitled to a share of personal property. In later times a daughter also took her father's interest in land in circumstances where there were no male heirs up to the third degree of relationship. Earlier it had been the position that a father could appoint property to his daughter who was however compelled to marry a relative within the extended family. The question of inheritance was further complicated by the prevalence of polygamy, which appears to have been dictated by economic considerations and which continued long after the arrival of Christianity in the fifth century. A concubine who bore a child was recognised as a lawful wife with a consequential conferring of inheritance rights on the offspring.[1]

References

1   The summary of early Irish conditions has been extracted from the more detailed information available in *Life in Ireland*, L. M. Cullen (Batsford); *Early Christian Ireland - Introduction to the sources*, K. Hughes (The Sources of History); *Early Christian Ireland*, M. and L. de Paor (Thames and Hudson); *The Course of Irish History* (Moody and Morton Editors) (The Mercier Press).

The Norman period

Primogeniture

1.03 The conquest of England by the Normans in the latter half of the eleventh century was complete and decisive. As a consequence, the concept of a central power took over from the more local jurisdictions. Feudalism implied a dominant sovereign with unrestricted powers which were exercised in favour of subordinates and vassals subject to various reserved rights.

The king was the ultimate owner of all of the land of the realm and any grants made were designed to support his power base. There was recognition of subsidiary rights created by holders of direct and indirect grants also subject to reserved rights in a vertical pyramidal structure with the king at the apex.

The Norman Conquest of England had far reaching legal effects. There was the introduction of primo-geniture or descent by date of birth with a priority for male successors in respect of land. Furthermore, under the feudal system, an overlord was entitled to rights and payments arising from succession, marriage and wardship. The property reverted to the overlord or sovereign in the absence of successors (escheat). It was only from 1540 onwards that land could be passed on under a written will.

Travelling justices

1.04 Central control was reinforced by social and legislative measures that applied consistent basis throughout the jurisdiction. The old Saxon Courts of the Shires and Hundreds[1] became obsolete and were replaced with travelling justices. The enforcement of this revised mode of justice became known as the common law as it was the law in common use. The formal courts we now recognise evolved over subsequent centuries.[2]

The common law

The common law was an improvement on the earlier systems in force as it recognised certain defined forms of action. However, this system also was criticised because:

(*a*)   the causes of action were limited in scope;

(*b*)   accessibility was restricted because petitions had to be presented in writing;

(*c*)   a favourable judgement resulted in damages which could be inadequate compensation for a plaintiff's grievance, particularly in relation to transactions concerned with land; and

(*d*)   the independence of the courts could be compromised by pressure or influence.

These inadequacies led to anomalies and dissatisfaction with the operation of the common law courts. The Sovereign, the ultimate feudal authority, could overturn any judicial decision. Inevitably, this gave rise to royal petitions.

Equity

Because the English kings were more concerned with military power, survival and financial support than the administration of a legal system, petitions against the judgements of the common law courts came to be examined and decided by the Chief Minister, the Lord Chancellor. This official, who up to the post-reformation period, was invariably a cleric introduced moral considerations into his deliberations enforcing an equitable code which was distinct from the common law principles. The evolution of general governing procedures and practice by the Lord Chancellors was gradual and ill-defined. The separate judicial rules applied by the Lord Chancellor's Courts is now known as the equity system, as it sought to temper the occasionally inflexible common law rules with fairness (equity).

References
1 A Hundred was the corresponding part of a Shire.
2 The first formal central court of justice was The Court of the Exchequer which was established in the reign of Henry I (1100 - 1135) and dealt with disputes concerning royal entitlements.

Common law and equity in Ireland

1.05 The Normans and later settlers in Ireland imported the current English principles of justice from their homeland. This process was encouraged and supported by a controlling structure with a Lord Deputy responsible to the English Sovereign for the management of the country's affairs. While this should have led to the absorption of the English legal system in Ireland it was not so in practice.

In the first place, the Normans only half conquered Ireland. They were never successful in the more northern part of the country controlled by the O'Neills. In both Munster and Connacht after initial supremacy they failed to maintain their numbers and became integrated with the native population. There remained, however, at all times part of the east coast and hinterland around Dublin subject to English authority, rule and custom.[1] The extent of the authority claimed to be exercised from this enclave over the centuries was, while not immediate enforceable over the whole country, historically of para-mount significance. A parliament was established in the thirteenth century which proceeded to make laws that were theoretically applicable to the overall jurisdiction. This continued until 1801 when the parliaments of Great Britain and Ireland were integrated.

References
1 Dublin was never an Irish town in its development phase. It was built up by the Vikings as a trading centre. Its proximity to England and its natural river outlet was a controlling gateway to the rest of the country and recognised as such by the later settlers. Authority was never ceded back to the native Irish from the twelfth century onwards.

The Tudor period

Poynings' law

1.06 In a parliament summoned by Edward Poynings, the Lord Deputy, at Drogheda, in December 1494 it was enacted that all statutes made earlier in England were to be effective in Ireland. While this famous Poynings Law was presumptuous, in that at the time it was enacted the scope of the English writ ran to less than four counties, it was important because after the surrender of Hugh O'Neill in 1603, when the power of the feudal Irish chiefs and their Norman counterparts was finally broken, it became effective over the whole country. The Drogheda Parliament also restricted the scope for independent Irish legislative measures by agreeing that future parliaments could only be summoned by Royal permission and further that the King and Council had a right of veto over the measures which could be introduced and legislated. The restrictions were modified to a post-legislative veto in 1782.

The Statute of Wills

1.07 It was only in the nineteenth century that the dominance of the ownership of rights and interests in land came to be diminished as the effect of the Industrial Revolution expanded the growth of personal property and the use of chattels. The paramount nature of land holdings as the measure of wealth and status in earlier times had led, in the nature of things, to devices which were designed to overcome or reduce any charges or superior rights charged on the tenure and also to preserve succession rights.

It was only after the Statute of Wills (1540) came into force that land could be devised by will under English law.[1] The "use" in what in modern times would be regarded as a tax-avoidance scheme was the measure which came into being in various forms to achieve this effect.

Example

Under the common law if A transferred his complete (fee simple) interest in land to B for the use of A and his heirs, B acquired the legal right to the property and the exclusive right to dispose of it. The rules of Equity, looking at the intent rather than the form of the settlement, intervened to create a separate superimposed interest in favour of A and his heirs.[2]

References
1 The corresponding Irish legislation is contained in the Statute of Wills 1634.
2 The example outlines the clear distinction between the common law and the rules of equity. The legal rights of B under the common law code are retained but a further equitable right in clarification and restriction of these rights has been super-imposed.

Uses

Introduction

1.08 The earliest form of the use was to transfer freehold land to monasteries for the use of the settlor and his heirs. The conveyance was on the lines of a devise to the superior of a monastery A, the use of B and his heirs. The transfer vested the legal right to the land under the common law in A. The legal owner of land was the person obliged under feudal law to perform or supply the reserved rights in favour of an overlord but such rights were not enforceable against church property (*libera eleemesyna*). This procedure became known as mortmain (*mortuus manus*) as it superimposed a "dead hand" on the previously existing feudal rights and entitlements. A statute enacted in 1259 at Westminster provided that it should not be lawful for men of religion to enter the fee of any one without the licence of the lord from whom the fee was immediately held. A further Act in 1279 sought to curb continuing abuses.[1] The position was further clarified by the Statute of Westminster II in 1285.[2]

The King and the other overlords whose interests were affected by mortmain settlements could in practice bind themselves to take no advantage of the statutory reliefs and licences were easily available on payment of an adequate fine (qui libet potest renunciare jure pro se introducto). Legislation in 1299 prescribed the manner in which rights attached to land could be amortised.[3]

The efforts to protect rights and interests in land both on an inter-vivos basis and for succession purposes continued over the following centuries with the utilisation of the use as the corner stone for the avoidance procedures.

References
1 Statute of Mortmain (7 Edw. I, st. 2 c. 13) (De Viris Reliesis).
2 13 Edw. I, st. 1 (De Donis Conditionalibus). The effect of this and the earlier legislation concerning mortmain were confirmed by the Statute of Westminster III, 1290 (18 Edw. I c. 3) (Quia Emptores)
3 27 Edw. I, st. 2 c. 1.

The Statute of Uses

1.09 In 1535 the Statute of Uses was enacted at Westminster. [1] The legislation provided that where a legal interest was held in freehold land to the use of another the latter's equitable interest was converted into a legal interest thus alienating any priority interest.

Example

If A settled freehold land on B to the use of C then B had no statutory interest in the land while C had both an equitable and legal interest.

Furthermore the common law did not recognise the imposition of a use upon a use.

Example

In a disposition where A transferred a freehold or fee simple interest in land to B and his heirs to the use of C and his heirs to the use of D and his heirs, the last gift over to D and his heirs was disregarded.

However, the rules of equity, while recognising the effect of the Statute of Uses, intervened to provide relief from the mischief which the Statute created. This was based on a formula derived from a decision handed down in Jane Tyrell's case in 1557. The Chancery Courts were prepared to recognise the existence of a beneficial equitable interest where the legal interest was held

Historical review   **1.12**

in a fiduciary capacity. In circumstances where A had settled freehold land unto and the use of B and his heirs in trust for C and his heirs, the legal interest was regarded as being held by B while C and his heirs had an equitable interest. This procedure nullified the effect of the statutory conversion and execution of the legal interest imposed by the 1535 Act and gave rise to the legal device we now know as "the trust".

References
1   27 Hen. VIII, c. 10.

1.10 Technically, up to the end of the 1400s English laws had no force in Ireland as the country had its own Parliament with independent legislative powers. In 1320 this Parliament re-enacted a number of earlier English statutes including the provisions of the Statute of Westminster 1285 concerning mortmain. The Parliament continued to cater for the special interests of Norman and later settlers until Poynings Law (1494) imported the effect of earlier English statutes.[1]

References
1   As an example of the continuing effect of Poynings Law the Mortmain (Repeal of Enactments) Act 1954 repealed English Statutes dating from 1279, 1285, 1344 and 1391.

The Statute of Uses (Ireland)

1.11 The next bench mark as far as Irish legal equitable legislation is concerned came after the arrival of Viscount Wentworth as Lord Deputy in 1633. During 1634 he introduced and had approved a number of legislative measures which re-enacted English post-Poynings provisions. Included amongst these was the Statute of Uses (Ireland). This Statute, in section 1, provided for the execution of uses in respect of freehold land as in the earlier sixteenth century English counterpart, but, likewise, could be by-passed by the intervention of a trust.[1] The utility of the use was further minimised by the contemporaneous enactment of the Statute of Wills (Ireland) under which land could be bequeathed under a written will.

References
1   The Statute of Uses (Ireland) 1634 s 1 still remains effective in Ireland. Sections 5, 6 and 7 of the Act were repealed by the Succession Act 1965.

The 1600s

1.12 The seventeenth century witnessed the disintegration of feudal power in England. The execution of Charles I in 1648 led to a short period of absolute parliamentary rule until a constitutional monarchy was restored in 1660.[1] Estates

9

confiscated in the inter-regnum period, which in many cases had been substantially increased in size from royal grants and purchases after the previous mid-century dissolution of the monasteries, reverted to or were re-acquired by the previous owners.

After the Restoration the rules of equity began to flourish with an emphasis being placed on precedent. In the 1676 case of *Cook v Fountain* an attempt was made to classify trusts on the basis of whether they arose from the actions of parties or under the law. This gave rise to the modern concept of express, implied and constructive trusts (see Chapter 3).

1.13 Conditions in Ireland in the 1600s were very different from those in England. The flight of the Ulster Earls (O'Neill and O'Donnell) to Europe in 1607 left the native Irish population leaderless and unprotected. Their lands and the lands of their dependants were confiscated to the Crown and planted with settlers mainly of Scottish origin (James I on the throne of England at the time had earlier reigned as James VI of Scotland). The planters, local town dwellers and the native rural Irish had different loyalties, objects and intentions. An attempt by the O'Neills to re-establish their supremacy in Ulster, despite a decisive defeat of Crown forces at Benburb in 1646, petered out from a lack of general support. Cromwell's short but effective Irish campaign in 1649 led to a further plantation, mainly as a benefit for serving officers, which continued the break-up of native Irish land holdings. The power of English based law was thus considerably strengthened. By the end of the century, after the Irish support for the ousted James II had been overcome, the supremacy of the English legal system as effective throughout the whole island was unchallenged.

References

1   On the European mainland feudalism continued in force up to the middle of the nineteenth century. The Treaty of Westphalia signed in 1648 provided that the religion of the overlord was to be that of his subjects (cuius regio eius religio).

The 1700s

1.14 In eighteenth century Ireland, land was the primary source of wealth. General economic conditions were deplorable and there were restrictions placed on the agricultural based enterprises by the London Parliament. As a result of statutory restrictions imposed by the Irish Parliament in 1778 only 5% of the country's land was held by the majority Catholic population grossing £60,000 out of a national rent roll of £4,000,000.[1]

References

1   *The Course of Irish History* (Moody and Morton, Editors) (The Mercier Press).

The 1800s

1.15 In 1801 the Parliaments of Great Britain and Ireland were united and after that time legislation enacted by the Imperial Parliament concerning trusts, unless specifically excepted, applied in both countries. Several important measures were brought into force in the 1800s:

    (*a*)   An executor of an estate became a statutory trustee for the next-of-kin.[1] Previously an executor was entitled to take the surplus personal property not covered by the testamentary bequests.

    (*b*)   Gifts to charitable trusts were not recognised when such gifts were made under a will within three months of a death.[2]

    (*c*)   The legislation included in previous Trustee Acts was consolidated in 1893.[3]

    (*d*)   In 1894 a short measure was introduced to make changes perceived to be necessary to the main Trustee Act and included in its provisions a power given to the High Court in Ireland to make vesting orders for land and personal property as had been originally allowed to its English counterpart.[4]

Three later Acts passed by the Imperial Parliament[5] did not apply to Ireland. Important later English legislation enacted after 1921 referable to trusts [6] have no effect in the Republic of Ireland.

References

1   The Executors Act 1830. Repealed by the Succession Act 1965 Sch 2 Pt III.
2   Charitable Donations and Bequests (Ireland) Act 1844 s 16. This legislation followed on the lines of the earlier Charitable Uses Act 1735, effective in England. The specific Irish legislation was repealed by the Schedule to the Charities Act 1961.
3   Trustee Act 1893 (consolidating Trustee Acts 1830, 1852, 1888 and 1889). There was a saver for the 1850 and 1852 provisions concerning the jurisdiction in lunacy in Ireland. The Lunacy Regulation (Ireland) Act 1871 dealt with the general position. The current jurisdiction in this area is exercised by the President of the High Court in accordance with the Courts of Justice Act 1936 s 9. As regards the Trustee Act 1888, ss 1 (defining, inter alia, a trustee) and 8 (setting out statutory limitation periods for actions against trustees) were also saved as recited in the Schedule to the Trustee Act 1893. These two sections were repealed by the Statute of Limitations 1957 s 9 and Sch Pt II.
4   Trustee Act 1893, Amendment Act 1894 s 2.
5.   The Judicial Trustees Act 1896, the Land Transfer Act 1897 (Sections 1 to 5 dealt with the position of a personal representative as trustee for real property) and the Public Trustee Act 1906.
6.   The Law of Property Act 1925, the Trustee Act 1925, the Variations of Trusts Act 1958 and the Recreational Charities Act 1958.

Unified court system

1.16 In 1877, a unified superior court system dealing with both common law and equity principles was established. Where the common law rules conflict with the rules of equity, the rules of equity prevail.[1]

In 1922, a separate court system was established for the newly independent Irish Free State.[2] The courts of first instance included a High Court invested with original jurisdiction in and with power to determine all matters and questions, whether of law or fact, civil or criminal. A Supreme Court with appellate powers on High Court decisions was also established.[3] The power of the Supreme Court was not to be absolute however as the article provided specifically for a right to petition the King.

References

1 Judicature (Ireland) Act 1877 s 28(1).
2 Courts of Justice Act 1924 ss 17 (High Court) and 18 (Supreme Court). Constitution of the Irish Free State (Saorstát Éireann) Act 1922; Constitution of Saorstát Éireann 1922, art 64.
3 Art 66. The later 1937 Constitution of Ireland, enacted by the People on 1st July 1937, did not continue this right of petition (Article 34.4.1).

Charities

Meaning of "charitable"

1.17 The preceding paragraphs have discussed the evolution of the judicial equity system in the context of its relevance to private or individual trusts. A parallel development from the seventeenth century onwards also took place in respect of public or charitable trusts under English law.

In the re-distribution after the Norman Conquest of England the Church received over a quarter of the land. Its wealth and holdings continued to expand with time despite the restraints imposed under the thirteenth century Mortmain Statutes. When Henry VIII, following his dispute with the Papacy on the question of succession, had declared the independence of the English church much church land was confiscated between 1536 and 1538.

This produced an enormous change in the country's social structure and economy. The monasteries and other church institutions had previously been responsible for the relief of poverty amongst the population. Additionally, a local Bishop had historic rights concerning the distribution of intestate personal property for charitable purposes.[1] The new lay owners of former church lands did not have the corresponding social or moral obligations of their predecessors. In consequence, a locally controlled system sponsored by the Crown was set up to oversee works for the poor.[2]

The Preamble to the Elizabethan Statute listed a number of objects which were to be considered as charitable. These listed objects were subsequently used as a benchmark by the Chancery Courts to determine what is considered "charitable". In modern times they have generally been superseded by the four part classification set out by Lord McNaghten[3] but the technical meaning of the wording included in the Preamble to the Fourth Statute of 1601 remains relevant.

References

1   *Irish Land Law* by J. C. W. Wylie.(Professional Books), Chapter 15 (Intestacies).
2   43 Eliz. I, c. 4 1601. This statute was repealed by the Mortmain and the Charitable Users Act 1888 but the repeal excluded the Preamble. On the overall decline of the influence of the Catholic Church in England see *A Social History of England*, Briggs, (Weidenfeld and Nicholson).
3   *Pemsel v Commissioners for Special Purposes of Income Tax* 3 TC 53; [1891] AC 531.

The Statute of Charitable Uses (Ireland) 1634

1.18 The Westminster Statute of 1601 did not apply in Ireland but the Earl of Wentworth in his reforming zeal to harmonise Irish and English laws had a similar (but not identical) measure passed by the Irish Parliament in 1634.[1] This Statute was analysed by Sir E. Sugden, Lord Chancellor:

> I must consider the Statute of Charles as a legislative enactment upon the pattern of the 43 Eliz and whatever validity the 43 Eliz gave, by recognition of uses of charitable uses, and consequent to the inherent jurisdiction of Courts of Equity in England the same will be available and is equally true in this country, in the case of the Statute of Charles.[2]

This case established that the legal and technical meaning of the term "charitable" was to be the same in both England and Ireland.

In a later case[3] Judge Hanna delivering the unanimous decision of the High Court declared:

> The law has been built up upon the preamble of the Statute 43 Eliz 4 which corresponds to the Irish statute, the 10th of Charles 1, Sess 3 c.1. The 43rd of Elizabeth, c.4 being subsequent to Poynings' law, did not extend to Ireland; but in *Attorney-General v Delaney* (1 IR 10 CL 104 at p 125) Pallas, C. B. was of the opinion that the charitable purposes in Ireland were identical with the charitable purposes in England.

References

1   The Statute of Charitable Uses (Ireland) 1634. It was repealed by Statute Law Reform (Ireland) Act 1878.
2   *Incorporated Society v Richards* Drury and Warren Reports (Ireland) Chancery Reports 1841-1843 at p 326.
3   *Pharmaceutical Society of Ireland v Special Commissioners of Income Tax* 2 ITC 157; [1938] IR 202 (HC) at p 320.

UK Charities Act 1960

1.19 The area which historically has given rise to the greatest difficulties in determining a charitable status relates to gifts made for religious purposes. Distinctions by the English Courts between religious purposes and the advancement of religion have been fatal to a number of claims. Since 1922, the independent Irish judiciary has not always followed English precedents concerning the disallowance of gifts made for contemplative orders.[1] Since 1961, a gift for the advancement of religion is to be construed in accordance with the laws, canons, ordinances and tenets of the religion concerned and must be conclusively proved as having a public benefit.[2]

The English charity legislation[3] has provided for the establishment of a Charity Commission which is empowered to determine a legal charitable status. A decision to refuse a claim at executive level can be formally appealed by a written submission to the Board of the Commission. An adverse decision by the Board may be appealed directly to the High Court.[4] The Charity Commissioners also maintain a register of charity cases which have been given the advantage of "permanent endowment" or perpetual succession.[5] A charity included in the Commissioners' Register is recognised, by virtue of this inclusion, as qualifying for exemptions from national and local taxes.[6]

References

1 Leading decisions by the English courts are contained in *Cooks v Manners* [1871] LR 12 Eq 574; *Gilmour v Coates* [1949] AER 242 (HL). Judge Gavan Duffy, President, refused to follow *Cooks v Manners* in *Maguire v Attorney-General* [1943] IR 238 (HC) when approving as charitable a gift to the Order of Marie Reparatrice. However, in *The Estate of Michael Keogh* [1945] IR 13, Judge Overend, also in High Court, accepted the relevance of the *Cocks v Manners* decision.

2 Charities Act 1961 s 45(1)-(2).

3 Charities Act 1960 (UK).

4 (UK) Charities Act 1960 s 5 sets out the appeal procedures.

5 (UK) Charities Act 1960 s 45(3).

6 (UK) Charities Act 1960 s 5(1).

The Charities Act 1961

1.20 The Irish charity legislation is more limited in its effect than the UK law and is mainly concerned with outlining powers of the Commissioners of Charitable Donations and Bequests as a regulatory body.[1] The Board of the Commissioners has no power to determine or register charities. It may give an opinion or advice to the trustees of a charity concerning the application or administration of property.[2] Proceedings may be instituted by the Board for the recovery of charitable gifts improperly withheld or misapplied.[3] The Board, in a public trustee capacity, may accept land or other property in trust for charitable purposes.[4] It also has power to frame schemes applying property cy-pres, where the original objects or purposes cannot be effected [5] and can authorise (or make when it is the trustee) the sale, exchange, surrender of any land or the raising of mortgages thereon,[6] or the sale of periodic payments arising out of land.[7] The Board also has power to appoint new trustees to a charitable trust.[8] Finally, the Board is authorised to frame a scheme for the incorporation of a charitable body. The Board also has power to modify the scope and administration of charitable bodies regulated by a statute or charter.[9]

References
1   Charities Act 1961 ss 5-44; as amended by the Charities Act 1973 ss 2-17.
2   Charities Act 1961 s 21.
3   Charities Act 1961 s 23.
4   Charities Act 1961 s 31.
5   Charities Act 1961 s 37.
6   Charities Act 1973 s 11 in substitution for Charities Act 1961 s 34.
7   Charities Act 1961 s 35.
8   Charities Act 1973 s 14, replacing Charities Act 1961 s 43.
9   Charities Act 1973 s 4.

1.21 The Irish charity legislation contains a number of relieving provisions concerning the technical aspects of determining a charitable status and these are examined in Part 3.[1] The legislation also contains administrative provisions covering:

(*a*)   a scheme to establish a common investment fund for charities;[2]

(*b*)   the occasions where the doctrine of cy-pres is to be applied;[3] and

(*c*)   power for the Board to apply to the High Court for directions.[4]

References
1   Charities Act 1961 Pt III and Sch 1.
2   Charities Act 1961 s 46.
3   Charities Act 1961 ss 47-48.
4   Charities Act 1961 s 51. This power can also be exercised by any other person with the consent of the Attorney-General. Under s 53 the Board must be advised and supplied with information on any proceedings in relation to any charity except where the proceedings are taken by the Attorney-General. There does not appear to be any statutory penalty for failure to keep the Board advised.

Report of the Committee on Fundraising Activities for Charitable and Other Purposes

1.22 A Committee was established by the Minister for Justice in 1989 to examine the adequacy of the existing statutory controls over fund-raising activities for charitable and other purposes. The Committee, in its Report, did not regard itself as competent to recommend a statutory definition for either a charity or charitable purposes, pointing out that there were many decided cases both in this country and the United Kingdom on what constitutes "charity" or "charitable status" and what purposes can be regarded as "charitable".[1]

The Committee's Report lists in Appendix 3 categories which the Revenue Commissioners accept as established for charitable purposes by virtue of being beneficial to the public.[2] Finally, as regards the supervision and regulating of the administration of charities the Committee's report (in the introduction to Chapter 4) makes it clear that there is no authorisation for any liaison between the Commissioners of Charitable Donations and Bequests and the Revenue Commissioners to deal with possible abuses by charitable bodies.

References

1   *Report of the Committee on Fundraising Activities for Charitable and Other Purposes* 1990 (Stationery Office). In Ch. 1(4)(*a*) (Definition of Terms), a specific reference is included to the classification introduced by Lord MacNaghten in *Commissioners of Income Tax v Pemsel* 3 TC 53 [1891] AC 531: see Chapter 7.
2   This matter is considered in more detail in Chapter 6.

Part 2

General trust provisions

Chapter 2

Private trusts

Meaning of "trust"

Introduction

2.01 Although there is no statutory definition of a trust, the expression "trust" does not include the duties incident to an estate conveyed by way of mortgage. With this exception, the expression "trust" and "trustee" include implied and constructive trusts and cases where the trustee has a beneficial interest in trust property, and the duties incident to the office of personal representative of a deceased person.[1]

Furthermore, no notice of any trust, express, implied or constructive may be entered on a company register or be receivable by the Registrar of companies.[2]

2.02 The absence of a statutory meaning for a trust is not surprising because the concept developed from deficiencies in the principles of the common law. The court of equity, originally exercised by a religious Chancellor as the representative of the English Sovereign, sought to provide reliefs for injustices not covered by the common law code. This was achieved by looking at the intent rather than the form of transactions. There was, from the beginning, a moral and social ethos in the exercise of equitable jurisdiction which reflected and mirrored, in a positive manner, the evolving mores of society. This moral and social ethos has continued up to the present day.[3]

References

1 Trustee Act 1893 s 50.
2 Companies Act 1963 s 123.
3 Arising from a number of trust settlements which required to be interpreted by the English Courts following challenges by the Commissioners of Inland Revenue a new classification (automatic resulting trusts) was proposed by Megarry J. in the case of *Vandervill's Trusts* (No. 2) [1974] Ch 269 at (pp 294) where the whole or part of the successive beneficial interests have not been provided for in the trust.

Definition

2.03 Inevitably, commentators have tried to define the indefinable. Lewin,[1] having initially declared that "no definition of a trust appears to have been

19

accepted as both comprehensive and exact" then proceeds to try with a definition which is somewhat imprecise in its wording. A definition quoted by Lewin and also accepted judicially[2] is that set out by Sir Arthur Underhill:[3]

> A trust is an equitable obligation binding a person (who is called a trustee) to deal with property over which he has control (which is called the trust property), for the benefit of persons (who are called the beneficiaries or cestuis que trust) of whom he may himself be one — and any one of whom may enforce the obligation. Any act or neglect on the part of the trustee which is not authorised or excused by the terms of the trust instrument, or by law, is called a breach of trust.

This definition has been criticised as being too loose in that it does not cover gifts for public purposes (which are regarded as charitable) and because it ignores purpose trusts, (that for example relate to specific animals or monuments) where there is no beneficiary capable of enforcing the provisions. However, it is possible to claim that Underhill's definition also extends to charities in view of the power of the Commissioners of Charitable Donations and Bequests, with the consent of the Attorney-General, to sue (on behalf of the beneficiaries) for the recovery of any charitable gift which is improperly withheld, concealed or misapplied.[4] The later contributors to Underhill claim that purpose trusts are of marginal relevance and should be ignored as anomalous.

References

1 *Lewin on Trusts* Ch I (Sweet and Maxwell).
2 *Re Marshall's Will Trusts* [1945] Ch 217; [1945] 1 All ER 550; *Green v Russell* [1959] 2 All ER 525; [1959] 2 QB 226.
3 *Underhill's Law of Trusts and Trustees*. Division I, Article I (Butterworths).
4 Charities Act 1961 s 23. A similar principle applies under English law and the later contributors to Underhill have made a similar argument in support of the general application of Sir Arthur's definitions.

Elements of a trust

2.04 A trust involves a transfer of an interest in property. The persons involved are: a settlor, a trustee, and a beneficiary.

Settlor

The settlor is the person who supplies or furnishes the property. The gift or transfer involved may arise under an inter vivos (between living persons) or testamentary settlement (by will, on a death). Property passing under an intestacy may be subject to a secret trust. The property that is subject to a trust may be personalty (chattels, portable assets) or realty (land or buildings) and, furthermore, the trust may apply to both legal and equitable interests in such property.[1]

References

1 Transfers by means of the feudal concept of the "use" (the forerunner of the trust) were, in practice, confined to freehold land. The Statute of Uses (Ireland) 1634 s 1 sought to execute an interest held in seizen (freehold) to the use, confidence or trust of the person in whose favour a further interest was

created. The Statute recognised the creation of limited interests by a disponer of freehold land but without increasing the measure of the donee's interest converted an equitable interest into a legal interest. (An inter vivos gift of land by A, a freeholder, to B for life created a legal life interest under the Statute.) Section 1 of the 1634 Statute is still in force and must be taken into consideration in drafting inter vivos conveyances of freehold land.

Trustee

The trustee is the person who holds the transferred property in trust (in a fiduciary capacity) and not beneficially. A settlor may nevertheless act as trustee.

Beneficiary

The beneficiary (cestui que trust) is the person who has either a legal or equitable interest in the property comprised in the settlement. The beneficiary has a right to sue the trustee for the enforcement of the trust's provisions. A trustee may also be a beneficiary under the settlement but this could involve a conflict of interests especially in connection with trusts where the trustee has a power to appoint income or capital on a discretionary basis. There is nothing to prohibit a settlor being included as a beneficiary under a trust made by himself, for example, A transfers property to A for life, with remainder to B.

Other transfers of property

2.05 A trust must be distinguished from other arrangements or agreements which may involve the transfer of property.

Contracts

A contract is the agreement made between contracting parties where there has been an offer and an acceptance of that offer. It is a common law concept. While a contract may be concluded for the benefit of a third party that party has no right to have the contract terms enforced and the rules of equity may not be used to assist such a person. Under a trust, however, a beneficiary has a right to seek enforcement of the relevant provisions. There must be evidence of a trust rather than a contract.[1]

References
1 In *Vandesitte v Preferred Accident Insurance Corporation of New York* [1933] AA 70 the Court of Appeal refused to accept the existence of a trust where a judgment was unsatisfied against the authorised nominee of an insurer under a third party motor risks policy. It followed that the successful litigant against the nominee could not enforce the judgment against the insurer.

Estates in the course of administration

A trust arises in respect of the duties incident to the office of personal representatives of a deceased person.[1] The personal representative is the representative of the deceased and holds the real and personal estate of the deceased as trustee for the persons who are entitled to it by law.[2] It has been held by the Courts that the persons who are entitled by law to the estate are not necessarily the persons entitled to it under the deceased's will or those entitled to it under the rules of intestate succession. In the case of an insolvent estate the personal representative will hold it in trust for the creditors of the estate.[3]

The Irish courts have approved dicta of the UK courts to the effect that a residuary legatee had no interest in any of the property of a testator until the residue had been ascertained.[4] It follows, therefore, that a trust (in the course of administration) cannot exist for residuary property until the residue has been ascertained. The rules concerning specific devises and bequests are unclear. While generally a year is allowed for a personal representative to wind up an estate ("the executor's year"), the personal representatives must distribute the estate of the deceased as soon as possible after the death having regard to the nature of the estate, the manner in which it is required to be distributed and all other circumstances.

The personal representative should assent to and release property when it is clear that the property is not required to meet the expenses of the administration or required to be retained to cover the legal right of a surviving spouse.[5] After the time allowed, which is a matter to be decided by the Courts, where there is a dispute with a beneficiary on the facts of the individual case the personal representative would appear to be a trustee de son tort (of his own wrong) for the specific devisee or legatee.

References

1 Trustee Act 1893 s 50 (see 2.01). Similar provisions were first included in the Executors Act 1830 (11 Geo 4 and 1 Will 4). Before that executors were entitled to the unappropriated surplus of personal assets (other than land or buildings) under a will. Real property (land or buildings) would have devolved outside the testamentary provisions to the heir-at-law.
2 SA 1965 s 10(3).
3 *Moloney v Allied Irish Banks Ltd* [1986] IR 67 (H.C.)
4 *Barnardo's Homes v Special Income Tax Commissioners* [1921] 2 AC 3 at P. 8.
5 SA 1965 ss 52-54 sets out provisions governing the assent of land by a personal representative. SA 1965 s 111 provides that a surviving spouse of a testator leaving children is entitled to a one third share of the estate which is increased to a half share where there are no surviving children. Rights of distribution on an intestacy are outlined in SA 1965 Pt VI ss 67-75.

Agency

This common law concept involves an agreement giving rise to a relationship between a principal and another person, the agent, who acts under the power, control and direction granted to him by the principal. There is no agreement between a trustee and the beneficiaries of a trust as they both function independently and disjunctively. An agent is restricted to his delegated powers and functions (*delegatus non potest delegare*). A trustee has a title to property which an agent does not have. Furthermore, a trustee is not a representative of the beneficiaries in his transactions, whereas an agent is at all times acting for his principal.

Bailment

This common law concept need not necessarily arise under a contract. It involves the delivery of goods to a bailee, which are to be restored to the bailor as soon as the object of the arrangement has been achieved. It arises frequently in commercial operations connected with the carriage and storage of goods. The bailee is entitled to a fee for the carriage or storage, but unlike the position of a trustee as regards a trust, the bailee has no interest in the property of which he has possession.

Bailment only applies to personal property whereas a trust can relate to all types of property. Bailment was used extensively by the poorer section of the community up to about thirty years ago in the form of redeemable pledges of personal property with pawnbrokers. (A short term loan was given by the bailee pawnbroker against the security of the property lodged. The property had to be retained by the bailee and returned to the bailor on redemption of the loan.)

Powers

While a trust deed as a matter of prudence includes enabling powers for the proper and efficient administration of the trust property on behalf of the beneficiaries, a power to appoint property may exist outside the framework of a trust. The essential difference between a trust and a power is that trustees *must* perform the duties imposed on them whereas the exercise of a power is discretionary. Furthermore, under a trust a beneficiary has an equitable interest in the trust property but no interest arises at the time a power is created and any change of an existing interest only occurs when the power is exercised.

A *general power of appointment*, which enables property to be transferred without restriction by the holder of the power, does not give rise to a trust as there is no beneficiary until the power is exercised. This is in contrast to a *special power of appointment* which restricts the beneficiaries to a designated class of persons. Such a power may constitute a trust.[1]

Example

A, by will, left all his property to his widow B for life with remainder as B may by will or deed appoint.
There is no beneficiary in remainder until B exercises her power of appointment. A trust may be created by B at that time. If she fails to exercise the general power given to her the property reverts to the estate of A.[2]

Example

A, by will, left all his property to widow B for life with remainder over amongst his children as B by will or deed appoints or in default of such appointment to be divided amongst the children equally.[3]

There is a trust for the children from the date of death of A as they have a present right of ownership of their father's property on the death of B subject to the exercise of the special power of appointment which may exclude some children.[4]

References

1   CATA 1976 s 2 defines "general power of appointment" as including "every power, right or authority whether exercisable only by will or otherwise which would enable the holder thereof to appoint or dispose of property to whomsoever he thinks fit or to obtain such power, right or authority, but exclusive of any power exercisable solely in a fiduciary capacity under a disposition not made by himself, or exercisable by a tenant for life under the Settled Land Act 1882 or as mortgagee".

     The same section defines a "special power of appointment" as a power of appointment which is not a general power of appointment.

2   *Re Mills* [1930] 1 Ch 654; *Chambers v Fahy* [1931] IR 17 (HC).

3   These examples ignore the effect of SA 1965 s 111 (legal right of surviving spouse) and SA 1965 s 117 (provision for children) on testamentary dispositions.

4   If a child of a testator predeceased him but left a child (or children) and B failed to exercise her power of appointment that issue (the child or children) is entitled to stand in place of its deceased parent as if the child had survived the testator (SA 1965 s 98). The entitlement is to divide (per stirpes - by the stem) the share which would have passed to the deceased parent if he had survived the testator.

Written documents

2.06 An inter vivos trust may, generally, be created by the expression of an intention to bring it into being. Where land is transferred into a trust signed evidence in writing is required for a trust to be valid.[1]

A will that creates a trust must comply with the requirements of the Succession Act 1965 in respect of capacity, signature and witnessing. It follows that deeds of trust cannot contain clauses that purport to exclude the trusts' provisions from the rules of equity.[2]

References

1   Statute of Frauds (Ireland) Act 1965 s 4.

2   *National Anti-Vivisection Section Society v Commissioners of Inland Revenue* 28 TC 311, [1948] AC 31.

The "three certainties"

Introduction

2.07 "Three certainties" are required to support the existence of a valid private trust:[1]

(*a*)   The words used, upon the whole, ought to be construed as imperative.

(*b*)   The subject of the recommendation or wish must be certain.

(*c*) The objects or purposes intended to have the benefit of the recommendation must be also certain.

References
1   *Knight v Knight* [1840] Beav 3 148 at p 173 (Lord Langdale M. R.).

The words used must be certain

2.08 One of the maxims of equity is that it looks at the intent rather than the form of action and this procedure of "looking through" is used by the Courts to evaluate and determine whether the terms of a settlement create an imperative obligation. It is of interest that the "three certainties" outlined by Lord Langdale shortly after the Executors Act 1830 had become law. Before that legislation personal representatives were entitled to take all unappropriated personal property under a will. As this behaviour was not necessarily in accordance with the unexpressed wishes of the testator and the Courts in earlier times tended to imply words of hope, trust, confidence or desire as indicators that a trust had been created against the rights of an executor. This "look through" approach was overturned by the application of the "three certainties" rule. However, the inclusion of precatory words (hope, trust, confidence etc) in a will does not preclude the existence of a trust where there is other evidence in the document that indicates an *obligation* is being imposed by the document.

The Irish courts have held, applying the "three certainties" rule, that a bequest made by a testator to his brother "with full power to dispose of it as he thinks fit for the use and benefit of my wife and children" constituted the creation of a trust.[1]

In contrast where a testator bequeathed all his property to his wife but expressed a *wish* that she should by deed or will appoint part in favour of a named son, the judicial decision was against the existence of a trust.[2] Judge Ross, having reviewed the precedents, concluded that words concerning the existence of a trust must be interpreted in their ordinary sense unless there is something in the terms of the documentation from which a court ought to infer that a trust is intended.

References
1   *Charles v Fahey* [1931] IR 17 (HC)
2   *In re Humphrey's Estate* [1916] 1 IR 2 Ch D

The subject matter must be certain

2.09 In order to provide the certainty required in respect of the subject matter of a trust there must be a vesting of the appropriate property in the trustees.

A trustee in his fiduciary capacity must be aware of the limitations of the functions to be exercised and it follows that there must be certainty as to the extent and nature of the interest involved.

The certainty of the subject matter also concerns the interests to be taken by the beneficiaries. Thus, although the subject matter of a gift, wish or settlement may be defined and the persons included as objects may be identifiable and certain there may be no quantifiable measure of the benefit to be allocated and no enabling discretionary power capable of being exercised by the trustees in favour of the beneficiaries.

Example

A, by will, appoints all his property to his widow B to be used by her for the benefit of herself and the children of the marriage.

B, in these circumstances, would be regarded as taking an absolute interest in the property as there were no defined or ascertainable rights in favour of the children.[1]

References

1 The example is based on the decision given in *Curtis v Rippon* [1820] 5 Madd 434.

The objects must be certain

2.10 Historically, it was essential that a valid private trust should be certain in its objects.[1] This requirement was logical in that the trustees, when exercising administrative powers or applying the income or capital to the beneficiaries (as directed) should be aware of the nature and extent of all the interests. Otherwise there was the possibility that, if they overlooked or miscalculated the interest of a beneficiary (especially where no discretionary powers of allocation were available under the trust provisions) they could be sued and held liable for negligence or mis-application.

The rules of equity recognise a distinction between the exercise of an appointment which creates an interest that had not previously been in existence and an appointment (see 2.05), made by trustees to beneficiaries who already had a vested interest under the terms of a trust. It was sufficient, in relation to a power of appointment, to be able to ascertain whether a person was covered or excluded from benefiting under the terms of that power. In the case of a trust, however, the beneficiaries and the extent of their entitlements must to be established.

Under English law there is at present some doubt as to whether it is necessary to be able to ascertain all the beneficiaries under a settlement in order to have trust (see 2.11). As in this jurisdiction fewer requirements apply to powers of appointment.[2]

References

1 This does not apply to trusts established for charitable purposes only. In the event of uncertainty in the objects of such a trust a scheme to be framed by the Commissioners of Charitable Donations and Bequests (CA 1961 ss 29 and 48(6)) or by the Courts (CA 1961 s 48) for property to be applied on a cy-pres (as near as possible) basis. CA 1961 s 48 sets out other occasions for the application of the cy-pres rule. CA 1973 s 8 amended CA 1961 s 29.

2 *Re Gestetner's Settlement* [1953] Ch 388; *Barnet v Blumka* [1953] 1 All ER 1150; *Re Gulbenkian Settlement* [1970] AC 508. The test to be applied is whether a postulant is or is not a member of a class of beneficiaries.

Discretionary trusts

Application of property in favour of beneficiaries

2.11 Most modern trusts which are reduced to writing contain, as a matter of prudence, discretionary powers that allow the trustees some flexibility in administering the provisions of the trust.[1] A discretionary trust, like any other trust, must:

(*a*) be imperative in the nature of the settlements,

(*b*) be certain as regards the property involved.

Such a trust will also normally concern a named class, or classes, of beneficiaries. The trustees are empowered, at their discretion, to appoint income on capital to or for the benefit of any one or more of the class or classes of beneficiaries.[2]

The members of the classes each have an equitable right to be considered for distributions by the trustees, but they have no entitlement to any benefits until a discretion is exercised directly or indirectly in their favour.

The distinction between a special power of appointment (which limits the scope of the holder in its exercise) and a discretionary trust is a fine one and has been the subject of a number of judicial decisions which are difficult to reconcile. This distinction has been eliminated for English legal purposes by a recent House of Lords decision[3] that a trust operates where any "given postulant" qualifies as a beneficiary under exercisable discretionary powers of appointment. The court thereby put the test used to determine a discretionary trust on a par with that used for special powers of appointment and removed the requirement that the objects of the trust be certain (i.e. identifiable persons etc). The court considered whether references to "relatives" and "dependants" were "uncertain" and thus allowing the disposition to be construed as a trust. The House of Lords majority decision was based on the grounds that the appropriate test was to be by reference to the conceptional uncertainty of the wording rather than difficulties arising on the practical application of a disposition. However, the judgments recognised the need to exclude from the application of this wide principle any provisions which were administratively unworkable, for example, a gift to all the citizens of Greater London. There is doubt as to whether the decision generally applies to all trusts.[4]

The decision is important because it implies that:

(*a*)   An unquantifiable interest under a special power of appointment does not create any right or lien against the holder of the power.

(*b*)   A beneficiary under a trust has the right to challenge the trustees in respect of the operation and management of the settlement. In the case of a discretionary trust, while a legal challenge could be successful in forcing the trustees to make distributions there is no consequent guarantee that the challenging beneficiary will reap any advantage.

(*c*)   Where only a single survivor of a class of beneficiaries under a discretionary trust remains that person takes an absolute interest in the property of the trust.

(*d*)   The exercise of a power of appointment is optional.

Under a discretionary trust the trustees must act within the powers conferred on them and at some point are required to distribute the income and capital of the trust fund. Despite their discretionary nature the trust provisions may, in exceptional cases, provide for a full distribution of income without any power of accumulation (an exhaustive trust).

References

1   Trustee Act 1893 (TA 1893) s 3 reads: "Every power conferred by the preceding sections shall be exercised according to the *discretion* of the trustee, but subject to any consent required by the instrument (if any) creating the trust with respect to the investment of trust funds".

TA 1893 ss 1 and 2 are concerned with powers of investment by trustees. They have been updated by the provisions contained in the Trustee (Authorised Investments) Act 1958 ss 1, 2 and 6 and Statutory Orders extending the scope of authorised investments made under the power conferred by s 2(1) of that Act.

2   The term "discretionary trust" is defined in CATA 1976 s 2 as amended by FA 1984 s 105, for the purposes of the ("once off") discretionary trust tax introduced by FA 1984 ss 104-109 and the annual discretionary trust tax imposed by FA 1986 ss 102-108.

3   *McPhail v Doulton* [1971] AC 424.

4   In *Baden's Will Trusts* (No 2) [1973] Ch 9, the Court of Appeal judges had differing views as to the approach to be applied in determining a postulant to establish the existence of a trust.

Secret trusts

Illegitimate children

2.12 Over the centuries, secret trusts were used mainly to benefit the external party in a continuing intimate relationship outside marriage by allowing the children (issue) of such illicit relationships (who had no statutory right of descent to real property (land or building)) or any general entitlement under an intestacy of their parents to share the other assets.

Since 1987 the relationship between a person and his father and mother must be determined for succession purposes irrespective of whether the father and mother have been married.[1] This means that a child born outside marriage (or the issue of such a child) may share with the other children (or remoter issue) of a common parent on an equal footing (pari passu). While a will may include a secret trust for the benefit of the outside party in a triangular domestic relationship, the value of any such gift would be subordinate to the succession rights available to the testator's legitimate surviving spouse.[2]

References
1   The Status of Children Act 1987 s 3 provides the basis of the general determination of a relationship. The Status of Children Act 1987 s 29 inserts a new SA 1865 s 4A which provides that the meaning of a relationship between a child and his parents is to be determined in accordance with Status of Children Act 1987 s 3 for succession purposes.
   The earlier position was that an illegitimate child, (except for rights conferred under Legitimacy Act 1931 s 9, where the mother of the child had died without legal children or issue) had no entitlement to share in a parent's estate. That position was upheld by the Supreme Court in *O'B v S* [1984] IR 316, where the plaintiff challenged the constitutionality of SA 1965 ss 67 and 69. Similar restrictions also applied in respect of claims by children for support under SA 1965 s 117.
2   SA 1965 s 111.

2.13 It appears that the courts have recognised secret trusts because the failure to apply a settlor's intentions could create an unintended right in favour of a person or give rise to fraud.[1]

A secret trust can be made either by an inter vivos settlement (A to A for life with remainder to B, the secret trustee) or under a will. In practice, as the desire is to conceal the source of the devolution of property they almost invariably arise on a death. The contents of wills are available for public inspection whereas no such right is attached to inter vivos settlements. An agreement *not* to make a will leading to an intestacy which would result in the distribution of the estate amongst the next-of-kin can form the basis of a secret trust.

References
1   *McCormick v Grogan* [1868] LR 4 HL 82; *Blackwell v Blackwell* [1929] AC 318.

2.14 An important feature of secret trusts which has been recognised by the Courts in numerous decided cases is that they are considered to be independent and separate in their operation from the arrangement or settlement under which they were set up. Secret trusts have been classified into two categories depending on whether or not the existence of such a trust is disclosed by direct evidence.

Fully secret trusts

2.15 Fully secret trusts arise where gifts are made (or property is transferred) by a settlor in favour of another person unconditionally without any reference (or disclosure) being made concerning the creation of a further interest in the gift or property. However, the named beneficiary of the gift or transfer must have agreed earlier with the settlor to hold the advantage given to him for the benefit of a third person.[1]

The following requirements have been considered necessary to support the existence of a fully secret trust:

(a) There must be independent evidence (since there is none in the governing agreement) of the existence of the trust. While supplementing documentation is desirable it is not absolutely necessary.

(b) The trustee must agree to accept the property and carry out the settlor's wishes. Acceptance by a trustee can be made before or after a will is made provided it is given in the lifetime of the testator. [2] Where there are two or more trustees notice must be given to all the trustees. However, where a trustee is a joint tenant of property, notice to one of the tenants (in contrast to the position applicable for tenants in common) binds all the joint tenants on the grounds that they have non-severable interests.[3]

(c) The trust must be certain as regards the property involved and the objects of the trust. Thus a transfer of property under a will to a person who had agreed to its further disposal or transfer at the testator's wish was held to be void for uncertainty (despite the availability of indirect evidence supporting the existence of a secret trust) as the testator had during his life failed to communicate directly his intentions to that person.[4] In these circumstances no benefit accrues to the named beneficiary or potential trustee as clearly there was no intention (animus) by the testator to benefit him and, accordingly, the property reverts to form part of the residue of the testator's estate.

References
1   *R. C. v Stapleton* [1937] IR 225.
2   *Moss v Cooper* [1861] 4 LT 790.
3   *Geddis v Semple* [1903] 1 IR 73.
4   *Re Boyes* [1884] 26 Ch D 531.

Half-secret trusts

2.16 Half-secret trusts arise where the trustees are appointed to hold property but the nature of the trusts is not specified.

Example

A, by will, bequeaths his Irish Government Stocks to B to be applied by B in the manner advised to him by A previously.

As in the case with fully secret trusts, the trustee must agree to accept the property (and carry out the settlor's wishes) and the trustee must be certain as regards the property involved, and the objects of the trust.

The main difficulty with half-secret trusts is the nature and time of notice needed by trustees under a will. Several English cases have held that agreement by a trustee in respect of a half-secret trust is necessary *before* the date of the will.[1]

While the technical distinction is a fine one (as all secret trusts are considered to be separate and operative outside the effects of a will) the basis of the judicial restriction in half-secret trust cases has been that where property has been included in a will the devise (or bequest) must be complete, because the testator cannot reserve a future power to complete an earlier testamentary devise (or bequest).

References

1   *Blackwell v Blackwell* [1929] AC 318; *Re Keen* [1937] Ch 236.

2.17 The Irish courts may support the existence of a half-secret trust where the trustee was only advised of the testator's intentions after the date of a will.[1]

The Irish courts have also held, on the facts of a particular case,[2] that a half-secret trust does not operate outside (dehors) the will. The gift involved a bequest of a sum of money in the following terms:

> I will bequeath eight hundred pounds to my executors to be disposed of by them as I shall verbally direct them.

It was accepted in the High Court that a half-secret trust existed in favour of the testator's widow and that relevant directions to this effect had been given to the executors at the time of the making of the will. However, while the widow was the admitted beneficial recipient of the legacy outside the terms of the will it was held that, under specific Revenue legislation concerning the duty on property within a secret trust, the executors were liable to legacy duty in respect of any such property passing from the deceased's estate.[3] The Judge made it quite clear that the effect of his ruling was limited and that he was distinguishing other cases on the basis that he was concerned immediately with the application of specific statutory law.

2.18 Where a nominated trustee under a testamentary half-secret trust predeceases the testator, the basis for the trust disappears and, accordingly, the bequest or devise (which forms part of the residuary estate of the testator) fails.[4]

References

1   *Re Browne* [1944] IR 90; on the facts of the case Judge Overend held that a fully secret trust existed thus leaving the question of the timing necessary for a half-secret trust still to be clarified under Irish law.

2   *Revenue Commissioners v Martin Stapleton (as executors of the will of William Stapleton deceased)*
      [1937] IR 225.
3   Succession Duty Act 1853 s 8.
4   *Re Maddock* [1902] 2 Ch 220.

Donatio mortis causa

2.19 The literal meaning of this Latin phrase is a gift made in contemplation of death. It relates to a gift by a donor whereby the donee is to have the absolute title but only if the donor dies.[1] The gift stands on its own and a valid "donatio" can be enforced against the personal representative of the donor.

The main distinguishing feature of a donatio mortis causa as compared with other inter vivos gifts is that if the immediate risk of death disappears the gift reverts to the donor. However, even during the risk period, if the donor wishes to re-claim the gift he has the right to do so.

In any interval between the date of a donatio and the date of death of the donor, the donee holds possession of the property but has no equitable right to enforce rights or interests. It is thus an imperfect gift. While it is a maxim of equity that it does not assist a volunteer, this does not apply to a donatio mortis causa and the courts will enforce a qualifying gift after the death of a donor.

2.20 The courts have recognised a number of features which are necessary to constitute a donatio mortis causa:[1]

(*a*)   There must be delivery of the property. It follows that the property must be capable of delivery. No difficulties should arise with respect to items such as furniture, jewellery or personal effects (choses in possession). A valid donatio was held to have been made where a father gave a son land to build a house without a conveyance and did not object to the erection of the building.[2] Problems generally arise regarding the title to property which is placed in joint names.

The intention of the donor, as manifested by his actions, must be considered. In a leading Irish case,[3] an elderly man had a number of bank deposit receipts in the joint names of himself and two other relatives. He frequently cashed and relodged the receipts in different amounts and there was no evidence that the other joint holders were aware of the existence of the deposit receipts. Shortly before his death he again changed the amounts held in the joint names and advised the bank manager that the receipts were to be handed over to the surviving joint holders if anything happened to him. The manager was told to maintain absolute secrecy about the existence of the accounts. The Supreme Court unanimously ruled against the claims of the surviving joint account holders that there had been a donatio mortis causa.

(*b*)   There must be a danger (but not necessarily an expectation) of death, apart from the inevitable mortality of all individuals.

(*c*)   The gift must be made and the intention expressed that the absolute and final transfer of the gift is conditional on the death of the donor.

(*d*)   A donee must be prepared to supply evidence to support his claim if possession of the donatio is challenged by a personal representative.

(*e*)   The death may occur from a condition other than that which the donor contemplated.[4]

References
1   *Re Beaumont* [1902] 1 Ch 889; *Re Craven's Estate* [1937] Ch 431. See generally judgment of Molony C. J. in *Re Mulroy* [1924] 1 IR 98.
2   *Dillwyn v Llewelyn* [1862] 4 De G F & J 517.
3   *Owens v Greene* [1932] IR 225.
4   *Wilkes v Allington* [1931] Ch 104.

Chapter 3

Categories of private trusts

Introduction

3.01 An early classification of trusts declared:

> All trusts are either, first, express trusts which are raised or created by act of the parties, or implied trusts, which are raised or created by act or construction of law.[1]

This classification has since been refined and nowadays, four main types of private trusts are recognised:

(a) *Statutory trusts*: these are trusts which are impressed on transactions by provisions of statutes.

(b) *Express trusts*: these arise directly from the intended deliberations or actions of a settlor of property.

(c) *Implied (or resulting) trusts*: these trusts are inferred from the language and circumstances used in (or relating to) a settlement.

(d) *Constructive trusts*: these cover trusts which arise by operation of law irrespective of the intentions, declaration or wishes of the parties to a settlement.

While it could be said that the distinction between the meaning of statutory and constructive trusts is somewhat artificial, it can be justified on the basis that statutory provisions are usually mandatory whereas constructive trusts are governed by the application of the rules of equity by the courts.

References
1   *Cook v Fountain* [1676].

Statutory trusts

3.02 Examples of statutory trusts are:

(*a*)   The personal representatives of a deceased are statutory trustees for the next-of-kin.[1]

(*b*)   Certain profit-sharing schemes for company employees will not be approved unless a trust is established to hold the shares for a period before they can be released to the employees.[2]

(*c*)   Certain unit trust schemes whereby a trust must be created on behalf of the unit holders. [3]

(*d*)   Where a person dies and his estate is insolvent, a trustee may (by agreement) be appointed to wind up the insolvent estate. [4]

References
1   SA 1965 s 10(3) re-enacting provisions of the Executors Act 1830.
2   FA 1982 Pt IX and Sch, para 3; FA 1992 s 17.
3   Unit Trust Act 1990 s 1; Unit Trust Act 1990 s 20 repeats in the full Unit Trust Act 1972.
4   Bankruptcy Act 1990 s 10.

Express trusts

Introduction

3.03 Express or declared trusts can be made either orally (by parol) or in writing. However, in relation to transfers of land between living persons (inter vivos transfers) there must be evidence in writing of the transaction.[1]

It is not essential that the appropriate declaration of trust must itself be in writing, and, even if it is in writing, it is not essential that it be signed provided there is a connection with a document signed by the settlor setting out the conditions of the trust. The transaction must be:

(*a*)   certain as regards the property being transferred,

(*b*)   certain as regards the persons (or objects) that will benefit from the trust, and

(*c*)   be imperative.[2]

Secret trusts (see 2.12), discretionary trusts (2.11) and donatio mortis causa (2.19) may qualify as express trusts.

References
1   Statute of Frauds (Ireland) Act 1695 s 4. On a death property devolves under a will or under the rules of intestacy (SA 1965 Pt VI) and consequently no independent evidence is necessary.
2   *Forster v Hale* 3 Ves 696.

Executed trusts

3.04 Express trusts may be categorised as either (*a*) executed trusts or (*b*) executory trusts.

An executed trust is a trust that has been executed (perfected). Such a trust requires no intervention by the courts to clarify its application or intent. An executory trust requires some action to carry out the settlor's intentions:

> Every trust is in a sense executory; when, however, there is a mere trust giving just a legal estate to the trustee, who has a certain trust to perform, we are not in the habit of calling it an executory trust. In the proper sense, an executory trust is a trust in which something more is to be done. Executory trusts may thus be of two kinds, one in which something is to be done, yet where the testator has acted as his own conveyancer as it is called and the Court has nothing to do but to follow out the limitations. Such trusts do not differ from ordinary estates. They must be construed accordingly to the clear intent of the settlor. The other species of executory trust is, when the testator intended something beyond what is effected by the words creating an estate and has imperfectly stated what is to be done; and the Court is thus invested with a larger discretion, other than if the words were used by themselves.[1]

References
1   Lord Sugden in *Boswell v Dillon* [1844] Ir Eq R 389.

Executory trusts

3.05 When a court intervenes to apply proper and legal wording to a settlor's imprecise arrangements the court will follow the doctrine of equity and look at the intent (rather than the form) of the transaction. The court will not introduce any new concepts.[1] It is solely concerned with putting a legal gloss on the informality or impreciseness of the settlor's expressed wishes.

Thus, where the sole defect is a specific further requirement by the settlor, the only discretion allowed to the court is to decide whether that specific is to be executed (or performed).

Where a settlor's expressed intentions are unclear, or do not make sense, the court has wider discretion.

References
1   *Re Flavel's Will Trusts* [1964] 2 AER 232.

Incomplete trusts

3.06 An express trust, whether executed or executory, may be distinguished from an incomplete trust. An express trust is complete even though an executory trust may require the assistance of the courts to ensure that the settlor's intentions are carried out.

An incomplete trust on the other hand refers to a transaction which, while not unlawful or void in itself, does not create a valid trust as the property which is the subject of the transaction has not been properly vested in the trustees.

For example, to be effective, a transfer of land to the trustees by the settlor must be evidenced in writing.[1]

Similarly, a transfer of ownership of private company shares must be recorded in the company's register (and notified to the registrar of companies). If this is not done, the transfer of shares in incomplete.[2]

3.07 Under a trust, a beneficiary generally has the right to have the trust's provisions enforced (see 2.04). No such right prevails if the trust is incomplete.[3]

It is a maxim of equity that the court will not give a beneficiary something that he is not properly entitled to under the settlement's provisions (i.e. the court does not perfect an imperfect gift). Nevertheless, the courts have occasionally departed from this principle to assist a claimant. For example, where a loan was repayable by a borrower but during her life the lender had informally foregone her right to instalment repayments by paying the borrower sums she owed him in full. The lender appointed the borrower executor of her will. The court decided that this appointment perfected the imperfect gift (the absolving of the debt owed to the deceased while the deceased was alive) and thus permanently recognised the forgiving of the debt.

References

1   See para 3.03.
2   *Mulroy v Leeds* [1862] De G. F. and J. 264; decision applied in *Re Wall* [1956] 1 WLR 1346.
3   Under the common law if consideration is given by the beneficiary under a contract there is a right, as a participating party rather than a stranger, to enforce the agreement.
4   *Bird v Strong* [1874] 18 Eq 315.

Implied trusts

Resulting trusts

3.08 Implied trusts are also known as resulting trusts, because with the exception of trusts arising under mutual wills, there is usually a reversion of the interest in the trust property to the settlor (or to his estate). An implied trust is therefore different from an express (executory) trust because a court will enforce such a trust to give effect to the implied (but unexpressed) intention of the settlor. On the other hand, a court will only intervene to give effect to an express (executory) trust when it is necessary to determine the meaning of expressed but imprecise intentions.

3.09 An implied trust usually arises where there is a failure by the settlor to provide for the final vesting of a beneficial interest, for example, where there is a cesser of a limited interest, and no provision has been made for the creation of a further interest. The result is the property reverts back to the settlor or his estate. Such trusts have been described as automatic implied trusts[1] as the reversion follows from the internal provisions of the trust and there is no need for a court to interpret the trust provisions.

Example

A, a bachelor, by his will left an interest in his farm to his brother B for life and provided that the unspecified remainder of his property was to be divided amongst named nephews and nieces.

On the death of B, which took place after that of A, the interest in the farm reverted to A's estate for division amongst the residuary legatees. Even if there had been no bequest of the residue by A giving rise to a partial intestacy or if the transfer to B with the same consequences was by way of a written inter vivos settlement, on B's death the land would still have gone back to form part of A's estate for distribution amongst A's next-of-kin (including B's estate).

References
1   *Re Vandervell's Trust* [1974] Ch 269.

3.10 It may also happen that a settlor fails to provide for an absolute vesting of property, for example, where a trust fails in respect of successive secondary objects.

Example

A bequest of property by A to B and C in successive life interests without any further gift over in remainder will revert to A or his estate on the death of B if B is predeceased by C.

Property purchased with consideration provided by others

3.11 An implied trust also arises when property is purchased in the name of a person with funds supplied by another.[1] In such circumstances the purchaser is presumed to hold the property in trust for the provider of the funds.[2] This positive presumption can be rebutted by evidence supporting a gift of the consideration to the purchaser.

The law does not require written evidence of the existence of an implied trust in favour of a person supplying the consideration.[3] This follows because an implied trust arises through the unexpressed acts, or the lack of direction from, a settlor. An implied trust does not arise where an advance is made by way of loan or mortgage to a purchaser of property as there is an enforceable separate contract under common law between the grantor and the grantee of the loan. The doctrine of implied trusts is important in determining the interests of spouses in the matrimonial home where domestic difficulties lead to a separation (see 3.17).

References

1   It is not unusual for solicitors to bid for property at auctions on behalf of clients. Where successful they are commercially known to have made the purchase "in trust". However, the so-called "trust" is really only an agreement to purchase as the authorised agent for the ultimate purchaser.
2   *Dyer v Dyer* [1788] Cox Eq 92.
3   Statute of Frauds (Ireland) 1695 s 4.

Mutual wills

3.12 Mutual wills made by agreement in complementary terms by persons to provide for the creation of interests in favour of the same ultimate beneficiaries give rise to implied trusts. Nevertheless, an implied trust does not arise if there has been no agreement between the testators even where the ultimate beneficiaries are the same under both wills.[1]

Mutual wills are usually made by husbands and wives (or brothers and/or sisters). Such wills provide, generally, but not necessarily, a priority life interest to the survivor in the property of the earlier deceased before the vesting of the overall property of both testators in the same beneficiaries. An agreement to draw up mutual wills can be revoked during the joint lives of the parties concerned as a will only takes effect from a date of death and no trust comes into effect until the first testator dies. However, advice of any revocation must be given to the other party as the arrangement to make mutual wills is based on the joint intentions.[2]

There can be no renegotiation of the terms of an agreement by a survivor and any disposition, whether between living persons or by way of a will, which contradicts the mutual agreement may be challenged in the courts.

A surviving testator under a mutual will agreement cannot be forced to accept any limited interest benefits conferred on him by the will of the earlier deceased. In these circumstances the joint agreement still subsists but the interest of the later beneficiaries in the deceased's property may be advanced to by-pass and ignore the surviving testator's priority limited interest.

References

1   *Re Oldham* [1925] Ch 25.
2   *Stone v Hoskins* 54 WR 64; 21 TLR 528.

Jointly held property

The doctrine of advancement

3.13 Where a single named holder of property, freely and without payment, causes another name to be added to his own as the joint holder of property a resulting trust is presumed to have arisen. In other words, if the new joint owner dies, the property reverts to the original single named holder. This principle, which applies to both real and personal property, may be rebutted by evidence to the contrary.[1]

In the case of joint deposit accounts, an essential requirement to support a claim for advancement is that the added joint holder must:

(*a*)   be aware of the existence of the joint account, and

(*b*)   have been directly concerned with the management or administration of the jointly held property.

Evidence up to the time the property was put into the joint names may be taken into account by the court, in considering whether there is a presumption of a resulting trust.[2] Subsequent acts or declarations will only be considered against the party who made them, and not in his favour. Thus the circumstances at the time the property is placed in joint names are important. Subsequent actions are less important and may be used only to rebut a claim.

References
1   *Owens v Greene* [1932] IR 225 (SC); see 2.20.
2   *Shepherd v Cartwright* [1955] AC 431.

Gift of property from husband to his wife or child

3.14 Where a husband makes an inter vivos gift of property to his wife, his child (or someone to whom he is in loco parentis) by adding the recipient's name to property previously held in the husband's sole name, the husband is presumed to have advanced the property to the recipient. In other words, the doctrine of advancement may displace the presumption of a resulting trust in favour of the settlor. The gift by the father is presumed to take immediate effect, in contrast to the position when property is, without any consideration being given, put into joint names. The presumption that property has been advanced may be, however, rebutted. The person to whom the property is advanced must:

(*a*)   be aware of the existence of the property that is to be advanced, and

(*b*)   have been directly concerned with the management or administration of the property.

The placing by the husband of property in the joint names of himself and his spouse to create a joint tenancy has the following advantages:

(*a*)   the property passes outside any will to the survivor;

(*b*)   court costs are saved in probate applications;

(*c*)   inheritances taken on and after 3 January 1985 by a surviving spouse from the deceased partner are exempt from inheritance tax;[1]

(*d*)   inter vivos gifts between spouses taken after 30 January 1990 are exempt from gift tax.[2]

A husband, when considering joining a child of his as the joint holder of property, should bear in mind that any advancement made to a child of a deceased is, subject to any contrary intention being disclosed, to be taken as made towards the satisfaction of the share of such child from the father's estate apart from any further specific testamentary bequests made to the child.[3]

References
1 FA 1985 s 59.
2 FA 1990 s 127.
3 SA 1965 s 63.

Gift of property from wife to her husband or child

3.15 The principal of advancement does not apply to gifts made by a wife to her husband or her children which create joint interests and, accordingly, there is a presumption not of advancement but of a resulting trust arising on the death of the wife. The difference in treatment between gifts by husbands (presumption of advancement) and wives (presumption of resulting trust) appears to contradict Article 40.1 of the 1937 Constitution which provides for equality of treatment before the law.[1]

References
1 *Equity and the Law of Trusts in the Republic of Ireland*, Keane J, (Butterworth) at 12.05 and 12.09.

Real property

The Statute of Uses (Ireland)

3.16 Where freehold land is transferred (between living persons or by will) to the use, confidence or trust of another person, that person is to stand and be "seized, deemed and adjudged" to be in possession with a legal interest.[1]

Nevertheless, the rules of equity provide for the existence of a superimposed interest which negates the effects of the statute.

Example

Thus where, after the Statute of Uses came into force, A made a disposition of freehold land unto and to the use of B in trust for C the *Statute* created a legal interest in favour of B but the courts[2] considered that C's interest was not similarly executed. C has created a separate equitable interest.

References
1 Statute of Uses (Ireland) Act 1634 s 1. This has not been repealed (see 1.09-1.11). The 1634 Statute also applies in Northern Ireland. The corresponding English Statute of Uses 1535 was repealed by the Law of Property Act 1925.
2 *Re Jane Tyrrell* [1557].

The matrimonial home

Joint tenancy

3.17 Problems should not normally arise where the home is purchased in joint names and all the consideration is paid by the husband as there is a presumption of advancement in favour of the wife to support the creation of a joint tenancy. This will also be the case where the purchase is or has been made out of a fund which is supplied or fed by both parties. There may be problems if the wife provides all the purchase monies as the doctrine of advancement is not relevant (see 3.15).

3.18 A disposition of the family home cannot take effect without the agreement of both spouses.[1] Any disposition made by a spouse who has the legal interest in the matrimonial home without the prior written consent of the other spouse is void.[2] In consequence, irrespective of the rights between themselves in the domestic premises, they are each considered to have a joint priority title against third parties.[3]

References

1 Family Home Protection Act 1976 s 3 as amended by Family Law Act 1981 s 10.
2 *Somers v Weir* [1979] IR 94 (SC).
3 The High Court, when granting a decree of judicial separation, may:
   (*a*) confer on one spouse either for life or for such other period (definite or contingent) as the Court may specify the right to occupy the family home to the exclusion of the other spouse;
   (*b*) order the sale of the family home.
   (Judicial Separation and Family Law Reform Act 1989 s 18).

Property in husband's name

3.19 When title to the matrimonial home is vested in the sole name of the husband problems can arise in the event of a separation if the wife claims to have acquired an equitable interest in the property. The law merely provides for the determination of any question between husband and wife as to the title to or possession of any property.[1]

The judiciary takes the view that it has the power to consider the existence of an implied or resulting trust in favour of the wife for any direct or indirect contributions made by her towards the purchase of a matrimonial home made in the sole name of the husband. The criteria necessary for the existence of an implied trust in favour of a wife against the interest of a husband holding the title to the matrimonial home in his sole name are:

(*a*) Where direct contributions are made by the wife to the purchase price or the mortgage repayments the measure of the wife's interest is to be determined on a proportionate basis. The contribution made by the wife must be of such a size to justify a conclusion that the home was acquired by the joint efforts of both spouses.

(*b*)   Where the wife's contributions are indirect (such as contributing by means of her earnings to a family fund) the inference to be drawn is that she has relieved her husband of a corresponding liability.

There has been some disagreement at the High Court level as to whether the Supreme Court's ruling requires the existence of a formal family fund to meet purchase commitments or whether general contributions to household expenses qualify.[4]

References
1   Married Women's Status Act 1957 s 12.
2   *D McC v M McC* [1986] ILRM 6.
3   *Conway v Conway* [1976] IR 254.
4   *Family Law in the Republic of Ireland* (Shatter) (Wolfhound Press) pp 491-513.

Contributions by wife

3.20 A contribution by a wife to the cost of acquiring *furniture* for the matrimonial home does not give rise to an equitable interest. Neither do payments made by a wife for an already acquired home which is in the sole name of the husband. In these circumstance there is merely a common law right to recover the amounts spent. In converse circumstances the husband would not have a right to be compensated as he is presumed to have advanced the property to the wife.

Unpaid domestic services supplied by a wife should not be considered as creating a resulting trust in her favour. However, in *B. L. v M. L.*[2] Judge Barr in the High Court has held that under the 1937 Constitution a wife has a beneficial interest in the family home irrespective of whether she had contributed any money or money's worth. The Supreme Court has overturned this decision holding unanimously that a declaration of a wife's beneficial interest in the family home based on the value of her domestic contribution would be a usurpation of legislative functions.[3] This decision is in line with earlier House of Lords decisions.[4]

References
1   *Equity and the Law of Trusts in the Republic of Ireland* (Keane) (Butterworth) Ch 12 at 12.12-12.17.
2   [1989] ILRM 528.
3   ITLR 13 January 1992.
4   *Pettitt v Pettitt* [1971] AC 886; *Gissing v Gissing* [1970] AC 777.

Matrimonial Homes Bill

3.21 In September 1992, the Minister for Justice, in a *White Paper on Marital Breakdown* proposed that new legislation be enacted to give each spouse an equal share of the family home and household chattels, as of right, irrespective of contributions made by either spouse. The resultant Matrimonial Home Bill 1993 was referred by the President (under article 26 of the Constitution) to the Supreme Court to decide whether the Bill was in accordance with the Constitution. On 24 January 1994 the Supreme Court decided that the Bill was unconstitutional because it could indiscriminately reverse many "joint decisions validly made within the authority of the family concerning the question of the ownership of the family home".

Constructive trusts

Unjust enrichment

3.22 In more recent times a doctrine of unjust enrichment has been developed as the basis for a constructive trust. The underlying principle is that a direct or indirect liability exists where a benefit is taken by a person at the expense of another and does not arise from a contract involving consideration.

> The fundamental principle upon which the doctrine of constructive trusts proceeds is that no person in a fiduciary capacity shall be allowed to retain any advantage gained by him in his character as trustee. [1]

The Supreme Court of Canada has adopted the doctrine of unjust enrichment as the basis of the liability of a constructive trustee.[2] Measuring the extent of the enrichment may require looking at the application of the property. Problems may arise:

(*a*)   where the property has been passed to a third party,

(*b*)   where there are several independent acts or transactions, and

(*c*)   where it is uncertain that any advantage has accrued.[3]

References

1   Lord Chatterton, Vice Chancellor, in *Gabbett v Lawder* [1883] 11 LR Ir 295 (CD).
2   *Sorachan v Sorachan* [1986] 29 DLR (4th) 1.
3   In a separate development the Australian High Court (*Baumgariner v Baumgariner* [1987] 164 CLR 137) has been developing a doctrine of proprietary estoppel whereby the court attempts to determine the real (or actual) position, rather than the legal law.

Separate personality

3.23 In the "Romford Market" case[1] a lease held in trust for an infant expired. The lessor refused to renew the lease but granted a separate lease to the trustee of the infant in his personal capacity. The court held that the benefits of the new lease were to be held for the infant's trust. The principles underlying this decision are still relevant but must not be taken to effect third parties or strangers. Thus where a renewal of a yearly lease of a business premises was refused to a widow who was administratrix of her husband's estate but a new lease was given to her son who was helping his mother in the running of the business the court refused to recognise the existence of a constructive trust for the benefit of the estate.[2]

A trustee is also a legal person (as an individual) independent of his fiduciary status. Therefore, a trustee who set up a business similar to that of which he was a trustee was held not to be in breach of trust.[3]

Similarly, a limited liability company that has been properly incorporated under the Companies Acts 1963-1990 is a separate legal person . It is distinct from the directors who are administrators but not trustees of the corporate property. They can, however, be liable to the company as constructive trustees where internal knowledge of the company's activities is used for personal advantage.

References

1   *Keech v Sandford* [1726]. The principle was restated and approved in *Gabbett v Lawder* (see 3.22).
2   *Re Biss* [1903] 2 Ch 40.
3   *Moore v McGlynn* [1894] IR (CD).

Agents

3.24 As previously discussed, the common law concept of agency involves an agreement giving rise to a relationship between a principal and another person, the agent, who acts under the power, control and discretion granted to him by the principal. An agent must account to his principal for non-contractual profits. An agent must not only account on special payments related to the disposal of property (choses in possession) but on payments relating to services provided. In the leading UK case[1] a solicitor for a trust together with a beneficiary of the trust, and with the apparent permission of the trustees and the other beneficiaries, bought all the shares in a company (other than those already owned by the trust) and made a substantial profit for the two investors and the trust. Subsequently, another beneficiary of the trust claimed that he had been misled as to the effect of the transaction. This objection was upheld by the court. A constructive trust was deemed to exist on the basis that the knowledge available to the two investors concerning the affairs of the company in which the investments had been made arose from the trust's shareholding in that company.

References

1   *Boardman v Phipps* [1967] 2 AC 46.

Third party liability as trustee

3.25 A third party may be liable as a constructive trustee for inter-meddling in trust property in the following circumstances:

(*a*)   Where property is received with notice, actual or constructive, of the existence of the trust and where knowledge of the abuse of the trust is only received after the transfer.

(*b*)   An agent is liable where he is aware that a breach of trust is being committed by the transfer of the property to him.

(*c*)   A stranger to a trust who knowingly assists in furthering any fraud is liable for the consequences of any such fraud.

Thus, a banker who accepted trust monies on deposit was held not to be liable as a constructive trustee when the monies were subsequently and illegally transferred abroad because, at the time of the transfer, the bank had no reasonable grounds to suspect that the trust provisions still applied. The relevant knowledge required to make the defendant bank, as a stranger to the trust, accountable as constructive trustee was knowledge of the facts, not of mere claims or allegations. Such knowledge could be actual knowledge or knowledge that the bank could have obtained from the circumstances or from making reasonable enquiries. The onus of establishing that the bank did not satisfy these conditions was placed on the plaintiff.

A stranger is not to be made liable as a constructive trustee for assisting in the fraudulent breach of a trust, as opposed to the receipt of a trust property, unless knowledge of the fraudulent design can be imputed to him. There must be dishonesty or a want of probity on his part. Constructive notice of a fraudulent design is not enough although knowledge may be inferred in the absence of evidence by the alleged trustee, if such knowledge would have been imputed to an honest or reasonable man.[3]

References
1   *Agip (Africa) v Jackson* [1989] 3 WLR 1367.
2   *Baden v S G Dévelopment du Commerce SA* [1992] 4 All ER 161.
3   *Eagle Trust plc v SBC Securities Ltd* [1992] 4 All ER 488

Vendors of land as trustees

3.26 Where a vendor has agreed to sell land (or buildings), but the contract has not been finally completed, he is regarded while still in beneficial occupation as a constructive trustee for the purchaser and he is entitled to any profits arising during the interim.[1] If the sale falls through, the purchaser has not acquired any interest in the property. Thus, the purchaser has an equitable interest in the property from the date of the agreement of sale up to the date of completion. While this offers protection to the purchaser in that the vendor is liable for any wilful damage to the property in the interval to the completion of the sale it also imposes obligations.[2] The purchaser should insure for the risks involved and if a business is being bought he should arrange for the continuance of lines of credit and the giving of commercial guarantees.

References
1   *Raynor v Preston* [1881] 18 Ch 1; *Rideout v Fowler* [1904] 2 Ch 93.
2   *Phillips v Silvester* [1872] 8 Ch 173.

Void and voidable trusts

Void trusts

3.27 A void trust is a trust that never existed in the eyes of the law and therefore never came into effect. A voidable trust is a trust that does exist in the eyes of the law. Such a trust contains provisions that appear to be effective but may be challenged in court.

3.28 Any illegal terms of a settlement are void. A settlement in favour of two living illegitimate children of the settlor was valid, but a provision to benefit an illegitimate child after the date of the settlement was void. This ruling does not apply to dispositions or settlements on or after 14 June 1988 which are to be construed as if the parents of a child were not married.[2]

The High Court has also held that provisions settling property on grandchildren of a settlor on condition that the children were brought up in the Roman Catholic faith, were void. The mother of the children had been a practising Church of Ireland adherent since her marriage. The decision was made on the grounds that the restrictions imposed on the beneficiaries went against the rights of the parents to bring up their children under the 1937 Constitution and were, accordingly, against public policy.[3]

References
1   *Thompson v Thompson* [1891] 27 LR Ir 457 (CD).
2   Status of Children Act 1987 ss 3 and 27.
3   *Re Blake* [1955] IR 89.

The rule against perpetuities

3.29 A trust settlement (other than for bona fide charities or pension funds)[1] cannot indefinitely postpone the transfer of property rights. This restriction is expressed as the law against perpetuities:

Where the vesting of any interest in property, whether real or equitable, is postponed for a period exceeding a life in being at the date of the instrument creating it, or where the disposition is a will, at the date of death of the testator and twenty one years after the expiration of such life or lives, such interest is void.[2]

The period is extended to take into consideration a conceived but unborn child (en ventre sa mere) at the time of the disposition or death.

References
1 The governing provisions relating to superannuation funds are set out in the Perpetual Funds (Registration) Act 1933 s 6.
2 *Cadell v Palmer* [1833] Cl and Fin 172. The combined effect of the Age of Majority Act 1985 s 2 and FA 1986 s 12 is to reduce the attainment of full legal age from 21 to 18. It remains to be seen whether the Courts will apply the 21 year age limit or seek to reduce to 18 years of age time periods of existing dispositions.

3.30 It is not essential that the trust property be finally distributed during the perpetuity period. The property may be vested if:

(*a*)   all the qualifying beneficiaries exist,

(*b*)   their interests can be qualified,

(*c*)   any conditions or contingencies imposed are satisfied.

Under Irish procedures no distinction is made between interests in capital or income.

3.31 Furthermore, under Irish law, unlike that in England,[1] is that the rule against perpetuities is concerned with possibilities rather than probabilities. A theoretical look is taken at what could or might happen in the future irrespective of what eventually transpires.

Example

A, a married man, provided by an inter vivos gift that funds were to be held in trust to accumulate the income arising and to distribute the settlement property equally amongst his named sons who attained 18 years and his named daughters at that age or on their earlier marriage.
As the interests of all the beneficiaries will be identifiable and quantifiable without any unfilled conditions before the expiration of 21 years from the date of death of the settlor the gift is not caught by the rule against perpetuities.

Example

A provided under his will that all his grandchildren living at the time of his death were to share in a trust for his residual property. The trustees were empowered to appoint all the income arising at their discretion and to accumulate any surplus not expended. The capital was to be divided amongst all such grandchildren on attaining 25 and appropriate power was given to the trustees to advance anticipated shares to qualifying beneficiaries on attaining that age.
The rule against perpetuities is not satisfied because, by the perpetuity date, some of the qualifying grandchildren may only have a conditional interest in the income arising subject to the discretion of the trustees.

Class gifts are regarded as contingent until all the names of potential beneficiaries are ascertained but such gifts must also provide for an ascertainable share of the property to each beneficiary on an unconditional basis.[2]

Example

A, by an inter vivos settlement, provided that his daughter, B, was to take a life interest in his private company shares with remainder over to the eldest or successive male child of B on attaining 21. A pre-deceased his daughter.

Under the equitable rule, there was the possibility at the date of the disposition that a grandchild would not fulfil the conditions by the expiration of the perpetuity period and, accordingly, the gift-over is void. However, the common law provides that the gift-over is valid if a qualifying grandchild is the required age at the time of the disponer's death. The interest, in such circumstances, is regarded as properly vested.[3]

References

1 Under the Perpetuities and Accumulations Act 1964 s 3 the rule is only considered in England at the expiration of the perpetuity limitation period applicable and, accordingly, trusts are not struck down as ineffective from the commencement date of the provisions.

2 *Pearks v Moseley* [1880] 5 AC 714.

3 *Andrews v Partington* [1790] Cox 223. See 5.04 for non-application where the governing document applies an exclusion.

Freedom to dispose of property

3.32 A beneficiary, other than a charity, receiving an interest in property must be free to dispose of that interest. The fact that a company can retain property for an indefinite period (not depending on the duration of human life) does not invalidate any benefit taken as the company may divest itself of the property at any time.[1]

References

1 If, however, a restriction on alienation is included in any benefit taken by a company, other than a charity, the gift is void. *Re Ward* [1949] Ch 498.

Fraud or misrepresentation

3.33 Trusts made on the basis of fraud or misrepresentation are void. The courts have set aside settlements where the settlor claims that he was not aware of the effects of the settlement due to ignorance or a mistake. If the settlor's true intentions are not expressed in the document(s) creating an inter vivos settlement, the settlor may ask the court to rectify the situation.

3.34 A trust made to avoid payment to creditors is voidable. The trusts' provisions stand until challenged. A potentially defective trust must be shown, by the circumstances of the case, to have been drawn up with fraudulent intent.[1]

References

1 *Thompson v Webster* [1859] 4 Drew 628.

Bankruptcy

3.35 A conveyance or transfer of property within a period of two years before the adjudication of bankruptcy not made in good faith and for valuable consideration is void.

If the settlement's provisions are voidable the relevant provisions will also be void if a bankruptcy occurs within five years from the date of the settlement unless the beneficiaries can show that, at the time of the settlement, the settlor was able to meet all his debts without recourse to the settlement property. Furthermore, benefits payable to the wife and children of a settlor which were not in the ownership of the settlor at the time of the marriage are restricted.[1]

References
1   Bankruptcy Act 1988 s 59.

Variation of a trust's provisions

3.36 As outlined in 3.33 a settlor who creates an inter vivos settlement may ask the court to rectify the situation where his wishes or intentions have not been effectively interpreted. The court's help[1] may also be sought to deal with administrative emergencies. Thus, an authorisation was given to trustees, which was not available under the terms of the governing deed, to exchange shares for a more valuable holding.

The court will not intervene to create new rights for beneficiaries but it will determine the rights of the beneficiaries among themselves. It follows that a court will generally not intervene to vary the terms of an expressed trust (see 3.03). In a 1954 House of Lords decision[2] a majority decided that it should not follow earlier practice whereby the terms of an express trust *could* be varied with the consent of all beneficiaries who were of full age.

Irish law has not developed like its English counterpart and at this time there appear to be no proposals to update the relevant legislation. When a private Bill was introduced in the Senate on 21 November 1990, to amend the terms of an express trust on the basis that no other action was open to the settlor under Irish law, as would have been available to him under the English legislation, it was attacked on the grounds that the official concern should be to have the general trust law amended and not to confer an exceptional benefit on an individual settlor.[3]

References
1   *Re New* [1901] 2 Ch 534.
2   *Chapman v Chapman* [1954] AC 429. New legislation was introduced by the Variation of Trusts Act 1958 to counter the effects of this decision.

3 The Altamont (Amendment of Deed of Trust) Bill 1990. The 1963 settlement provided for the eldest son of the settlor to benefit. However, there was no male heir and a variation was being sought to enable benefits to be transferred to the wife and five daughters of the settlor.

Termination of a trust

3.37 It is in the nature of a trust that a settlor has divested himself of an interest in property to the confidence of trustees to carry out the settlor's intentions. However all the beneficiaries who are of full age may agree to terminate a trust.[1] The trustees have no function in this matter despite any restrictions imposed by the settlement. Again, such beneficiaries, if they are not satisfied with the current trustees of a settlement, can terminate the trust and set up a new trust on the same terms with different trustees.[2] Beneficiaries however, have no general right to appoint new or additional trustees (see 4.05).

References
1   *Saunders v Vautier* [1841] Cr and Ph 240.
2   *Re Brockbank* [1948] Ch 206.

Chapter 4

Trustees

Legislation

The Trustee Act 1893

4.01 The main statutory provisions governing the administration of trusts under Irish law are contained in the Trustee Act 1893 (TA 1893: see Appendix I). This statute was not enacted to show the rights and duties of trustees but rather to generally facilitate the operation of trusts while allowing the courts to apply the rules of equity.

The Act has four main parts:

(*a*)   Part I (sections 1-9) deals the investment rights and powers of trustees.

(*b*)   Part II (sections 10-24) deals with the appointment of new trustees; the purchase and sale of property; the appointment of agents; the giving of receipts and the indemnification of trustees for actions done in good faith.

(*c*)   Part III (sections 25-46) enables the courts to intervene when necessary to appoint new trustees; to vest property where contingent interests arise; and to receive and give a discharge to trustees for money or securities paid in to the Court at the behest of the majority of the trustees.

(*d*)   Part IV (sections 47-54) contains miscellaneous provisions including definitions for terms used in the Act (s 50).

Legislative changes since 1893

4.02 While much legislation has been enacted in England since 1893 concerning trusts,[1] in Ireland the Trustee Act 1893 has only been marginally amended as follows:[2]

(*a*)   *Section 1.* A substituted section[3] expanded the categories of authorised investments to cover:

(i) Irish government stocks (including savings certificates) and securities guaranteed by the Minister for Finance;

(ii) securities in a number of semi-State companies;

(iii) real securities in the State;

(iv) securities or mortgages on local authorities and statutory bodies;

(v) British government securities inscribed or registered in the State;

(vi) debentures not exceeding the share capital of a company which has paid a dividend of at least 5% on its ordinary shares in each of the preceding five years;

(vii) deposit accounts with the commercial banks, the Post Office and the Trustee Savings Banks.

(*b*) *Sections 16 and 45 (in part).* The original section 16 authorised a married woman acting as a bare or inactive trustee to convey or surrender an interest in any freehold or copyhold hereditaments as if she were unmarried (a femme sole) while the reference in section 45 was to income over which she had no power of anticipation. These provisions are now repealed. [4]

(*c*) *Section 21 (in part).* This section, in so far as it allows a personal representative to compromise rights in respect of both real and personal property, has been repealed.[5]

(*d*) *Section 25.* The High Court has power to appoint a holder of an office (or the holder for the time being of an office) as a new trustee in place of an earlier holder of that office. The court may also appoint, nominate or consent to a new trustee where the trust property is vested in the holder of an extinct office.[6]

References

1 See 1.15.

2 Special limited amendments of sections 42 and 41 (as substituted in 1958) in the Dublin and Blessington Steam Tramway (Abandonment) Act 1932 s 15 and the National Bank Transfer Act 1966 s 8 respectively have been ignored.

3 Trustee (Authorised Investments) Act 1958 s 1. The list has been widened to include a number of credit institutions and the major building societies under Ministerial Statutory Orders made under Trustee (Authorised Investments) Act 1958 s 2(1):
Trustee (Authorised Investments) Order SI 285/1967;
Trustee (Authorised Investments) Order SI 241/1969;
Trustee (Authorised Investments) Order SI 377/1974;
Trustee (Authorised Investments) Order SI 41/1977;
Trustee (Authorised Investments) (No 2) Order SI 344/1977;
Trustee (Authorised Investments) Order SI 407/1979;
Trustee (Authorised Investments) Order SI 58/1983;
Trustee (Authorised Investments) (No 2) Order SI 366/1983;

Trustee (Authorised Investments) Order SI 224/1985;
Trustee (Authorised Investments) Order SI 372/1986.
4   Married Women's Status Act 1957 s 19 and Sch.
5   SA 1965 ss 8, 9 and Pt III. A personal representative of a deceased is now authorised to accept any composition or security for any debt or property claimed by SA 1965 s 60(8)(c).

Duties of trustees

4.03 The duties of a trustee, under the legislation, and according to the rules of equity, are as follows:

No conflict of interest

A trustee before accepting an office should determine that no conflict of interest is likely to arise because of his personal activities or circumstances. Such a conflict could arise for example, where the appointed trustee is the only other tenant in common of property. Thus a trustee who set up a *business* similar to that carried on by a trust was not considered as having a conflict of interests.[1]

References
1   *Moore v Glynn* [1894] 1 IR 74.

Capacity to undertake the terms of the trust

Any trust documentation should be examined to ascertain the nature of the obligations being undertaken. The trustee must have the capacity to carry out the terms of the trust. Incapacity may arise from either physical or mental infirmity. Legal incapacity may arise for example in the case of an individual aged under 18. While such an infant is not prohibited from being appointed a trustee as a trustee he cannot exercise any power which requires prudence and discretion before he becomes of full age (sui juris).[1] A trustee removed by the courts during infancy may be restored to his office on the coming of full age.

It appears that where a person is appointed both an executor and trustee under a will but declines to act as executor for the winding up of the estate he may still be a trustee for any separate trust which commences to operate on the completion of the administration.[2]

References
1   *Jevon v Bush* 1 Vern 342.
2   See 2.05.

Due care and diligence

A trustee must use due care and diligence in administering the general affairs of the trust as he is accountable to the beneficiaries for any breach of trust. The main distinction between a contract (which is subject to the rules of common law) and a trust which is subject to the rules of equity is that the beneficiaries are entitled, despite being strangers to the settlement, to seek performance of the trust's provisions.[1]

References
1   See 2.05.

Personal liability

A trustee may be held personally liable if he does not adhere strictly to the terms of the trust. Liability in respect of money or securities received by a trustee is to be confined to the value of any such receipts without prejudice to any trust instrument.[1]

References
1   TA 1893 s 24.

Vesting of property

A trustee must verify that property has been transferred and vested as part of the trust. If there is no vesting there is no trust.[1]

References
1   *Knight v Knight* [1840] 3 Beav 148.

No remuneration

A trustee is a volunteer and unless the trust document specifically provides for payment to him for his services, he is not entitled to be remunerated for such services. Nevertheless, a trustee is not to be at a personal loss for expenses incurred. A trustee may reimburse himself, or pay or discharge out of trust premises, all expenses incurred in the execution of the trust.[1]

References
1   TA 1893 s 24.

No advantage to be derived from the trust

No action should be taken by a trustee to acquire any advantage or benefit, directly or indirectly, at the expense of the trust (see 3.25-3.26).

Authorised investments

In the absence of more extensive powers set out in the trust instrument, the trustees may only make certain authorised investments.[1]

References

1   Trustee (Authorised Investments Act) 1958 s 1 (see 4.02).

Cessation of trust

If there is a sole absolute beneficiary the trustee must hand over the trust property as the trust provisions are then exhausted.[1] A trustee must relinquish his office where all the beneficiaries who are of full age agree to the termination of the trust despite the differing nature of the interests concerned. Such beneficiaries may also agree to appoint the trust property to another person and the trustee must accede to this agreement. Additionally, the beneficiaries may set up an identical trust for the trust property with new trustees but they are not entitled to look for an amendment of the original trust provisions.[2]

References

1   *Saunders v Vautier* [1841] Cr and Ph 240.
2   *Re Marshall* [1914] 1 Ch 192.

Confidence in trustee cannot be delegated

The basis of the selection of a trustee is in the confidence imposed in him by the settlor or the courts. This confidence cannot be delegated by the trustee unless he has been given specific authority to do so.[1]

References

1   *Turner v Corney* [1841] 5 Beav 515. *Pilkington v CIR* [1964] AC 612.

Interests of beneficiaries

A trustee must consider the interests of the beneficiaries and ensure, as far as possible, that no preference is being exercised in favour of any beneficiary at the expense of his fellows (see Chapter 5).

Co-trustees

A trustee must act in harmony with his co-trustees in the administration of the trust. Where there was a disagreement between trustees with the result that one of the trustees refused to complete a conveyance of land the High Court intervened to remove the recalcitrant trustee and appointed a new trustee in his place who was amenable to the transfer.[1]

References
1   *O'hUadhghaidh v O'Loinsigh* 109 ILT 122.

Information regarding the affairs of the trust

A trustee must supply the beneficiaries with information concerning the affairs of the trust. The High Court has held [1] that a beneficiary under a discretionary trust was entitled to seek and be given copies of the trust accounts and details of the investments comprising the trust fund.

References
1   *Chaine-Nickson v Bank of Ireland* [1946] IR 393.

Charitable trusts

The trustees of a trust for charitable purposes must take steps to apply property cy-pres (ie as near as possible to the settlement's provisions) where the objects of the settlement no longer exist.[1]

References
1   Charities Act 1961 s 47(4).

Rights of trustees

4.04 A trustee has certain rights and entitlements which, although numerous, are rather limited in their scope and effect.

Refusal of appointment

A trustee is a volunteer and can refuse an appointment. However, having accepted an appointment, a trustee cannot then renounce it. Separate sets of trustees may be appointed for different parts of a property.

Payment for services when authorised by settlement

A professional trustee is entitled to charge for services undertaken on behalf of the trust where authorisation is given by the governing deed.[1]

References
1   *Bray v Ford* [1896] AC 44; *Dale v CIR* [1954] AC 11; 34 TC 468.

Retirement

Where there are more than two trustees a trustee may, subject to any restrictions in the deed of trust and with the consent of his co-trustees, retire and be discharged from all obligations.[1]

References
1   TA 1893 s 11.

Reimbursement of expenses

A trustee is entitled to be reimbursed for costs and expenses incurred (see 4.03).

Authorised investments

A trustee, unless forbidden by the trust provisions, is authorised to invest in certain government and other securities (see 4.02).

Ascertainment of rights

A majority of the trustees of a trust may pay in to the High Court money and securities held.[1] When the rights of the persons entitled to the money or securities are ascertained the court may direct payment or transfer to be made to the persons entitled.[2]

References
1   TA 1893 s 42.
2   Rules of the Superior Courts 1986 Order 73.

Sale of property

Where a trust contains a power for the sale of property the trustee is authorised to take any necessary action (including agreement to sell) to effect the sale.[1]

References
1   TA 1893 s 13.

Power to accept composition

A trustee, unless otherwise restricted under the trust deed, is empowered to agree a settlement of outstanding debts ie accept a composition of both real and personal property.[1]

References
1   TA 1893 s 21(2) as amended by Succession Act 1965 ss 8, 9 and Pt III.

Power of attorney

A trustee acting or paying money under a power of attorney is protected and incurs no liability when he is operating in good faith and without knowledge of any defects in the power. Any causes of action in respect of the trustee's activities must be made against the person receiving the payment.[1]

References
1   TA 1893 s 23.

Appointment of solicitor as agent

A trustee may appoint a solicitor to be his agent without incurring any liability for such appointment.[1]

References
1   TA 1893 s 17(1). Under 17(2) a banker may be an agent for trustees in respect of the proceeds of life assurance policies.

Insurance of land and buildings

A trustee has power to insure buildings and other immovable property of a trust up to three quarters of the value.[1]

References
1   TA 1893 s 18.

Renewal of lease

A trustee has a discretionary power to renew a lease and to raise money for this purpose.[1]

References
1   TA 1893 s 19.

Issue of receipts

A receipt in writing given by a trustee for any money, securities or other personal property payable, transferable or deliverable to him is a sufficient discharge and there is no need to look behind the receipt to see how the trustee applied the property.[1]

References
1   TA 1893 s 20.

Survivor of joint trustees

Where there are two or more joint trustees under a settlement the survivor or survivors may, unless limited by a contrary expressed intention by the settlor, exercise or perform all the necessary functions and actions. [1]

References
1   TA 1893 s 22.

Appointment and retirement of trustees

4.05 A trustee appointed by the original settlor is termed "an original trustee". A trustee appointed later is described as "a substituted trustee". A trustee must be identifiable but need not be specifically named. Thus, an appointment by a settlor of trustees to be those acting under the trusts created by her father's will was held to be valid.[1]

Where a trustee, irrespective of the method of his appointment,

(*a*)   dies;

(*b*)   remains out of the jurisdiction for more than twelve months;

(*c*)   desires to be discharged from his fiduciary office; or

(*d*)   refuses or is unfit or incapable of action;

then the appointing authority under any governing documentation or, in turn, the surviving trustee or trustees (or the personal representative of the last surviving trustee) may, by writing, appoint another one or more trustees.[2]

The number of the trustees may, unless restricted by the provisions of the settlement, be increased when this power is being exercised. Where only one original trustee was appointed a single replacement can be made otherwise there must be at least two trustees to carry out the trust obligations.[3]

Where there are at least two remaining trustees and one trustee desires to be relieved of his duties he must declare his intention by deed and obtain the consent, also by deed, of his co-trustees and any other person entitled to appoint trustees.[4]

A trustee cannot retire from only some of his duties nevertheless where there are separate trusts for different parts of the property a trustee may retire from all duties relating to the separate trusts.[5]

References
1   *Rivers v Waidanis* [1908] 1 Ch 123.
2   TA 1893 s 10(1).
3   TA 1893 s 10(2)(*c*).
4   TA 1893 s 11.
5   *In re Lord and Fullerton's Contract* [1896] 1 Ch 228.

Professional trust

4.06 There are advantages in appointing a professional trust company to act as a trustee. As the company cannot "die" no changes will arise as a result of deaths or retirement of trustees. Further, the bank or other institution acting as trustee will administer the terms of the trust objectively according to the prescribed provisions.

4.07 The statutory powers (see 4.04) to appoint solicitors or bankers, to insure property and to renew leases are all discretionary powers which the trustees are not compelled to use. They would, however, be well advised to accept any professional help and assistance available to protect the trust property. Any expenses incurred in connection with such services are payable out of the trust property.

Intervention by the courts

4.08 As discussed in Chapter 1, the trust evolved over several centuries, and the concept was clarified by the courts of equity. The decisions of these courts were aimed at equalising rights and remedying wrongs by looking at the intent rather than the form of transactions. The rules of equity are not restricted by legislation which, instead, is designed to facilitate the operation of the general trust procedures by giving the High Court power to appoint new trustees and vest property.[1] Provision is also made for the payment into court of trust monies.

4.09 The High Court may also appoint new trustees where it is found difficult or impractical to do so without the assistance of the court. The court can substitute a new trustee for one who has been convicted of a felony, or is bankrupt.[2] Separate sets of trustees can be appointed for distinct trusts.[3] A trustee appointed by the court has the same powers, authorities and discretions as if he had been originally appointed by a settlor under any governing instrument.[4] An estate in the course of administration is not a trust and the High Court cannot appoint an executor or administrator using these powers.[5]

References
1   TA 1893 Pt III.
2   TA 1893 s 25(1).
3   *Moss's Trusts* 37 Ch 513.
4   TA 1893 s 37.
5   TA 1893 s 25(3).

4.10 The High Court has a discretionary right to vest land [1] where:

    (*a*)   a new trustee has been appointed by the court;

    (*b*)   a trustee:
        (i)   is an infant,
        (ii) is out of the jurisdiction, or
        (iii) cannot be found;

(*c*) the rights of a trustee are uncertain; or

(*d*) a trustee refuses to release a right to a person entitled to that right.

The High Court also has power to vest rights in stocks and the income thereof and in other rights to property (choses in action).[2]

4.11 Where land is subject to a contingent right in favour of an unborn person the High Court may release the land from the right or may make a new vesting in any person in respect of the entitlement which the unborn person on coming into existence would have been entitled.[3] Furthermore, where there is a contingent right to land held as a security by an infant mortgagee the High Court may vest, release or dispose of the land or the right as if it were the trustee of the infant.[4]

4.12 Where money or securities are paid in to the High Court at the behest of all or the majority of trustees the court is to make orders in accordance with the Rules of the Superior Courts for the management and disposal of the property.[4]

References
1   TA 1893 s 26.
2   TA 1893 s 35.
3   TA 1893 s 27.
4   TA 1893 s 42.

Chapter 5

Beneficiaries

Introduction

5.01 One of the "three certainties" required to support the existence of a valid trust is that there must be certainty as regards the objects (or beneficiaries) of the trust (see 2.07, 2.11). The beneficiary can seek the enforcement of the trust provisions, a right which is not available to a stranger or third party to a contract.[1]

While a settlor is not prohibited from retaining a reduced interest in the disposed property, the essence of a trust is the transfer and delivery of an interest in property to trustees to be held in a fiduciary capacity for the beneficiaries or objects of the trust. A trustee can assume the office of trustee (see 4.03). It would generally be unwise to appoint a beneficiary as trustee because of a possible conflict of interests. Nevertheless, in practice a settlor will not nominate himself as trustee but will reserve to himself an exclusive power to appoint new trustees.

References

1   In the case of a discretionary trust a person named in the class of beneficiaries can require the trustees to consider exercising their discretion in his or her favour or in favour of another object (*In re Mamisty's Settlement* [1973] 2 All ER 1203).

No beneficiaries

5.02 If there is no object (or beneficiary) of a trust then the trust is void. It is therefore essential that the governing document states clearly and unambiguously who the beneficiaries are.

Rights of beneficiaries

5.03 If all the beneficiaries are of full age they may require the trustees to wind up the trust.[1] On the other hand, the High Court, on due application by the trustees, may order the removal of a contingent right of an unborn beneficiary.[2]

5.04 A beneficiary with a vested interest in the income of a trust is entitled to receive particulars of the trust's financial activities, subject to the beneficiary bearing the cost of supplying the information.[3]

References
2   *Saunders v Vautier* [1841] Cr and Ph 240; see 3.36.
3   TA 1893 s 27.
4   *Chaine-Nickson v Bank of Ireland* [1976] IR 393.

Absolute interest on attainment of specified age

5.05 Where a trust instrument that provides benefits for an indefinite number of objects (for example, grandchildren as a class) entitles each qualifying beneficiary to take an absolute interest in part of the trust property on attaining a specified age, the number of the qualifying beneficiaries is closed off when the first beneficiary attains the specified age.

This rule is not a rule of law but one of construction and its effect can be displaced by a specific contrary intention expressed in the governing trust document.[2]

References
1   *Andrews v Partington* [1790] Cox 223.
2   *Williamson v Williamson* [1976] Ch D 92 (NI).

Kinds of beneficial interests

5.06 A beneficiary's interest under a trust may be classified as being:

(*a*)   vested,

(*b*)   vested liable to be divested,

(*c*)   contingent, or

(*d*)   discretionary.

Vested interest in possession

5.07 A beneficiary may have an interest in possession which gives him a present right to the income of the trust.[1] In these circumstances the beneficiary has an interest which can be both claimed and enforced.[2] The enforcement of any such claim is subject to the exercise of the administrative functions of the trustees concerning expenses, costs, duties and taxes payable on behalf of the trust liabilities.

Vested interest in expectancy

A vested interest in expectancy occurs where possession depends on some *certain* future event. The certainty involved is usually (but not necessarily) related to the life span of a priority interest holder.[3]

When a vested interest in expectancy comes absolutely into possession but the trust still continues to function because either the trustee or the beneficiary has not sought a winding up, the continuing trust is regarded as transparent for taxation purposes and the beneficiary is directly chargeable on the trust income arising.[4]

Example

A, by will, settles property on his widow B for life with remainder over to his son C absolutely. On A's death, B takes a vested interest in possession having acquired a present right to the income arising during her life. C has a vested interest in expectancy which will come into possession on his mother's death either directly or to his estate if he predeceases his mother but survives his father.

References
1   *Gartside v CIR* [1968] AC 553; 1968 1 All ER 121.
2   *Pearson and others v CIR* [1980] 2 All ER 479 (HL).
3   A gift may be related to the life of a third party (pur autre vie), for example A to B during the life of C with remainder over to D on the death of C.
4   *Hamilton-Russell Executors v CIR* 25 TC 200; 1 All ER 474. *Spens v CIR* 46 TC 276; [1970] All ER 295.

Vested interest liable to be divested

5.08 A vested interest liable to be divested occurs when the governing deed excludes a beneficiary from entitlement in certain circumstances.

Example

Thus, in the example shown in the preceding paragraph, if the continuance of B's limited interest was conditional on her not re-marrying her interest would become divested and her benefit would be withdrawn if she took another husband.

Contingent interest

Nature of contingent interest

5.09 A contingent interest is an interest which is conditional and uncertain. The distinction between interests vested in possession and contingent interests is important for income tax purposes because, when the interest held is contingent, the beneficiary under a trust is only liable on the actual payments of income out of the trust whereas if the interest is vested in possession the beneficiary is liable to income tax on his full income entitlement.

Example

A, by inter vivos gift, settles property on trustees to hold until B attains his majority when he is to take absolutely in possession. During the trust period income is to be accumulated subject to the exercise of the trustee's discretion to make payments out of such income for the maintenance and education of B.

B has a contingent interest in both the income and capital of the trust. Any payment made out of income is subject to the exercise of the trustees' discretion while there is no vesting of capital unless and until B comes of age.

5.10 The creation of settlements on the basis shown in the example was quite common up to 1974 with provision for the full accumulation of income. When the accumulated income vested in the beneficiary on attaining a specified age or on marriage, if earlier, the beneficiary was entitled to claim personal allowances and reliefs against the trust income with effect from the settlement.[1]

If the income was substantial payment of sur-tax could be avoided as the income arising was only charged to income tax. Furthermore the existence of such a settlement in favour of a child did not debar a claim for child allowance. This relief was withdrawn for 1973-74 and subsequent years.[2]

References
1   ITA 1967 s 154 re-enacting provisions in ITA 1918 s 25 and FA 1925 s 9(1).
2   FA 1925 s 9(1).

Failure of objects

5.11 Because of the limited tax avoidance benefits now available it is unusual nowadays to find settlements created which are similar to those described in the preceding paragraphs.

In the event of the failure of the objects there was a resulting trust of the property in favour of the settlor or his estate. Continuance of the trust was ensured as is the present practice, by providing for other objects.

5.12 Historically, where real property was settled by a trust that provided in the event of failure of an object for a gift of the property, the settlement was regarded as having created a vested interest.[1] This rule was designed to protect succession rights to freehold land so that an interest would not be destroyed by a contingency which left the land without an owner, as required under common law.

The Irish courts have held that this rule should be treated as a rule of construction rather than a rule of law. When applied to a residuary clause of a will, the rule is based on fallacious reasoning, and a testator is free to include provisions in his will that by-pass the rule.

5.13 More recently, the courts have held that the rule (whereby a gift over — future interest — of *real* property created a vested interest) does not to apply to a gift over of *personal* property until it comes into possession. The litigants had agreed that where, under settlement provisions which allowed for a gift over of the property in the event of the failure of primary objects, income was to be accumulated in full until the main beneficiary attained a specified age. A vested interest (in the fund's *income*) was only to arise from that time onwards. Neither the High Court nor the Supreme Court overturned the settlement provisions.

The *capital* of the fund was to be paid to the main beneficiary at a later date. The trustees claimed that the vested interest did not arise until the *capital* of the trust funds (which was not yet in the possession of beneficiary) was transferred to the beneficiary. This point was successfully disputed by the Revenue Commissioners in the Supreme Court. The beneficiary was entitled to a present enjoyment of the trust fund's income.

References

1   *Phibbs v Acker* [1842] Cl and F 583.
2   Kenny J in *Murphy v Murphy* [1964] IR 308 (HC); see also *Revenue Commissioners v Royal Trust Company (Ireland) Ltd*, unreported, HC, 1970 (No 147 Sp).
3   *Jacob v Revenue Commissioners*, unreported, HC, 1981 (No 28A).

Discretionary trusts

5.14 Because a beneficiary of a discretionary trust (see 2.11) is not entitled in possession until the trustees appoint some property to him, it would appear that such a beneficiary is in an equivalent situation to the holder of a contingent interest. However, the following differences arise:

(*a*)   A beneficiary within the qualifying class of a discretionary trust may seek enforcement of the trust provisions although the result of any such action may not result in any benefit arising to him on the resulting exercise of the trustees' discretion.

(*b*)   The trustees of a discretionary trust must at some time appoint the property of the trust to a member (or members) of the qualifying class of beneficiaries. In the case of a contingent interest where the qualifying conditions have not been satisfied there is no appointment by the trustees and, accordingly, no subsequent interest in the funds of the trust arises to the contingent interest holder from such failure.

Holder of limited interest and holder of absolute interest

Apportionment of entitlements

5.15 A trust by its nature is the repository of property held for the benefit of identifiable persons. In the normal course it would be unusual to have a trust in operation where absolute interests are involved as in these circumstances a vested interest in possession arises to the interest holder. Such a trust may be used, however, to protect the property of persons who suffer from physical or mental infirmities or the property of infants.

A beneficiary who has acquired an absolute interest in trust property may, for convenience and with the concurrence of the trustees, allow the property to continue to be managed by the trustees. These are the exceptions and normally the beneficiaries of a trust will have entitlements of differing degrees, for example, present limited or future absolute interests. It is the duty of the trustees to balance the rights of the interests concerned. This involves consideration of two basic principles:

(*a*)   Does the nature of the property held discriminate between the present and future interests?

(*b*)   What profits or gains are to be apportioned to income and treated as referable to the limited interest holder, and what sums are to be apportioned to capital and treated as referable to the interest in remainder?

Inevitably, there have been disagreements regarding the allocation of property between the holder of a limited interest (usually a life interest) and the holder of a future interest (the remainder interest), and there have been several court decisions clarifying these matters.

5.16 The courts have held that where a settlement gives trustees power to vary the nature of the investments held with the consent of the life tenant, the trustees can, against the life tenant's wishes, compel a change if the property of the trust is threatened.[1]

References
1   *Costello v O'Rourke* 3 Ir R Eq 172; *Re Hotchkins's Settled Estates* 35 Ch D 41.

Life tenant and remainderman

5.17 A life tenant is entitled to the income arising on trust property on and from the date the limited interest vests in possession. If the interest arises under a will (as part of the residue), after the death of a settlor there are usually liabilities and debts due against the property. The question then arises as to what proportion of these debts is chargeable against the limited interest (the life tenant's interest) and what proportion is chargeable against the future interest (the remainderman's interest). Under the rule in *Allhusen v Whittel* [1] the life tenant is charged for the benefit of the remainderman with the interest on the amounts paid by the estate for debts, funeral and testamentary expenses and also legacies as if they had been paid at the date of death. The basis of the rule is that the life tenant is only entitled to benefit from the net value of the residue. The modern form of the rule, which can in practice only be determined after the completion of the administration of an estate, requires an apportionment to be made by reference to the following criteria:

(*a*)   the date of payment of the debt or expense,

(*b*)   the income of the estate after income tax chargeable from the date of death to the completion of the administration computed on a day to day basis over the full period.

Accordingly, where the successive limited and remainder absolute interests are concerned with residuary property, they must be treated as paid out of a mixed fund of capital and income.

For the purpose of adjusting rights as between a tenant for life and the remainderman of a residuary estate, debts, legacies, estate duties, probate duties and so forth are to be deemed to have been paid out of such capital of the testator's estate as will be sufficient for the purpose, when to that capital is added interest on that capital from the date of death to the date of payment of the legacy or debt, or whatever it may have been, interest having been calculated at the average rate of interest earned by the testator's estate during the relevant period.[2]

Example

A testator died on 5 October 1987. The administration was completed on 5 April 1989. The net value of the estate as at date of death was £10,000. The gross income arising over the full administration period was £1,500. Funeral expenses of £1,500 were paid on 5 April 1988. The following is the apportionment of the funeral expenses between the life tenant and the remainderman:

	£	£
Value of residue at date of death		10,000
Proportion of residuary income arising up to date of payment of funeral expenses (1,500 x $^1/_3$)	500	
Less income tax @ 35%	175	325
		10,325
Proportion of expenses applicable to capital $\frac{10,000 \times 1,500}{10,325}$		1,453
Proportion of expenses applicable to income $\frac{325 \times 1,500}{10,325}$		47
		1,500

A similar apportionment should be made for all other relevant debts and expenses payments. The theoretical and equitable justification for the application of the rule can lead to practical problems.

The dicta quoted is qualified by an earlier decision[3] which provides that it is the net income of the estate after deduction of tax that must be taken into consideration.

Example

A, a testator, left his full estate, which included let property, to his widow for life with remainder over to his children equally. A, arising from a dispute, had failed to meet mortgage payments due for a number of years. The mortgagee obtained a court decree for £2,000 against the estate nine months after the date of death. The property was valued at £40,000 for capital acquisitions tax purposes and the annual rental was £4,000. The income tax basic rate was 25%.

Apportionment of liability

Average rate of net income arising

$$\frac{4,000 - 1,000}{40,000} = 7.5\%$$

Charge on life tenant

$$2,000 \times \frac{15}{200} \times \frac{9}{12} = £113$$

71

The rule in *Allhusen v Whittel* can be excluded by appropriate provisions in a will. The rule is impossible to apply in practice for small liabilities. Its use is generally confined to debts and liabilities which will give rise to worthwhile benefits to the residuary legatee after the cost of making the apportionment have been met.

References

1   (1867) 16 LT 695.
2   *Corbett v CIR* 21 TC 449; [1937] 4 All ER 700. The direct point at issue in this case concerned whether payments made to a residuary legatee before the date of the ascertainment of the residue were liable to tax when made in the hands of the legatee. The Court of Appeal unanimously held they were not. Subsequently, legislation was enacted both in the United Kingdom and Ireland to counter the effect of this decision, see ITA 1967 Pt XXIX.
3   *In re Oldham* [1925] Ch D 75, 132 LT 788.

Apportionment of income

5.18 While the rule in *Allhusen v Whittel* is concerned with the apportionment of debts and liabilities arising from the creation of successive interests in a residue it may also be necessary to apportion income accrued up to the date of a death but paid afterwards.

Prior to the enactment of the Apportionment Act 1870 interest on money lent was apportioned on a time basis under the common law, but this did not apply to rents or other periodic payments in the nature of income. The Apportionment Act provided that rents, annuities, dividends and similar payments were to be regarded as arising on a day-to-day accrual basis. The apportionment of dividends, however, is to be made by reference to the basis or accounting period over which the income accrued rather than by reference to the date of payment.

Income accrued prior to a testator's death but paid afterwards forms part of the income of his estate. Thus, income paid to a deceased person's estate cannot arise to the holder of a limited interest unless the deceased person's will contained a provision to exclude the effects of the Apportionment Act.[1, 2]

Example

A, who died on 31 December 1990, left a life interest of the ordinary shareholding he had held in the family private company to his brother. Dividends for the company's year to 31st March 1991 were paid as follows:

	Distribution £	Tax credit £
Interim dividend 30 September 1990	700	300
Final dividend 30 June 1991	1,050	450
	1,750	750
Apportionment to estate of A		
(three quarters of accrual period)	1,387	562
Less received by A	700	300
Estate income	687	262

In practice, for income tax purposes, the income apportionment rules are ignored other than for the purposes of administration accounts submitted to the Revenue.

References
1 *CIR v Henderson's Executors* 16 TC 282.
2 *Stewart's Executors v CIR* 33 TC 184. *Wood v Owen* 23 TC 541, [1941] KB 92.

Mortgaged property

5.19 Where an individual holds a life interest in mortgaged property and the mortgage is not paid off, or there are arrears of mortgage payments, the property will normally be sold. If the sale proceeds are less than the outstanding principal and interest the interest arrears are apportioned between the owner of the property and the holder of the life interest in the property.[1]

Example

A, a testator, provided in his will that his widow B was to receive the interest arising on his loan of £20,000 to D, which was secured on mortgaged business premises. The mortgagor D, due a changing population pattern, was obliged to give up his business leaving all the principal unpaid and interest arrears of £4,000, of which £2,000 accrued after the death of A. The premises were taken over against the unpaid liabilities and were subsequently sold for £18,000.

Amount from sale due to life tenant B

$$18,000 \times \frac{2,000}{20,000} = £1,800$$

Amount of capital available for re-investment by trustees £16,200 (£18,000 - £1,800) B, during her lifetime, will be entitled to the income arising on the re-invested capital.

References
1 *Re Atkinson* [1904] 2 Ch 160.

Future interest in personal property of a wasting nature

5.20 The rule in *Howe v Earl of Dartmouth*[1] is concerned with reversionary interests in personal property (including leaseholds)[2] which is of a wasting[3] or hazardous nature. The rule aims to preserve the relative value of successive limited and absolute interests, to ensure that the value of the remainderman's interest is not eroded.

The executors/trustees must dispose of the property and re-invest the proceeds in authorised securities. Until this is done the life tenant is entitled to interest at 4% (this rate was used in an English case in 1962)[4] on the value of the property as at date of death. After the conversion the life tenant is entitled to the full income arising on the authorised investments. The rule does not apply to real property and its effect can be avoided by the expression of a contrary intention in a testator's will.

References
1 [1802] 7 Ves 137.
2 *In Re Trollope's Will Trusts* [1927] 1 Ch 596 interpreting the Law of Property Act 1925 s 28(2), it was decided under English law that the rule no longer applied to leasehold property.
3 Mining or other shares dealing with the extraction or the working of natural resources pay substantial dividends for a limited period when there is maximum production with a later tailing off of profits and the consequent diminution in the value of the shares.
4 Judge Keane in *Equity and the Law of Trusts in Ireland* (Butterworth) considers that if a case comes before the Irish Courts there seems to be no reason why the current rate of interest payable on judgment debts should not be applied.

Successive limited and future interests in personal property

5.21 The rule in *Earl of Chesterfield's Trust's*[1] sets out the procedure to be used when valuing (at the date of the testator's death) a future interest in personal property which only comes into possession at the end of a limited interest, for example, a life assurance policy on the life of another person.

In contrast with the *Howe v Lord Dartmouth* rule, this rule is designed to protect the limited interest holder. The rule requires the future interest to be valued as a capital sum, which invested at 4% compound interest[2] (after deduction of income tax) will produce the necessary income.

Example

A in 1989 loaned £12,000 to his brother B which was to be interest-free for a period of five years and subsequently subject to an 8% annual charge pending repayment of the principal after a further 10 years. A died in 1990 creating a life interest in the loan, or any re-investment of the capital sum, in favour of his widow. The loan was taken over by an investment company in 1992 in return for a payment of £10,000 to the trustees of A's estate.

Apportionment of interests[3]	£
Applicable to capital	
Sum required to be invested for 2 years @ 8%	
compound interest added yearly to provide £10,000	8,873
Payable to life tenant as income	1,427
	10,000

The life tenant will continue to benefit from the income arising on the re-investment of the capital in authorised securities.

References
1 [1883] 24 Ch 643.
2 See note 4 above concerning the rate of interest chargeable.
3 An 8% interest rate has been taken as appropriate which is the deferred rate chargeable on the loan.

Successive limited and absolute interest subject to charge

5.22 The rule in *Perkins v Brown*[1] applies where an obligation by a settlor while alive continues after his death and is charged on successive limited and absolute interests. The rule calculates the charge as being equivalent to a capital sum, if invested @ 4% simple interest from the date of death to the due date of payment of the annuity, amounts to the payment. The balance is referable to income. Thus the capital percentage after three years will be 89.3% calculated as follows:

$$X + (X \times \frac{4}{100} \times 3) = 100$$

where X is the capital sum to be invested @ 4%.

Example

A testator who died on 5 April 1990, charged an annuity of £500 against the residue of his estate which was left in successive limited and remainder interests. A payment of the annuity was due on 5 April 1992. The part apportionable to capital is £462.96 as follows:

Amount payable (X) + (X x rate of interest) x time = Annuity

$$\frac{X + (X \times 4)2}{100} = 500$$

$$X = £462.96$$

The rate of interest applied in a later case [2] was 3.5%.

References
1 [1907] 2 Ch 596.
2 *Re Poyser London v Poyser* [1908-1910] All ER 374.

Leasehold property

5.23 Where leasehold property is taken under a will in successive life and absolute interests any charge for maintenance or repairs of the property is allocated completely against the interest of the remainderman.[1] Such charges need to be distinguished from current liabilities such as rates, income tax and management charges which are charged on the life tenant's interest as they fall due.

References
1 *Brereton v Day* [1895] IR 518.

Other apportionment rules

5.24 The proceeds of the sale of investments made cum-dividend are regarded as wholly allocated to capital.[1] However, for Irish income tax purposes where securities (not including shares in a company) are held for a period of less than two years the cum-dividend element of the disposal is deemed to accrue from day-to-day as income of the disponer.[2]

Arrears of interest on cumulative preference shares are regarded as income arising on the date of payment.[3]

Dividends paid out of the capital profits of a company are income.[4]

Bonus shares of a company issued as authorised by the Articles are regarded under the rules of equity as being wholly on capital account on the basis that the property of the company is not reduced in value. On the other hand if a company has no authorised power to issue bonus shares any such issue is regarded as being in lieu of cash and therefore income.[5]

The value of all bonus shares issued by a company other than for consideration is Sch F income for income tax purposes.[6]

References

1   *Re McLaren's Settlement Trusts* [1954] All ER 414.
2   FA 1984 s 29.
3   *Re Walkey* [1920] 2 Ch 205.
4   CTA 1976 s 84(2)(*a*); *Re Kleinworth* [1951] Ch 860.
5   *Hill v Permanent Trustee Co of New South Wales* [1930] AC 720.
6   CTA 1976 ss 84(2)(*b*) and 86.

Part 3

Charities and imperfect trusts

Chapter 6

Nature of a legal charity

Meaning of charity

Statute of Charitable Uses 1601

6.01 In popular language the word "charity", in its widest sense, refers to a disposition of goodwill towards mankind generally and in a more restricted sense, relief of the poor. Arising from decisions of the courts the term has also acquired a technical meaning:

> Of all the words in the English language bearing a popular as well as a legal significance I am not sure that there is one which more unmistakably has a technical meaning in the strictest sense of the term, that is a meaning clear and distinct, peculiar to the law as understood and administered in this country, and not depending upon or co-terminous with the popular or vulgar use of the word.[1]

> This Court has adopted a very narrow construction in deciding what is deemed to be a charitable purpose. It must be either one of those purposes denominated charitable in the statute of Elizabeth, or one of such purpose as the Court construes to be charitable by analogy to those mentioned in that statute.[2]

The statute of Elizabeth — the Statute of Charitable Uses 1601 — was enacted in England to reform abuses arising by way of fraud, breaches of trust, negligence etc in connection with charitable activities. The Statute's preamble lists the following as charitable purposes:

> Relief of aged; impotent and poor people; maintenance of sick and maimed soldiers and mariners; maintenance of schools of learning, free schools and scholars in universities; repairs of bridges, ports, havens, causeways, churches, sea-banks and highways; education and preferment of orphans; relief, stock or maintenance of houses of correction; marriages of poor maids; support, aid and help of young tradesmen, handicraftsmen and persons decayed; relief or redemption of prisoners or captives; aid or ease of any poor inhabitants concerning payment of taxes. [3]

References
1   Lord MacNaghten in *Special Commissioners of Income Tax v Pemsel* 3 TC 53; [1891] AC 531.
2   Lord Langdale in *Kendall v Granger* [1842] Beav 300.
3   43 Eliz 1 c 4.

Statute of Charitable Uses (Ireland) 1634

6.02 The Statute of Charitable Uses 1601 has historically been construed by the English Courts in a very liberal spirit and many purposes not expressly mentioned therein have been held as charitable by coming with its "spirit and intendment".[1]

That statute did not apply in Ireland but in 1634, when the Earl of Wentworth was Lord Deputy, the separate Irish Parliament passed the Statute of Charitable Uses (Ireland) which contains very similar provisions.[2] This statute ("an act for the maintenance and execution of pious uses") was directed against Archbishops and Bishops of the Established Church and it created procedures whereby these dignitaries might be compelled to answer for any misappropriation of charitable funds entrusted to them. The Act applied to "lawful and charitable uses warranted by the laws in this realm now established and in force" and like its English counterpart it listed several specific objects which were regarded as charitable:

> The erection, maintenance or support of any college, school, lecturer in divinity, or in any of the liberal arts or sciences; the relief or maintenance of any manner of poor, succourless, distressed or impotent persons; the building, re-edifing or maintaining in repair any church, college, school or hospital; the maintenance of any minister and preacher of the Holy Word of God; and the erection, building, maintenance or repair of any bridges, causeways, cashes, paces and highways within the realm, or for any other like lawful charitable use and uses, warranted by laws established and in force.

References
1   *Morice v Bishop* of Durham [1805] 9 Ves 355.
2   10 Car I sess 3 CI.

6.03 The Irish statute was elaborately analysed by the courts:

> I must consider the Statute of Charles as a legislative enactment upon the pattern of 43 Eliz and that whatever validity the 43 Eliz gave, by way of recognition to cases of charitable uses, and consequently to the inherent jurisdiction of Courts of Equity in England, the same will be available and is equally true in this country in the case of the Statute of Charles.[1]

The consequence of this decision has been that the legal and technical meaning of the term "charity" is considered to be almost identical in Ireland and the UK. There have inevitably been some changes since 1922. In the United Kingdom, special legislation was introduced in 1958 to cover the provision of certain

public recreational facilities (see 1.19). On the other hand, the rigid interpretation by the English courts that the advancement of religion was invariably
charitable did not find favour with the Irish courts (see 1.19).

References
1   Sir E Sugden, Lord Chancellor, in *Incorporated Law Society v Richards*, 1 Dr and War 258; 4 Ir Eq
     177.

Legal definitions of a charity

6.04 One of the earliest attempts to define a legal charity [1] declared that the
concept related to:

> a gift to a general public use which extends to the poor as well as the rich [1]

Later judgments stated:

> It is probably impossible to define what is a charitable bequest; and it is certainly not
> advisable to attempt to do so. We must always go back to the analogy of the Statute, which
> furnishes the only test that can be applied, to see whether a gift is charitable or not.[2]

> The method employed by the Court is to consider the enumeration of charities in the
> statute of Elizabeth, bearing in mind that the enumeration is not exhaustive. Institutions
> whose objects are analogous to those mentioned in the Statute are admitted to be chari-
> ties and, again, institutions which are analogous to those already admitted by reported
> decisions are held to be charities. The pursuit of these analogies obviously requires
> caution and circumspection. After all the best that can be done is to consider each case,
> as it arises, upon its own special circumstances.[3]

The courts have also held[4] that it might be unproductive to have a definition for
the term "charity" as such a definition might form the basis for a set of further
artificial distinctions.

References
1   Lord Camden in *Jones v Williams* Amb 651.
2   Rigby L J in *Re Nottage (Jones v Palmer)* [1895] 2 Ch D 549.
3   Chitty J in *Cross v London Antivivisection Society* [1895] 2 Ch 501.
4   *Smith v Incorporated Council of Law Reporting for England and Wales* 6 TC 477; [1914] 3 KB 25;
     see also dicta of Viscount Simmons in *Baddeley v CIR* [1955] AC 572 at p 627.

Public benefit

6.05 In the late 1800s, it was held [1] that a charity must (in the mind of the
settlor) benefit the public, in other words the benefit must be one which the
founder believes to be of public (non-private) advantage and this belief must
be rational and not contrary either to the general law of the land or to the
principles of morality. This doctrine of a subjective test has not been
supported by more recent court decisions.

If a testator by stating that a trust was beneficial to the public could establish that fact, trusts might be established in perpetuity for all kinds of fantastic (though not unlawful) objects. The question whether a gift was, or might be, operative for the public benefit was a question to be answered by the Court by forming an opinion upon the evidence before it. [2]

6.06 In determining whether a gift is charitable the state of mind which influenced the donor to make a gift is wholly immaterial.

A testator's motive may have been quite other than of sincere charity. [3]

A gift, of which the necessary result is altruistic public benefit, does not fail to be charitable because it originates in an egoistic motive. In plain English, if nothing could be charitable which was done with the motive of obtaining a personal benefit, here or hereafter, few charitable acts could stand the test, and unless we hold that a self-interested motive is necessarily uncharitable we cannot deprive public benefits of a charitable character by inquiring into the motive which dictated them. [4]

Furthermore, the source of a gift is irrelevant in determining whether it is charitable. Whether a gift is funded by public or private finance is also irrelevant.

References
1 Fitzgibbon L J in *Webb v Oldfield* [1898] IR 431.
2 Russell J in *In Re Hummelenberg* [1923] 1 Ch 237.
3 Porter M R in *Perry v Twomey* 2 LRI 481.
4 Fitzgibbon L J in *Attorney General v Hall* [1897] 2 IR 426.

Establishment

6.07 To be officially recognised, a charity must be legally established within the State.[1] This requirement can give rise to problems because many charitable bodies, including both religious and lay organisations, increasingly have international relationships and affiliations. The Revenue Commissioners will recognise for income tax purposes the existence of a branch of a foreign organisation as charitable, if it is controlled in respect of its Irish activities, including financial management, wholly within the State.

Charitable objects

Introduction

6.08 The modern classification of charitable objects can be summarised as follows:

Charity in its legal sense comprises four principal divisions; trusts for the relief of poverty; trusts for the advancement of education; trusts for the advancement of religion; and trusts for other purposes beneficial to the community not falling under any of the preceding heads.[2]

References

1 *Gull v CIR* [1937] 4 AER 290; 21 TC 374; *Dreyfus (Camille and Henry) Foundation Inc. v CIR* 36 TC 126; [1956] AC 391.

2 Lord MacNaghten in *Special Commissioners of Income Tax v Pemsel* 3 TC 53; [1891] AC 531; a similar classification was earlier proposed by Sir S Romilly in *Morice v Bishop of Durham* 10 Ves 532.

Charitable trusts

6.09 A charitable trust is confined to public objects and is not applicable to private gifts. Additionally, such trusts must not provide for a resulting trust in favour of the settlor or his estate in the event of a failure of the objects. Most importantly, in contrast to other trusts, if the object of a charitable trust ceases to exist, under the cy-pres rule new objects, conforming as far as possible to the original intentions of the settlor, may substituted to continue the trust.

A charitable *trust*, except where it relates exclusively to the relief of poverty or is concerned with bequests for the benefit of a local area, must not be restricted in its application. Therefore the public must be entitled to benefit under the terms of the trust although they need not necessarily do so. A gift for the benefit of a local area must be made in general terms. If the objects are specific such a gift should not include any distinct non-charitable purposes.[1] Parochial endowments and bequests, like gifts for the benefit of a local area, should be made in general terms, and to qualify as charitable such gifts should not include non-charitable purposes.[2]

References

1 See Charities Act 1961 s 49 concerning the construction of gifts for mixed purposes.

2 *Morrow v McConville* [1889] 11 LRI 236; *Brannigan v Murphy* [1896] IR 418.

Public benefit

6.10 It is for the courts to determine whether a trust qualifies as charitable because it provides a public benefit. Thus, a trust for the benefit of children of over 100,000 employees (and past employees) of the British American Tobacco Co Ltd was held not to be constituted for public purposes.[1]

References

1 *Oppenheim v Tobacco Securities Trust Co Ltd* [1951] AC 297; following an earlier Court of Appeal decision in the case of *Compton, Powell v Compton* [1945] 1 All ER 198; 1945 Ch 123 where it was decided that a trust for the descendants of three named persons was not charitable.

Lord Greene, MR also declared that many "poor relations" cases had been decided at a time when the requirement for gifts to have a public character had not been clearly laid down. If such cases were now to come before the courts for the first time they would very likely be held to be invalid.

Lord Greene went on to concede, however, that it was too late to overrule existing "poor relations" precedents but added that they should be regarded as anomalous and not used to widen the meaning of charitable trusts generally.

Religious bodies

6.11 The House of Lords confirmed its technical and restricted interpretation of public purposes when in 1955 it refused to approve income tax exemption on charitable grounds for trusts which were designed to promote the moral, social and physical well-being of members or potential members of the Methodist Church in London suburbia.[1] This decision threw doubts on the status of a number of organisations with physical or moral social objects and caused the enactment of legislation[2] to validate the status of such organisations. While no corresponding legislation has been approved by the Oireachtas some gifts for mixed purposes may be relieved.[3] Bodies founded exclusively for the promotion of amateur games are exempt from income tax.[4]

References
1   *Baddeley v CIR* [1955] AC 572.
2   UK Recreational Charities Act 1958.
3   Charities Act 1961 s 49.
4   ITA 1967 s 349.

Friendly societies

6.12 Gifts to societies or institutions such as friendly societies,[1] trade unions,[2] credit unions[3] and mutual benefit societies which have as their *sole* object the private advantage of their members are not charitable but such bodies may have separate and identifiable funds for the relief of indigent or poor members of such organisations. Gifts for such purposes could therefore be classed as charitable.[4]

References
1   Both registered and unregistered friendly societies receive limited exemption from income tax: ITA 1967 s 335.
2   Trade unions who are restricted from assuring any person for a sum in excess of £2,000 or paying an annuity of more than £750, are exempt from income tax on certain interest and dividend income: ITA 1967 s 336.
3   Credit Unions registered under the Industrial and Provident Societies Acts 1893 to 1971 are exempt from income tax: FA 1972 s 43.
4   *Spiller v Maude* 32 Ch D 158; *In re Buck* [1896] 2 Ch 727; *In re Lacey* [1899] 2 Ch 149.

Illegal gifts

6.13 Where the objective of a gift is illegal, or contrary to public policy, the gift will not be upheld by the courts. Where only some of the objects are illegal, reference must be made to the terms of the trust. If all the objects are illegal the gift is void. If a distinction can be made between the legal and illegal objects the gift must also be apportionable between the legal and illegal objects.[1] A bequest for the purpose of paying fines of convicted persons was held to be void on the grounds that it would operate to encourage the commission of crime.[2]

References
1 *Chapman v Brown* [1801] 6 Ves 404.
2 *Thrupp v Collett* 26 Beav 125.

The doctrine of cy-pres

Intentions of the donor

6.14 Where a donor intends to donate property to charity by way of a trust, and the terms of the trust do not specify (or are unclear) how the property is to be applied, the trust is still valid and the court will attempt to carry out the donor's intentions as closely as possible. This is known as the doctrine of cy-pres:

> It is a doctrine merely for effectuating the intention, according to which, when it is once ascertained that the object of a gift is charity, but that the particular mode in which the testator intended to carry it out fails, from any cause, the court will not permit the benevolent intention of the testator to be defeated, but will apply the fund to some other charitable object, selected with a careful regard to the intention of the testator, and approaching as nearly as possible to what appears to have been his wish. In discovering this wish, of course, the court will consider the whole of the will and hold the nature of any other bequests he may have made a good key to his intentions.[1]

> The law of cy-pres requires the Court to substitute a practical plan for a charity as near as may be to the donor's own wishes, where these wishes, as formulated by the donor, cannot be carried out provided the will discloses a "general charitable intention.[2]

6.15 The doctrine of cy-pres also applies to charitable objects which have ceased to exist but which had originally been funded by the State.[3]

References
1 Napier L C in *Re Evans' Charities* 10 Ir Ch R 271.
2 Judge Gavin Duffy in *Re Ffrench* [1941] IR 49.
3 *Re Royal Kilmainham Hospital* [1966] IR 451.

Failure of the objects

6.16 The cy-pres rule is subject to any expressed wishes of the donor. Therefore, if it is clear that the donor wishes to exclusively benefit one charitable object and this object fails the cy-pres rule does not apply.

Thus where a testator bequeathed a sum of £200 in support of the Cork Female Orphan Society whose activities had been taken over by the Masonic

Female Orphan School before the date of the will the application of the cy-pres rule was refused by the court.[1]

Where a gift is made to a specific charitable object and this object ceases to exist before the gift becomes operative (ie before the death of a testator) the gift lapses and the cy-pres rule cannot be invoked to validate the gift.

Thus, a legacy to St Thomas's Seminary Westminster which had closed during the testator's lifetime was regarded as lapsed.[2]

References
1   *Makeown v Ardagh* IR 10 Eq 405; the earlier decisions in *Clarke v Taylor* 1 Dr 642 and *Russell v Kellett* 3 Sm and G 264 were followed.
2   [1895] 1 Ch 19.

Mis-description of the objects

6.17 A distinction must be made between circumstance where the original objects no longer exist (as in the preceding paragraphs) and circumstance where the objects are merely mis-described.

The cy-pres rule was applied in a case where a legacy to found a scholarship at Queen's College Belfast was made over in favour of its academic successor, the Queen's University Belfast, even though the later body did not exist at the date of the relevant will. [1]

Similarly a legacy to the Patagonian Chilean and Peruvian Missionary Society, a body which never existed, was applied cy-pres in favour of the South American Missionary Society. [2]

References
1   *Re Magrath* [1913] 2 Ch 331.
2   *In Re Kilvert's Trusts* LR 7 Ch 170; *In Re Geary's Trusts* 25 LRI 171; *In Re Raven* [1915] Ch 673.

Cy-pres rule applied by court

6.18 If a charitable object ceases to exist in the interval between the date of entitlement and the date the gift is available for payment the cy-pres rule can be invoked by the courts, but the gift must be of a general charitable nature. [1]

6.19 Thus where a testator devised a castle to the Irish nation to be used as a home for aged and infirm persons, and the State authorities were satisfied that the testamentary objects were impractical due to a lack of funds, the Attorney-General requested the High Court to have the property applied cy-pres (to an equivalent charity other than the State). This was refused on the grounds that the charitable objects were subordinate to the paramount intention of the testator to provide for the conservation of the castle.

References
1   *Re Slevin* [1891] 2 Ch 236; *Re Wokingham Fire Brigade Trusts* [1951] Ch 373.
2   *Re Ffrench* [1941] IR 49 HC.

When cy-pres rule may be applied

6.20 The original purposes of a charitable gift may be altered to allow property to be applied cy-pres in the following circumstances:

(*a*)   where the original purposes, in whole or in part:
   (i)   *have been fulfilled* as far as may be; or
   (ii)   *cannot be carried out*, or cannot be carried out according to the directions given and to the spirit of the gift; or

(*b*)   where the original purposes provide a use for *part only* of the property available by virtue of the gift; or

(*c*)   where *the property* available by virtue *of the gift and other property* applicable for similar purposes *can be* more effectively *used in conjunction*, and to that end can suitably, regard being had to the spirit of the gift, be made applicable to common purposes; or

(*d*)   where the original purposes were laid down by reference to *an area which* then was but *has since ceased to be a unit* for some other purpose, or by reference to *a class of persons* or to an area which has for any reason *since ceased*, either *to be suitable*, regard being had to the spirit of the gift, *or to be practical* in administering the gift; or

(*e*)   where the original purposes, in whole or in part, have, since they were laid down:
   (i)   been *adequately provided for* by other means; or
   (ii)   *ceased*, as being useless or harmful to the community or for other reasons, to be in law charitable; or
   (iii) ceased in any other way to provide a suitable and effective method of using the property available by virtue of the gift, regard being had to the spirit of the gift. [1]

Application of cy-pres rule to non-charitable gifts

6.21 While the application of the doctrine of cy-pres has traditionally been restricted to gifts of a general charitable nature the courts may apply the rule to both specific charitable or non-charitable gifts where property belongs: [2]

(*a*)   to a donor who, after such advertisements and enquiries as are reasonable, cannot be identified or cannot be found; or

(*b*)   to a donor who has executed a written disclaimer of his right to have the property returned.

In these circumstances, the court must have regard to the wishes of the trustees or other persons in charge of the property.[3]

Application of cy-pres rule by the Commissioners of Charitable Donations and Bequests

6.22 The Commissioners of Charitable Donations and Bequests have general powers to apply property cy-pres where the value does not exceed £25,000.[4]

References
1   Charities Act 1961 s 47(1).
2   Charities Act 1961 s 48(1).
3   The Commissioners of Charitable Donations and Bequests have a limited power to operate the cy-pres rule within the Charities Act 1961 s 48 where the value does not exceed £1,000. Special rules apply for land.
4   Charities Act 1961 s 29. Special rules apply in determining land and annuity values.

Chapter 7

Charitable purposes

The relief of poverty

Introduction

7.01 Gifts for the relief of poverty are ɔgarded as charitable.[1] Thus, the following gifts have been held to be charitable:

    (*a*)   gifts for the relief of the poor of a particular class or section of the community, for example, the poor of a parish or district;[2]

    (*b*)   gifts for the poor tenantry of a particular estate;[3]

    (*c*)   gifts for the poor of a town;[4]

    (*d*)   gifts for poor emigrants.[5]

    (*e*)   the pensioning off of old and worn-out clerks of a particular firm;[6]

    (*f*)   the provision of pensions payable to poor employees of a company;[7]

    (*g*)   the relief of indigent bachelors or widowers "who have shown practised sympathy in the pursuits of science in any of its branches"; [8]and

    (*h*)   the maintenance of a temporary house of residence for ladies of humble means.[9]

Even where no express reference is made to poverty in a gift an intention to relieve destitution is often inferred from the terms. Thus, a bequest to the "widows and orphans of the parish of L" was held to be charitable on the grounds that the wording necessarily implied that it was intended for the benefit of such widows and orphans as were suffering from privation.[10]

Similarly, bequests for the "maintenance, support, education or otherwise for the benefit of blind persons" resident in a certain district[11] and for "twenty aged widows and spinsters of the parish of P"[12] have been upheld as charitable by implying the relief of poverty. In the latter case the court was of the opinion that, although widows and spinsters were not specifically mentioned in the Preamble to the Statute of Charitable Uses 1601 the word "aged" would, if the matter depended on the Statute alone, have been sufficient to constitute the gift charitable.

A gift to the "poorest" of a particular class will not be held charitable unless it can be construed as a gift to those who are literally poor, and not merely to the least wealthy of a wealthy class.[13]

References

1   *Kenny v Attorney-General* 11 LRI 253; *In Re Darling* [1896] 1 Ch 50.
2   *Dillon v Reilly* IR 10 Eq 152; *In Re Swain* [1905] 1 Ch 669.
3   *Bristow v Bristow* 5 Beav 289. Compare *Browne v King* 17 LRI 448 where a bequest to a clergyman to apply income from property to children of tenants under the age of 12 years without any reference to material circumstances was held not to be charitable.
4   *Russell v Kellett* [1855] 3 Sm and G 264.
5   *Barclay v Maskelyne* 4 Jur (NS) 1298.
6   *In Re Gosling* 48 WR 300.
7   *Dingle v Turner* [1972] 1 All ER 878.
8   *Weir v Crum Brown* [1908] AC 162. Compare *In Re Cullimore's Trusts* [1891] 27 LRI 18 where a gift to widows who were resident on an estate for five years was not regarded as charitable.
9   *In Re Gordon* [1914] 1 Ch 661; see also *Clark v Anderson* [1904] KB 645, 5 TC 48.
10   *Attorney-General v Comber* 2 S and St 23. *In Re Dudgeon* 12 TLR 465.
11   *In Re Elliott* 102 LT 528.
12   *Thompson v Corby* 27 Beav 649.
13   *Attorney-General v Duke of Northumberland* 7 Ch D 745.

Poor relations

7.02 To be regarded as charitable, a *trust* must be for the benefit of the public, and not the donor's relations. A bequest for the benefit of a testator's "poor relations" does not benefit the public, but where such a bequest was in the nature of a perpetuity it was, in earlier times, accepted as charitable.[1]

More recently, however the English courts have held that where the qualification of a beneficiary was based generally on the relationship with the settlor the essential requirement that the charitable trust be for the benefit of the public was not present.[2]

Nevertheless, Irish legislation appears to uphold the decision in an old English case that a bequest to the poor, with a preference for the poor relatives of the testator, is charitable.[3]

References

1   *White v White* 7 Ves 423. *Gillam v Taylor* LR 16 Eq 581.
2   *Re Compton* [1945] 1 All ER 198; [1945] Ch 123. The decision in *Re Compton* was approved by the House of Lords in *Oppenheimer v Tobacco Securities Trust* [1951] AC 297, 1951 1 All ER 31.
3   Charities Act 1961 s 49; *Waldo v Caley*, 16 Ves 206.

Working classes

7.03 A gift to provide assistance for the holiday expenses of work people has been held not to be charitable.[1] Similarly, a gift for the "working classes" was not regarded as charitable because there was no limitation to poor people.[2] A hostel providing accommodation for persons of modest means met the requirement of relief of poverty and was regarded as charitable.[3] Similarly, a trust to provide a holiday home for members of the drapery trade at modest fees was held to be charitable.[4]

References
1   *In Re Drummond* [1914] Ch 90 30 TLR 429. This decision was quoted with approval in *In Re Compton* (see 7.02).
2   *Re Sander's Will Trust* [1954] Ch 265.
3   *Re Niyazi's Will Trust* [1978] 1 WLR 910.
4   *CIR v Roberts Marine Mansions Trustees*, 11 TC 335.

Friendly societies

7.04 A gift to a friendly society will be regarded as charitable if, under the rules of the society members to be recipients of the benefits must be poor in order to qualify for such benefits arising. Thus, a bequest to a society, the objects of which were the relief of orphan children of members, the supplying of medical assistance to poor sick members, the granting of annuities to poor members disabled by age or accident and the provision of accommodation for the poor at low rents were held to be charitable,[1] but if poverty is not a requirement the gift will not qualify as charitable.[2]

Charitable institutions

7.05 The establishment, maintenance and support of institutions such as hospitals, dispensaries, asylums, orphanages and night shelters have all been regarded as charitable.

In the case of the Mater Hospital, Dublin, where private fee-paying patients were cared for in an annex, it was held, although the hospital and the annex were administered as a joint undertaking, that the profits from the private patients were separate and were not charitable.[3]

A charity engaged in helping the relatives and survivors of the first and second world wars was regarded as trading and taxable on the profits of weekly dances.[4]

References
1   *Spiller v Maude* 32 Ch D 158; *Pearse v Pattison*, 32 Ch D 154. *In Re Buck* [1896] 2 Ch 727 and *In Re Sutton* [1901] 2 Ch 198.
2   *In Re Clarke's Trusts* 1 Ch D 497; *Cunnack v Edwards* [1896] 2 Ch 697.
3   *Davis v Superioress, Mater Misericordiae Hospital* [1933] IR 480; 2 ITC 1; see also *Governors of Rotunda Hospital v Coman* [1921] 1 AC 1; 7 TC 51.
4   *CIR v British Legion Peterhead Branch* 35 TC 509.

The advancement of education

7.06 The advancement of education is generally regarded as being for charitable purposes, and a bequest to trustees to be applied at their discretion "for the benefit, advancement and propagation of education and learning in any part of the world" was held to be charitable.[1]

References
1   *Whicker v Hume* 7 HLC 124.

Schools and scholarships

7.07 Bequests for the building, maintenance or endowment of schools,[1] or for the foundation or augmentation of fellowships, lectureships or scholarships are charitable.[2]

It is not essential that the educational establishment should be exclusively (or mainly) for the benefit of the poor.[3] Accordingly, bequests for the education of daughters of missionaries[4] and the sons of gentlemen[5] have both been accepted as charitable.

Nevertheless, in the case of a charitable trust, it is essential that the beneficiaries of the trust are clearly defined (see 2.09). Thus, a bequest of property "to be divided equally for the education of friends' children" was held not to be charitable.[6] Similarly, a trust created under a testator's will to come into force on the death of his wife, which provided for financial assistance to be given to the sons and daughters and male descendants of the testator's brother to enable them to attain professional qualifications, was regarded as being too narrow in its objects to be charitable. While the testator's motive may have been charitable, because the expressed intention was to benefit specific individuals there was no "public" purpose.[7]

References
1   *Attorney-General v Williams* 4 Bro CC 525; *Smith v Kerr* [1902] 1 Ch 744.
2   *Yates v University College London* 7 HLR 438; *In Re Magrath* [1913] 2 Ch 331.
3   *R v Special Commissioners* (ex parte University College of North Wales) 5 TC 408.
4   *German v Chapman* 7 Ch D 271.
5   *Attorney-General v Lonsdale* 1 Sim 105.
6   *Walshe v Downey* 43 ILTR 52.
7   *Re McEnery's Estate* [1941] 1 IR 323; see also *Attorney-General v Sidney Sussex College* LR 4 Ch 722; *Braund v Devon* LR 3 Ch 800; *In re Lavelle* [1914] 1 IR 194.

Education in particular subjects

7.08 Bequests for the promotion of education in particular subjects, for example:

(*a*) the advancement and propagation of education in economic science,[1]

(*b*) the study of maladies and injuries in animals useful to man,[2]

(*c*) the promotion of art,[3]

(*d*) to assist students to complete their musical education,[4] or

(*e*) to award prizes for essays in particular subjects,[5]

have all been held to be charitable.

While education relating to political matters is generally considered to be a charitable purpose this is not the case where the subject to be studied is a particular party.[6]

References
1 *In Re Berridge* 63 LT 470.
2 *University of London v Yarrow* 23 Beav 159.
3 *In Re Allsop* 1 TLR 4.
4 *In Re Harrison* 31 TLR 398.
5 *Ferrer v St Catherine's College* LR 16 Eq 19.
6 *Bonar Law Memorial Trust v CIR* 17 TC 508.

Museums, galleries etc

7.09 Bequests to public educational institutions such as museums and art galleries are generally regarded as charitable.[1] Thus a gift to establish an art museum in a particular town was held to be charitable,[2] but a bequest for the purpose of establishing a museum in Shakespeare's house, which was private property, was refused charitable status.[3]

A bequest to the Royal College of Surgeons in Ireland was held not to be charitable because one of the main objects for which the College was incorporated was the promotion of the interests of those practising surgery.[4] This decision is in line with those given in a number of Scottish cases which have been described as "portal" or "gateway" cases whereby membership is necessary to practice a specific profession. Thus a claim for exemption from income tax by the Pharmaceutical Society of Ireland on the basis that it was a body established for charitable purposes only was unsuccessful.[5]

References
1 *Beaumont v Oliveria* LR 4 Ch 309; *Thomas v Howell* 18 Eq 159; *British Museum v White* 2 S and St 594.
2 *In Re Holburne*, 53 LT 212.
3 *Thompson v Shakespear* 1 De G F & J 391.
4 *Miley v Attorney-General* [1918] 1 IR 455.
5 *Pharmaceutical Society of Ireland v Special Commissioners of Income Tax* [1938] IR 202; 2 ITC 157.

Public libraries

7.10 Bequests for the benefit of public libraries are charitable where there is public access to the library, but not where such access is restricted. Thus, a devise "to the trustees for the time being of the Penzance Public Library and their successors for ever, for the use, benefit, maintenance and support of the said library" was held not to be charitable as the library in question, despite its descriptive name, had been established and was supported by subscriptions of private individuals, and existed solely for their benefit with the general public being excluded.[1]

A gift "for the promotion of art and industry in Ireland" was held to be charitable[2] but a gift "to encourage artistic pursuits or assist needy students in art" did not receive approval.[3] Similarly, a gift of income arising out of land to be used to encourage young artists by erecting artistic towers and statues on the settlor's estate was refused charitable status.[4]

References
1   *Carne v Long* [1860] 2 De G F & J 75; 45 Eq 550.
2   *Attorney-General v Bagot* 1 CLR 48.
3   *In Re Ogden* 25 TLR 382.
4   *McCaig v Glasgow University* [1907] SC 231.

Public benefit

7.11 For an educational bequest to be regarded as charitable, it must be for the benefit of the public. Thus, where a testator had bequeathed all his property to trustees upon trust to pay discretionary sums

> towards the support and education in Ireland of any Roman Catholic boy or boys, man or men of the name of O'Laverty or Laverty, O'Lafferty or Lafferty being within the ages of eleven years complete and twenty three years complete until such boy or man shall have obtained a trade or profession

and the trustees were given clear discretion to select recipients and discontinue payments to such recipients the gift was not held to be charitable:

> In my opinion a valid charitable trust might be created for the advancement of education for persons of a particular surname, either by endowment of, or a gift to a school or college, or by a gift in the present case to trustees, if sufficiently definite. But is this bequest of that character? Having regard to the wide discretion given to the trustees, it seems that it might be worked, and might have been intended to work, as a mere matter of private bounty. For example, might not the trustees acting within the wide power and discretion conferred upon them by the will, carry out the trust by employing a governess or tutor for some wealthy young Laverty. Such a purpose could not be regarded as charitable in the legal sense. [1]

References
1   *Laverty v Laverty* [1907] 1 IR 9.

Profit making bodies

7.12 A company or institution founded for educational purposes with the aim of making a profit will not be regarded as a charity, because the education is not for the public benefit (but rather, only those who can afford to pay the necessary fees).[1]

References
1   *Birkenhead School Ltd v Dring* 11 TC 273.

Mixed gifts

7.13 Where discretionary powers were vested in the directors of a private company to apply up to 60% of trust property in relieving poverty among former employees of the company (or its associated companies) or for the further education of employees, ex-employees and their families, the resulting trust was held to be void on perpetuity grounds (see 3.29). Other provisions in the same document which created an award of a travelling scholarship for commercial students and also the advancement of commercial education were held to have created a valid charitable trust.

Mixed gifts involving partial charitable objects for Irish purposes are deemed to be charitable by law.[2]

References
1   *Blackwell and Ors, Trustees of George Dexter Foundation v Commissioners of Inland Revenue* [1965] 3 All ER 529; 42 TC 524.
2   Charities Act 1961 s 49, see Appendix II.

Education and charity

7.14 In the leading case on the inter-relationship between education and charity a trust was set up to organise and provide facilities which would enable students at schools and universities to play Association Football or other games or sports and thereby assist with both physical education and mental development.

The trust was accepted as charitable because:

> both the legal conception of charity, and within it the educated masses ideas of education are not static but moving and changing. Both change with changes in ideas about social values.

The playing of games or enjoyment of amusement or competition, are not, of themselves, charitable unless the games are part of the routine or curriculum of an educational establishment.[2]

In a recent UK judgment[3] the House of Lords held that a bequest for "use in connection with the Sports Centre in North Berwick or some similar purpose in connection with sport "qualified as a charity by virtue of being in the interests of social welfare under the Recreational Charities Act 1958 s 1. There is no corresponding Irish legislation.

References
1   *Lord Hailsham in Commissioners of Inland Revenue v McMullan* [1980] 1 All ER 884; 54 TC 413.
2   *Re Mariette* [1914]-[1915] All ER 794; 31 TC 536.
3   *Guild v Commissioners of Inland Revenue*, 27 February 1992.

Student unions

7.15 Although a student union may carry on ancillary educational, social, cultural and even political activities, such bodies generally do not qualify for any charity exemption available to the institution to which they are attached.[1]

References
1   *London Hospital Medical College v CIR* [1976] 2 All ER 113; 51 TC 365.

The advancement of religion

Introduction

7.16 Before the Reformation gifts for the advancement of the Roman Catholic Religion were regarded as charitable. When the Protestant religion became the State religion the only trusts which, by reason of their object being the advancement of religion, would have been recognised as charitable were trusts for the advancement of that religion.[1]

When the various Toleration Acts[2] rendered the practice of other religions lawful, trusts for the advancement of the religions of Protestant Dissenters, Roman Catholics and Jews came to be upheld as charitable by the courts.

Like the concept of charity itself the legal meaning of religion in that context has given rise to a number of problems:

> What is religion here? It cannot be abstract religion for no human being can hold that or even conceive an abstract idea of religion. I suppose Pantheism is the nearest approach to it. Religion for the purpose of the Statute of Pious Uses must be the aggregate of all the lawful forms of religion conscientiously held by the Kings subjects, with the practised limitation that each of them must be held by a number of persons sufficient to make that particular form of religion an appreciable component of the religion of the State, and so entitle those who hold it to take a benefit for themselves as a benefit to the public.

The exclusiveness, the vagueness or the self-sufficiency of the principles held by particular creeds, whether they rest on dogma, on doctrine or on conscience, cannot exclude those who profess any lawful creed from the benefits of charitable gifts.[3]

References
1   Statute of Charitable Uses 1601 (43 Eliz 1 c 4).
2   The more important of the relevant statutes applying to Ireland were 6 Geo I, c 5 (1719: Dissenters); 57 Geo III, c 70 (1817: Unitarians); 10 Geo IV, c 7 (1829) and 9 and 10 Vict, c 59 (1846-1847: Roman Catholics) and also 18 and 19 Vict, c 86 (1855-1856: Jews).
3   Fitzgibbon L J in *O'Hanlon v Logue* [1906] 1 IR 247.

Male religious communities

7.17 Although the penal laws (see 1.14) that imposed severe restrictions on Catholics were gradually repealed in the early 1800s, even in 1829 the foundation and operation of monastic male communities in the United Kingdom (which included Ireland) was still prohibited.[1] These discriminatory provisions did not apply to any religious order, community or establishment consisting of females bound by religious or monastic vows.[2]

The restrictions only applied against the male communities *as a religious community* and did not restrict the conferring of charitable status on objects carried on by such communities (for example, nursing, education) which were in themselves independently charitable.[3]

It appears that the prohibitions against male religious communities continued to apply until 1920 when they became clearly inconsistent and incompatible with the law of the new independent state.[4]

References
1   Roman Catholic Relief Act 1829 ss 26, 28, 29 and 33 (10 G IV c 7).
2   Roman Catholic Relief Act 1829 s 37.
3   *Carbury v Cox* 3 I CH 231; *Roche v McDermott* [1901] 1 IR 294. See also *In Re Greene* [1914] 1 IR 305.
4   Government of Ireland Act 1920 s 5(2) which provided that any existing enactment by which any penalty, disadvantage or disability is imposed on account of religious belief or on a member of any religious order as such shall cease to have effect. This position was confirmed by the Supreme Court in *Re Byrne*, *Shaw v Attorney-General* [1935] IR 795. Article 8 of the 1922 Constitution of Irish Free State provided for "the free profession and practice of religion subject to public order and morality". The 1937 Constitution in article 44, while effectively guaranteeing religious freedom to all denominations operating in the State when the provisions came into force, gave special recognition to the position of the Roman Catholic Church "as being the guardian of the faith professed by the great majority of the citizens". These preferential provisions were deleted by the Fifth Amendment to the Constitution in 1972.

English legal precedents

7.18 Although the wording in the preamble to the English Statute of Charitable Uses 1601 is different (in intent) from the wording in the preamble to the

Statute of Charitable Uses (Ireland) 1634 (see 6.01, 6.02) the courts have held that they have the same effect.[1] In other words, the legal meaning of the term "charity" is almost identical in Ireland and the United Kingdom. In practice, this means that the decisions of the English Courts up to 1921 are relevant when examining Irish charitable claims.

Later English decisions, while not binding on the Irish Courts, are useful in examining problems with a common background.

References
1   *Incorporated Law Society v Richards* [1841] 4 Ir Eq R 177; see also dicta of Judge Gavan Duffy in *Re McEnery's Estate* [1941] IR 323.

Non-Christian religions

7.19 The advancement of religion, notwithstanding the underlying Christian moral ethos of society, can be applied to non-Christian spiritual beliefs:

> ... it would seem that a trust for the purpose of any kind of monotheistic theism would be a good charitable trust, and that it is not illegal or contrary to public policy to deny the authority of the Old or New Testament.[1]

References
1   Lord Parker in *Bowman v Secular Society* [1917] AC 406.

Promotion of religion

7.20 Bequests for the purpose of promoting religion,[1] for the spread of the Gospel[2] and to the poor and the service of God[3] have all been upheld as charitable. However, a bequest for the Lords work[4] was held to be void because it was indefinite. Similarly a bequest most conductive to the good of religion[5] and a direction by a testator to his executors to dispose of his residuary estate to my best spiritual advantage as conscience and a sense of duty may direct did not create a charitable trust.[6]

All these cases (with a possible reservation on the circumstances of the last one quoted) would appear to qualify as mixed gifts under Irish law and would therefore be considered charitable.[7]

References
1   *Attorney-General v Stepney* 10 Ves 22.
2   *In Re Les* 34 Ch D 528.
3   *In Re Darling* [1896] 1 Ch 50.
4   *In Re King's Estate* 21 LRI 273.
5   *Dunne v Byrne* [1912] AC 407.
6   *In Re Gibbons* [1917] 1 IR 448.
7   Charities Act 1961 s 49.

Religious purposes

7.21 A gift for pious purposes or religious purposes will generally be construed by the courts as being confined to such pious or religious purposes as are in their nature legally charitable, unless a contrary intention appears from the relevant context.[1]

7.22 A bequest to trustees to be spent in such charities in Ireland and in such foreign missions as they should think fit was upheld as charitable.[2] Similarly a bequest for such missionary objects at home or in the colonies as the trustees should select was also regarded as charitable.[3]

References
1   *Wilkinson v Lindgren* LR 5 Ch 570; *In Re White* [1893] 2 Ch 41; *Arnott v Arnott* [1905] 1 IR 127.
2   *Dunne v Duignan* [1908] 1 IR 228.
3   *In Re Kenny* 97 LT 130.

7.23 Where a testatrix directed that her residuary estate should be held in trust for the General of the Salvation Army for the time being, to be used for corps purposes in Liverpool, it was held that the gift was charitable. The evidence showed that corps purposes meant the purposes of the religious branch, as distinct from the social branch of the Army.[1]

A bequest of £100 to the Christian Brethren (commonly known as the Plymouth Brethren and later as the Exclusive Brethren) was upheld as a gift for religious purposes and the other charitable objects carried on by the Society.[2]

Bequests for the distribution of bibles and for the printing and circulating of religious publications are also regarded as charitable.[3] In considering bequests for such purposes the court will not enquire as to the truth or soundness of any religious doctrine, provided that it is not illegal, contrary to public policy or opposed to the settled principles of morality.[4]

References
1   *In Re Fowler* 31 TLR 102.
2   *In Re Brown* [1898] 1 IR 423.
3   *Attorney-General v Stepney* 10 Ves 22.
4   *Thornton v Howe* 31 Beav 14.

Gifts to clergymen and preachers

7.24 One of the charitable purposes listed in the Statute of Charitable Uses (Ireland) 1634 was the maintenance of any minister or preacher of the Holy Word of God. No similar wording appears in the corresponding English Statute of Charitable Uses 1601. It seems that the omission from the English statute was deliberate because in 1601 when the statute became law religion was regarded as being variable according to the pleasure of the existing monarchy and that what were orthodox beliefs under one monarch might be accounted superstitious under another monarch.

The English Courts have historically accepted that gifts for maintenance or support of preachers or ministers are charitable.[1] A bequest to a trustee to be applied at his absolute discretion for the use of the Roman Catholic priests in or near London was held to create a perpetual charitable trust,[2] but, in contrast, a bequest of £200 to each of ten poor clergymen of the Church of England to be selected by a named individual was not regarded charitable.[3]

A gift to a clergyman and his successors, or to a clergyman or minister for the time being, even where specified distributions are to be made by the recipient, will be upheld as charitable and arising ex officio but not where the gift is to a particular clergyman or minister on a personal basis.[4]

References
1   *Pennington v Buckley* 6 Hare 451.
2   *Attorney-General v Gladstone* 13 Sim 7.
3   *Thomas v Howell* LR 18 Eq 198.
4   *Attorney-General v Cook* 2 Ves Sen 273; *Gibson v Representative Church Body* 9 LRI 1; *In Re Flynn* [1948] 1 All ER 541, 64 TLR 203; *In Re Rumball* [1955] 3 All ER 71 1956 Ch 105.

Maintenance of churches

7.25 The repair of churches is expressly mentioned in both the English Statute of Charitable Uses 1601 and the Statute of Charitable Uses (Ireland) 1634 as constituting a charitable purpose. Consequently the building, maintenance, repair and ornamentation of churches, chapels or meeting houses of any religious denomination recognised by the law are charitable purposes.[1] Similarly gifts for the provision and repair of church bells, organs, clocks and galleries and other general church expenses, are also charitable[2] as are gifts for the maintenance and repair of monuments including tombs and memorial windows forming part of the fabric of church fixtures.[3]

Trusts for the erection of monuments within a church to commemorate a deceased are voidable if they do not have an object or a beneficiary to enforce them.

References
1   *Attorney-General v Love* 23 Beav 499; *Dillon v Reilly* IR 10 Eq 152; *Morrow v McConville* 11 LRI 236.
2   *Dureur v Metteux* 1 Ves Sen 320; *Hoare v Osborne* LR 1 Eq 585; *Attorney-General v Day* [1900] 1 Ch 31.
3   *Hoare v Osborne* LR IR Eq 583; *In Re Barker* 25 TLR 753.

Maintenance of churchyards

7.26 The repair and maintenance of a parish churchyard and of the tombs within it is a charitable purpose.[1]

A bequest for the purpose of keeping certain burial grounds in good order, even though

(*a*) the use of the burial ground was restricted to the Society of Friends, and

(*b*) it specified the grave of the testator's late wife which was in one of the grounds

was held to be charitable. The directions regarding the grave of the testator's wife were considered not to create a separate trust but merely to impose a special obligation ancillary to the repair of the grounds.

In general, gifts for the erection, maintenance or repair of monuments or tombs to a testator or his relatives which are not within a church are not charitable. Such gifts are also void if they create a perpetuity (see 3.29).[3]

However, Irish law provides limited relief on expenditure for the provision, maintenance or improvement of a tomb, vault or grave or of a tombstone or any other memorial to a deceased person by treating it as charitable (where otherwise excluded) in so far as it does not exceed:

(*a*) in the case of a gift of income only, sixty pounds a year, or

(*b*) in any other case, one thousand pounds in amount or value.[4]

References
1 *In Re Vaughan* 33 Ch D 187; *In Re Douglas* [1905] 1 Ch 279.
2 *In Re Manser* [1905] 1 Ch 68.
3 *Roche v McDermot* [1901] 1 IR 394; *In Re Porter* 1925 1 Ch 68; *In Re Hooper* 1932 1 Ch 38.
4 Charities Act 1961 s 50.

Gifts for masses

7.27 Gifts for the celebration of masses are specifically regarded by Irish law as charitable.

The history of such gifts is complex. They were charitable before the Reformation. English laws passed in 1549 and 1559[1] made the celebration of masses illegal. Although these laws had no effect in Ireland the English courts held that the celebration of masses was to be regarded as superstitious and gifts for such purposes were void on the grounds of being contrary to public policy.[2]

It was not until 1919 that the House of Lords held that gifts for the celebration of masses were valid but the decision did not establish that such gifts were valid for charitable purposes.[3]

The current position under English law appears to be that only masses celebrated in public are regarded as for public benefit and thus qualifying as charitable.[4]

The imposition of penal restrictions on religions, other than the Established Church, by the Irish Parliament in the 1600s and 1700s meant that the question of the validity of gifts for the celebration of masses did not become relevant in Ireland until the early 1800s.

The courts then began to accept gifts for the celebration of masses as charitable despite expressing reservations on grounds of perpetuity (see 3.29) and public benefit.[5] Finally, in 1906[6] it was unanimously held by the Irish Court of Appeal that a bequest for masses in perpetuity is a good charitable gift, whether the masses are to be said in public or privately. That judgment is now enshrined in legislation.[7]

References

1   Act of Uniformity 1549 (2 & 3 Ed VI c 1) and Act of Uniformity 1559 (1 Eliz I c 2).
2   Preamble to Charities Act 1547.
3   [1919] AC 815; 121 LT 426. The court held that the Roman Catholic Relief Acts of 1829 and 1832 had effectively displaced the effect of the Charities Act 1547.
4   *Gilmour v Coates* [1949] AC 426; [1949] 1 All ER 848.
5   *Commissioners of Charitable Donations and Bequests v Walsh* 1823 7 I Eq R 36; *Attorney-General v Hall* [1897] 2 IR 426.
6   *O'Hanlon v Logue* [1906] 1 IR 247.
7   Charities Act 1961 s 45(2).

Limitations on religious gifts

7.28 The meaning of "the advancement of religion" has in recent times been interpreted in a widely varying manner by the Irish courts.

In 1940 a gift to be used in the best interests of religion as determined by the Chapter of the Diocese of Killala was held to be charitable.[1]

In 1944 bequests for the purposes of the Carmelite Order in the Irish Free State were held to be invalid as charitable gifts because they may have had both charitable and non-charitable purposes.[2]

Between these two decisions a gift to the Order of Perpetual Adoration of the Blessed Sacrament had been held to be charitable.[3]

These issues have now been clarified by legislation. A gift for the advancement of religion is presumed to be for the public benefit.[4] Furthermore, such gifts are to have effect and be construed in accordance with the laws, canons, ordinances and tenets of the religion concerned.[5] Where gifts, which include both charitable and non-charitable purposes, do not identify or apportion those purposes the terms of the gift are to be construed as having overall charitable objects.[6] There is no similar statutory relief under English law. The

House of Lords has held, following earlier precedents and in contrast with the Irish decision,[3] that a bequest to an English Convent of contemplative nuns lacked a public purpose and was not charitable.[7] The House also expressed reservations regarding the charitable status of masses held in private. Similarly, a bequest made to the Roman Catholic Archbishop of Brisbane and his successors to be used for purposes conducive to religion in the Diocese was not regarded as charitable.[8] A bequest to the Catholic Bishop of Nottingham for the promotion of the Catholic Church was held not to be charitable.[9] Gifts with combined religious, moral and recreational objects are generally not regarded as charitable.[10]

References

1 *In Re Howley's Estate* [1940] IR 109.
2 *In Re Estate of Michael Keogh* [1945] IR 13.
3 *Maguire v Attorney-General* [1943] IR 238. In the High Court Judge Gavan Duffy took the view that there was a good charitable bequest under the common law, and the provisions of the Toleration Act 1793 removed any statutory prohibition. This precedent was followed when a bequest to the contemplative Carmelite Convent to be applied for the repair and/or improvement of the Convent was held to be charitable in *Bank of Ireland Trustee Co. Ltd. v Attorney-General* [1954] IR 257.
4 Charities Act 1961 s 45(1).
5 Charities Act 1961 s 45(2).
6 Charities Act 1961 s 49.
7 *Gilmour v Coates* [1949] 1 All ER 848.
8 *Dunne v Byrne* [1912] AC 407.
9 *Ellis v CIR* [1949] 31 TC 178.
10 *Londonderry Presbyterian Church Trustees v CIR* [1946] 27 TC 431; *Cookstown Roman Catholic Church Trustees v CIR* [1953] 34 TC 350.

Gifts for the general public benefit

Introduction

7.29 A gift will be regarded as charitable if it has a charitable purpose ie:

(a) the relief of poverty (see 7.01),

(b) the advancement of education (see 7.06)

(c) the advancement or religion (see 7.16)

(d) if it is for the public benefit.

Gifts that qualify as charitable because they are for the public benefit are many and varied. [1]

References

1 See memorandum prepared by the Office of the Revenue Commissioners for the Committee on Fundraising Activities for Charitable and Other Purposes in 1990. Report published by the Stationery Office, Dublin; Appendix III.

Gifts for local areas

7.30 While in recent decades only gifts for the benefit of the public at large have been regarded as charitable[1] several older decisions have established that certain gifts to local areas are charitable. These decisions refer to gifts that benefit a parish,[2] county[3] or a town[4] even where no charitable purposes are specified in the gift.[5]

More recently a gift to a public hall was held to be charitable if the hall provided directly for the needs of the public; if public access is incidental, charitable status will be denied.[6]

A bequest to provide a municipal recreation ground was accepted as charitable,[7] while a trust formed to alleviate distress caused by floods in Devon and Somerset was also recognised as charitable.[8]

References
1   *Oppenheim v Tobacco Securities Ltd.* [1951] AC 297; *CIR v Baddeley* 1955 1 All ER 525, 35 TC 661.
2   *Attorney-General v Webster* LR 20 Eq 483; *Keane v Motherwell* [1910] IR 249.
3   *Attorney-General v Lonsdale* 1 Sim 105.
4   *House v Chapman* 4 Ves 541; *In Re Hann* [1903] 1 Ch 232; *In Re Allan* [1905] 2 Ch 400.
5   *Houston v Burns* [1918] AC 337; Charities Act 1961 s 49.
6   *Trades House of Glasgow v CIR* 46 TC 178.
7   *Tayport Town Council v CIR* 20 TC 191.
8   *In re North Devon & West Somerset Relief Fund Trusts* [1953] 2 All ER 1032; 1953 1 WLR 1260.

7.31 A gift to the State or to a local authority to be used for the benefit of the general population, or for the relief of public liabilities will also generally qualify as charitable.[1]

References
1   *Thelluson v Woodford* 4 Ves 235; *Attorney-General v Bushby* 24 Beav 299.

Non-charitable gifts

7.32 Not every gift for public utility or public advantage will qualify charitable. Gifts for "philanthropic purposes",[1] "benevolent purposes"[2] or "utilitarian purposes"[3] will not be regarded as charitable unless their purpose or objects are confined to those which are charitable. Although a gift "for public purposes" will not normally be regarded as charitable because of its uncertainty, a mixed gift for charitable and other public purposes will, if the objects are inseparable, qualify as charitable under Irish law.[4]

References
1   *In Re MacDuff* [1896] 2 Ch 451.
2   *In Re Jarman's Estate*, 8 Ch D 584; *In Re Barnett* 24 TLR 788. Under general Scottish law, however, a benevolent purpose is charitable: *Jackson's Trustees v Lord Advocate* 10 TC 460. English legal procedures apply for income tax: *CIR v Glasgow Police Athletic Association:* 34 TC 76; [1953] All ER 747.

3   *In Re Woodgate* 2 TLR 674.
4   Charities Act 1961 s 49. Gifts for specific existing public purposes in an area have been upheld as charitable in England, see *Blair v Dunne* [1902] AC 37; *Houston v Burns* [1918] AC 337.

Animals

7.33 The suppression of cruelty to animals is a good charitable purpose and bequests:

(*a*)   to a home for lost dogs;[1]

(*b*)   to the Dublin Home for Starving and Forsaken Cats;[2]

(*c*)   for founding and maintaining an institution for investigating the illnesses of animals or birds;[3] and

(*d*)   for the establishment of a slaughter house to prevent cruelty to animals[4]

have all been held to be charitable.

A society whose object was the total suppression of the vivisection of animals was refused relief as a charity by the House of Lords on the grounds that, on balance, the vivisection of animals was more beneficial to the community than its suppression and furthermore, the objects of the Society in seeking a change of the existing law were political.[5]

References
1   *In Re Douglas* 35 Ch D 472.
2   *Swifte v Attorney-General* [1912] 1 IR 132.
3   *University of London v Yarrow* 1 De G & J 72.
4   *Tatham v Drummond* 4 De G J & S 484.
5   *National Anti-Vivisection Society v CIR* [1947] All ER 217; 28 TC 311.

Vegetarian society

7.34 A bequest to a vegetarian society was upheld as charitable by an 1898 decision of the Irish Court of Appeal. The rationale for the decision was that the abstinence from all forms of animal flesh and increased use of vegetables lead to the improvement of health and the development of a more humane attitude towards all creatures.[1]

References
1   *In Re Cranston* [1898] 1 IR 431.

Political gifts

7.35 Gifts for purely political objects are not charitable.[1] The secularisation of education, the amendment of laws relating to religion or marriage are purely political objects and such objects have never been recognised as charitable.

A trust for the attainment of political objects is not illegal for everyone is at liberty to seek a change in existing laws but because the courts have no means of evaluating whether a proposed change will be for the public benefit there cannot be a decision to regard such objects as charitable. While provisions in a trust relating to the examination of political affairs may be regarded as educational they only qualify as charitable where any such examination is carried out as incidental to other more general educational purposes.[2]

References
1   *Bonar Law Memorial Trust v CIR* [1933] 49 TLR 220; 17 TC 508; *McGovern v Attorney-General* [1981] 3 All ER 493.
2   *Attorney-General v Ross* [1986] 1 WLR 252.

Sport

7.36 The encouragement of sport, games or recreational activities which are intended to promote the benefit of individuals, as distinct from the public, is not regarded as charitable.[1]

Since 1958, the provision of leisure facilities of a social nature has been officially recognised in the United Kingdom as a charitable purposes.[1]

While there is no corresponding Irish statute an exemption from income tax is available in this country for bodies established for the promotion of athletic or amateur sports or games.[2]

Gifts for sporting facilities at educational establishments had historically been considered charitable.[3] More recently, where the English Football Association had set up a trust to enable students at schools or universities to play football and other sports and thereby develop, both physically and mentally, the House of Lords, overturning decisions by the lower Courts, held these objects to be charitable.

References
1   Recreational Charities Act 1958.
2   *Glasgow Police Athletic Association v CIR* [1953] 1 All ER 747; 34 TC 76.
3   ITA 1963 s 349 as amended by FA 1984 s 9. The amendment was made following a High Court decision on a trust established for restricted private beneficiaries (*Revenue Commissioners v O'Reilly* [1983] ILRM 34). See Chapter 12.
4   *In Re Mariette* [1914-1915] All ER 794, 31 TLR 566; *In Re Mellody* [1918] 1 Ch 228.
5   *CIR v McMullan* [1980] 1 All ER 884, 54 TC 413.

Amateur societies

7.37 In recent times, the English courts have adopted a somewhat liberal approach to trusts and other bodies established for the benefit of the public.

The following have been held to be charitable:

(*a*)   a society founded for the general promotion of agriculture;[1]

(*b*)   a society devoted to the breeding and exhibition of cage-birds;[2]

(*c*)   a society formed to promote the practice and performance of choral works;[3]

(*d*)   a society for the printing and publishing of law reports;[4]

(*e*)   an association to promote craftsmanship;[5]

(*f*)   a trust founded to make awards to distinguished singers or composers;[6]

(*g*)   a non-profit making society formed for the promotion of cremation.[7]

References
1   *CIR v Yorkshire Agricultural Society* [1928] 1 KB 611; 13 TC 458.
2   *CIR v Glasgow Ornithological Association* 21 TC 445.
3   *CIR v Royal Choral Society* [1943] 2 All ER 101; 25 TC 263, where it was stated that whether a particular body is established for charitable purposes only is a question of law and in no circumstances can it be a matter of fact.
4   *Incorporated Council of Law Reporting for England v Attorney-General* [1971] 3 All ER 101; 47 TC 321.
5   *CIR v White* 55 TC 651.
6   *In Re Levien* [1955] 3 All ER 35.
7   *Scottish Burial Reform and Cremation Society Ltd v Glasgow City Corporation* [1967] 3 All ER 215; [1967] 3 WLR 1132.

7.38 In contrast to these positive decisions a society founded for the breeding of foxhounds was held not to be charitable.[1]

In Ireland exemption was refused to Ward Union Hunt Race Trustees because it was an agricultural society for activities in connection with an annual race meeting.[2]

References
1   *Peterborough Royal Foxhound Show Society v CIR* 20 TC 429.
2   937 2 ITC 152.

Chapter 8

Trusts of imperfect obligation

Purpose trusts

8.01 A purpose trust (a trust of imperfect obligation) is a trust which, while not illegal, is voidable and unenforceable as it does not have a beneficiary who is entitled to have the provisions of the trust enforced (see 2.07, 2.11).

If a trust of imperfect obligation is performed it will not be struck down by the Courts. Thus where a testator left a legacy to erect a monument to his memory in St Paul's Cathedral in Poet's Corner, in holding the gift to be valid the judge said:

> I do not suppose that there would be anyone who could compel the executors to carry out this bequest and raise the monument; but if the residuary legatee or the trustees insist upon the trust being executed my opinion is that the Court is bound to see it carried out.[1]

References
1   Lord Kindersley in *Trimmer v Danby* 25 LJ Ch 424; see also *In Re Astor's Settlement Trusts* [1952] Ch 534; 1952 1 All ER 1074.

The rule against perpetuities

8.02 The rule against perpetuities (see 3.29) means that the life of a trust, other than a charity or a superannuation fund, is determined by lives (of beneficiaries) in being at the time of the settlement or gift plus a period of 21 years. Only human lives can be considered for this purpose.[1] Accordingly, trusts of imperfect obligation have been held to have a lawful or valid life not exceeding 21 years.[2]

References
1   *In Re Kelly* [1932] IR 255.
2   *In Re Hooper* [1932] 1 Ch 38.

Purpose trusts that are charitable trusts

8.03 Whether a purpose trust is a valid trust (ie whether it has beneficiaries) is a distinct matter from whether the trust is a charitable trust (ie is for charitable purposes: see Chapter 7). Thus a gift for a tangible and useful monument in an area (for example, a recreational ground, a public park) would be regarded as charitable and have beneficiaries capable of seeking enforcement of the provisions, whereas a trust for the erection of a monument to a testator (outside church grounds) would not be charitable and would not generally have a beneficiary capable of enforcing the provisions (see 7.29).

Protection of animals

8.04 Trusts for the protection of animals are generally regarded as charitable by contributing to the moral and spiritual welfare of society.[1] A sanctuary for animals where no protection of species was provided and the animals were allowed to roam in natural conditions was refused recognition as a charity.[2]

8.05 While the English Courts have in recent times been widening the type of cases qualifying as charitable as being of benefit to the public the same liberality has not been applied to trusts of imperfect obligation.

A settlement aimed at promoting understanding, sympathy and co-operation internationally was declared void on the grounds of uncertainty.[3] A similar fate befell the testamentary trust of George Bernard Shaw which sought to have the present English alphabet reformed although the trust was limited to 21 years.[4] A trust to erect a useful memorial to a testator was also considered void as uncertain.[5]

References

1   *In Re Wedgwood* [1915] 1 Ch 113; see 7.33.
2   *In Re Grove-Grady* [1929] 1 Ch 557.
3   See 2 ante.
4   *Public Trustee v Day* [1957] 1 All ER 745 compromised on appeal as shown in [1958] 1 All ER 245. In contrast, a bequest by Shaw's widow of her residuary estate for the bringing within reach of the people of Ireland of all classes masterpieces of fine art was upheld as a valid charitable gift for the advancement of education: *In Re Shaw's Will Trust* [1952] Ch 163; [1952] 1 All ER 49.
5   [1960] Ch 232.

Part 4

Income tax

Chapter 9

The provisions governing trusts

Introduction

9.01 This chapter sets out brief summaries of the income tax provisions dealing with trusts. The application of these provisions is then explained (and illustrated) in chapters 11, 12 and 13.

Income Tax Act 1967

Body of persons, settlement

Section 1

9.02 This section defines "body of persons" as any body politic, corporate or collegiate and any company, fraternity, fellowship and society of persons, whether corporate or not corporate. The trustees of a trust are therefore a "body of persons".

Section 96(3)

9.03 A "settlement" for the purpose of charging profits on gains from dealing in or developing land within ITA 1967 Pt I Ch VII (now F(MP)A

1968 s 16) includes a trust. A "settlor" includes a person who provides, directly or indirectly, the funds of a settlement.

Section 105

9.04 This short section contains the general charge under Schedule D on bodies of persons (ie trustees) receiving or entitled to income.

Benefit in kind

Section 117(8)

9.05 This section, which is anti-avoidance in nature, provides that if a trustee of a settlement made by a company (*a*) has private (non-business) expenses paid by the company and (*b*) is "connected" with the company, then that person will also be regarded as connected with the company for the purposes of benefit in kind, and the benefit must be taxed by the company.

A person is connected with a company if he controls it, or if he can control it together with other persons who are connected to him. If two persons act together to secure control of a company, they are regarded, in relation to that company, as connected. (F(MP)A 1968 s 16(3)).

Returns by trustees

Section 176

9.06 Every person (including a trustee of a trust) who receives income belonging to any other person chargeable to tax thereon or who would be so chargeable if resident in the State, must deliver particulars of the person to whom the profits are payable when so required by an inspector of taxes. Since 28 May 1992, this information must be submitted to the inspector without an official request.

Married persons

Section 194

9.07 Where a wife's income is chargeable on her husband under the joint assessment election applicable under section 195 any such charge is to include any income assessable on the wife's trustees, guardian or committee.

Section 197

9.08 The separate assessment procedures set out in section 197 may be used by the Revenue Commissioners to apportion, determine and collect tax in circumstances where tax under a joint assessment within section 195 is unpaid and the wife's income included therein arises through a trustee, guardian, committee or personal representative.

Non-residents

Section 200

9.09 Assessments on a non-resident may be made and charged on a trustee, guardian, committee or agent of such person.

Guardians of incapacitated persons

Section 208

9.10 A trustee, guardian or committee of an incapacitated person, having the control of the property of the incapacitated person is chargeable to income tax on the basis of the liability which would arise to the incapacitated person.

Section 209

9.11 The trustee or other person chargeable on the income of an incapacitated person is to stand in place of that person for the assessment and payment of income tax due with a right to retain funds to meet any tax liability arising.

If payment is made directly to the incapacitated person, without passing through the hands of the trustee, then the trustee is not accountable to the Revenue Commissioners for the income tax of the incapacitated person, provided the trustee makes a declaration to this effect and submits the appropriate return to the Revenue Commissioners.

Retirement annuity schemes

Section 235

9.12 Retirement annuity schemes (pension funds for self-employed etc), including occupational trusts must (in order to be approved by Revenue) comply with the requirements of this section.

Section 238

9.13 The trustees of an occupational benefit scheme must furnish such information on the operation of the scheme to the Revenue Commissioners as they may reasonably require (subs (3)(*c*)).

Section 239

9.14 An annuity bought from funds of a settlement does not qualify as a purchased life annuity, the capital element of which may be determined by reference to the payment made (or consideration given).

Charities etc

Section 333

9.15 This section deals with trusts established for charitable purposes, hospitals, schools etc: (see Chapter 7).

Income from property vested in the trustees and income from interest and dividends (chargeable under Schedules C, D and F) is exempt from income tax.

Income applied to the maintenance and upkeep of graves, memorials etc (within the Charities Act 1961 s 50) is also exempt from income tax.

Section 334

9.16 Trading income arising to a charity that would be chargeable as a trading receipt within a charge to Schedule D is exempt from income tax.

The exemption is available to a charitable trust where such trading profits are applied solely to the purposes of the charity, and either:

(*a*)   the trade is exercised in carrying out a primary purpose of the charity; or

(*b*)   the work in connection with the trade is mainly carried on by beneficiaries of the charity.

However, profits from farming activities, while required to satisfy one of the alternative conditions, need not be applied solely for charitable purposes.

Section 349

9.17 Bodies established and existing for the sole purpose of promoting athletic games or sport are exempt from income tax.

Anti-avoidance

Section 367

9.18 The restrictions imposed for tax purposes on bond washing arrangements involving the purchase cum-dividend and subsequent ex-dividend sales of securities also apply to a body of persons, including, for example, the trustees of a trust.

Section 371

9.19 The income tax "dividend-stripping" provisions (ITA 1967 Pt XXIV) apply to bodies of persons and therefore apply to trustees of a trust (subs (7)).

Appeals

Section 432

9.20 The income tax appeals procedure may be used by the trustees of a trust for example, in relation to claims for exemption, relief etc where otherwise no right of appeal exists.

Revocable dispositions, dispositions for short periods and certain dispositions in favour of children

Section 438

9.21 A disposition that creates a power which allows the disponer to revoke the disposition is not recognised for income tax. For example, if a settlor covenants to pay £1,000 per annum to his nephew, but retains the power to revoke the covenant, the covenant will not be recognised for income tax purposes. The income will be regarded as that of the covenantor.

Section 439

9.22 This section is concerned with dispositions for short periods (covenants). Certain payments of income are to be regarded as annual payments which must be made under deduction of tax at the standard rate and are not to be regarded as applications of income. The relevant dispositions include payments:

(*a*)   to a university or college in the State for research purposes;

(*b*)   to any body of persons having consultative status with the United National Organisation or the Council of Europe;

(*c*)   to an individual or to persons for the benefit of a named individual;

(*d*)   to a university, college or school in the State for the teaching of the natural sciences or to a fund established for such purposes.

Section 440

9.23 Income under a disposition made, directly or indirectly, by a parent in favour of a child for a period less than the life of a child is, while the child is aged under 18 years and unmarried, to be the income of the parent settlor (see also s 443).

Section 441

9.24 A settlor who is required to deduct tax at the standard rate on income he has settled (ss 439, 440) is entitled to recover such tax from the trustees of the settlement.

Section 442

9.25 This section broadly defines "settlement" to include any trust, covenant, agreement or arrangement.

Settlements on children generally

Section 443

9.26 Under a disposition made by a parent in favour of a child while the parent settlor is living and the child is either under 18 years old or unmarried, any income payable to or for the benefit of the child is regarded as that of the parent for income tax purposes irrespective of the period of the disposition (see also ss 444-448).

Section 444

9.27 An irrevocable settlement of income made by a parent to a beneficiary who is his child, and under which the income is accumulated, may qualify as income of the child.

Section 445

9.28 "Irrevocable", in the context of s 444, is strictly defined to include any method by which the settlor can regain the income he has (allegedly) settled on the child.

Section 446

9.29 A settlor who is required to deduct tax at the standard rate on income he has settled (s 443) is entitled to recover such tax from the trustees of the settlement.

Section 447

9.30 This section broadly defines "settlement" to include any trust, covenant, agreement or arrangement.

Section 448

9.31 A transfer of an interest in a trade, whether carried on before the transfer was made by a sole trader or in partnership, to a child of the settlor is, while such child is either under 18 years of age or unmarried, regarded as a settlement on the child and, consequently, any income arising from the settled property to or for the benefit of such a child is regarded for tax purposes as the income of the parent transferor.

Estates of deceased persons

Section 454

9.32 Where the estate of a deceased is entitled to benefit from another deceased person's estate, the personal representatives acting for the first estate are to stand in place of the deceased beneficiary in respect of any income accruing from the second estate.

Where during the course of administration of an estate income from the residue is advanced to or for the benefit of a residuary legatee, whether directly or indirectly, through a trust or any other person, that advancement is deemed to be income of the tax year in which it is paid out.

Government securities

Section 466

9.33 The Minister for Finance is authorised to issue securities with a condition that any interest arising is paid without deduction of income tax. Where such securities are held (by a nominee) on behalf of another person, the Revenue Commissioners may request particulars of the beneficial recipients of such interest.

Schedule 4

9.34 While claims for allowances, deductions and reliefs are generally to be made directly by the claimant, such claims may also be made:

  (*a*)   by a guardian, trustee, attorney, agent or factor acting for the claimant, or

  (*b*)   by a person who is assessable on behalf of any other person.

Finance (Miscellaneous Provisions) Act 1968

Connected persons

Section 16

9.35 In determining profits from dealing in or developing land a trustee of a settlement is regarded as "connected" with both the settlor of the settlement, and any person "connected" with the settlor.

Finance Act 1973

Human rights bodies

Section 15

9.36 This section, by inserting ITA 1967 s 439(iia) provides that income covenanted to human rights bodies (s 20) is deemed to be the income of the covenantor unless the period for which the income is covenanted exceeds, or is capable of exceeding, three years.

Section 20

9.37 Internationally recognised bodies established for the promotion of human rights and the implementation of the European Convention for the protection of human rights and fundamental freedoms are entitled to the same exemptions to tax available to bodies established for charitable purposes only within ITA 1967 s 333.

Section 41

9.38 This section, by inserting ITA 1967 s 117(7)-(8) taxes benefits in kind receivable by a trustee of a trust.

Finance Act 1974

Standard rate of tax

Section 3

9.39 The charge to higher rates of income tax in excess of the standard rate is not applicable to income received by trustees of a trust as trustees of the trust.

Relieved dividends

Section 54

9.40 This anti-avoidance section provides that if employees are paid via export-sales relieved dividends (CTA 1976 Pt IV), or exempt Shannon dividends (CTA 1976 Pt V), in lieu of normal adequate emoluments the amount paid by such methods is taxed at normal income tax rates.

Transfer of assets abroad

Section 59

9.41 Solicitors, banks etc must supply information to the Revenue Commissioners regarding the transfer of assets abroad, and details of operations where they are involved in the management of transferred assets. This section might apply, for example where assets are transferred to a foreign trust.

Finance Act 1976

Surcharge on undistributed trust income

Section 13

9.42 This section is related to FA 1974 s 3, which provided that the income arising to trustees of a trust (in their fiduciary capacity) would be taxed only at the standard rate. This gave rise to tax avoidance in that if income was accumulated in a trust, it would not be taxed at more than the standard rate. There was therefore an incentive for high rate taxpayers to divert income into such trust, and allow the income to accumulate, knowing it would not be taxed at more than the standard rate.

This section, by imposing a 20% surcharge on income of a trust (that is not distributed to the beneficiaries within 18 months of the end of the income tax year in which it arises) removes the incentive to accumulate income in a trust. No repayment of or credit for the surcharge is available to beneficiaries when the income is distributed at a later date.

Bodies established for charitable purposes only and approved superannuation funds are specifically excluded from the effects of the surcharge.

Income accumulated by the trustees of an approved profit sharing scheme within FA 1982 Pt I Ch IX (see below) is not subject to the surcharge.

Finance Act 1982

Approved profit sharing schemes

Sections 50 to 58

9.43 These sections provide administrative rules whereby company employees who participate in a bona fide profit sharing scheme may legitimately avoid tax on share allocations up to a maximum of £2,000 for 1992-93 and later tax years.

The scheme must have a governing trust instrument, and the body of persons administering the scheme ("the trustees") must be resident in the State.

Finance Act 1983

Maintenance arrangements

Section 3

9.44 "Maintenance arrangements" in consequence of the dissolution or annulment of a marriage or the separation of the parties include relevant trust settlements.

Property returns

Section 20

9.45 Individuals, representatives and trustees must provide details of the description, location, cost and the nature of the interest held in any property when formally requested by the Revenue Commissioners.

Returns by nominee holders of securities

Section 21

9.46 Nominee holders of securities must reveal the identity of the beneficial owners of such securities when requested to do so by the Revenue Commissioners.

Finance Act 1984

Business expansion scheme

Section 27

9.47 While relief for investment in corporate trades (business expansion schemes) is primarily intended for direct investments by individuals, an indirect investment made by an individual through a qualifying trust fund which is established solely for investment in such schemes may also qualify for relief if the trust investment fund buys the eligible shares in a qualifying company.

Gifts for education in the Arts

Section 32

9.48 Gifts made to bodies engaged in third level education connected with the Arts or to non-profit making organisations which contribute to the advancement of such activities. The amount of any such annual gifts must exceed £100 but there is an upper limit of £10,000.

Finance Act 1985

Gifts to the President's Award Scheme

Section 16

9.49 This section was of limited effect and provided relief from income tax for payments made on or before 5 April 1987 to "Gaisce - The President's Award Scheme". Annual qualifying gifts must be in excess of £100 and not more than £10,000.

Finance Act 1986

Gifts to Cospóir

Section 8

9.50 This section provided income tax relief for gifts to the Minister for Education for the benefit of "Cospóir - The National Sports Council (An Chomhairle Náisiunta Spóirt)". Annual qualifying gifts must be in excess of £100 and not more than £10,000.

Deposit interest retention tax

Section 31

9.51 After 5 April 1986, financial institutions must generally deduct income tax at the standard rate from interest paid to deposit holders. However, bodies established for charitable purposes only are exempt from such deposit interest retention tax provided the necessary declaration is submitted to the Revenue Commissioners (FA 1986 ss 32, 38).

After 6 April 1992, deposit interest receivable by approved pension schemes and other bodies, including trusts relating to approved retirement annuity funds are not to be subject to retention tax at the time of crediting or payment. This effectively gives a full exemption to such persons from a direct charge to tax (see FA 1972 s 17(2)).

Finance Act 1988

Self-assessment

Section 9

9.52 Under the "self assessment" system, a "chargeable person" includes a person who is chargeable on account of some other person (see ITA 1967 s 176). Such chargeable persons must therefore pay preliminary tax due by that other person.

Finance Act 1989

Undertakings for collective investment in transferable securities

Section 18

9.53 This section changes the basis of the charge to be applied on income arising to registered unit trusts and Undertakings for Collective Investment in Transferable Securities (UCITS) approved under EEC Regulations.

In effect, the unit holder is to be the person chargeable to tax. Previously the trustees as the persons initially receiving the income were the persons chargeable (ITA 1967 s 105). However, payments of income made to Irish resident unit holders are to be subject to deduction of income tax at the standard rate.

Section 19

9.54 The trustees of an undertaking for collective investment in transferable securities must make a return of their dealings with each unit holder to the Revenue Commissioners. This is to ensure that the unit holder is including the relevant details in his return of income.

Finance Act 1990

Haemophilia HIV Trust

Section 7

9.55 Any payments made out of the funds of the Haemophilia HIV Trust to assist persons who had acquired the AIDS virus from blood transfusions are ignored for income tax purposes.

Undertakings for collective investment in transferable securities

Section 35

9.56 The trustees of an undertaking for collective investment in transferable securities need not withhold tax at the standard rate from the unit holder (FA

1989 s 18) if the units are linked to a life assurance policy and the units do not become the property of the policy holder.

Finance Act 1991

The Great Book of Ireland Trust

Section 13

9.57 Any income received by the Great Book of Ireland Trust Ltd or paid by it to designated companies is to be ignored for income tax purposes.

Undertakings for collective investment in transferable securities

Section 19

9.58 The definition of a collective investment undertaking in FA 1989 s 18 is extended to cover a unit trust scheme within the Unit Trust Act 1990 which repealed the earlier 1972 unit trust legislation. A company wholly owned by a collective investment undertaking which is used to transact investments and to limit liability on future contracts, options or other similar financial instrument is also to be regarded as a collective investment undertaking.

Finance Act 1992

Pension refunds

Section 6

9.59 After 28 January 1992 repayments of excess superannuation contributions to an approved or statutory scheme are subject to a tax charge of 25% in place of the previous 10% rate (FA 1972 s 21(2)).

The 10% rate is retained for chargeable amounts arising where a person's entire pension entitlement is commuted for a lump sum (FA 1972 s 22).

Foreign adoptions

Section 16

9.60 A child includes a child adopted abroad, where that adoption is legally recognised in the State by the Adoption Acts 1952 to 1991.

Approved profit sharing schemes

Section 17

9.61 The annual overall entitlement of an employee to benefit under the profit sharing scheme legislation introduced by FA 1982 Pt I Ch IX is reduced from £5,000 to £2,000 for years 1992-93 and later years.

Pension funds: deposit interest retention tax

Section 22

9.62 Approved pension funds and bodies concerned with retirement annuity contracts are excluded from deposit interest retention tax (see FA 1986 s 31).

Returns by intermediaries

Section 226

9.63 All persons concerned with letting or managing premises, payment of fees and commission, interest paid or credited, income received on behalf of others and intermediaries in relation to collective investment undertakings must supply information concerning the transactions to the Revenue. Previously, such information needed to be requested specifically by an inspector or the Commissioners.

Chapter 10

Tax treatment of trustees and beneficiaries

Trustees

Active trustees

10.01 A trust involves the transfer of an interest in property, whether legal or equitable, by a settlor to trustees to hold such property for beneficiaries thereby creating separate equitable interests. A settlor may be a trustee of a settlement created by him and also a beneficiary. A trust is not an individual in that an individual has rights and obligations under the common law. The trustees of a trust are regarded as a "body of persons" (see 10.05).

If the trustees have specific duties to perform they are described as active trustees. A nominal or passive trustee is a person who is a trustee in name only. Such a person is also know as a bare trustee. If all the trustees of a trust are bare trustees the trust is known as a bare trust. Examples of passive trusteeship arise in relation to bank deposit accounts placed in joint names where there is no question of advancement (see 3.13) or where stocks or shares are held by nominees on behalf of third persons.

Taxation

10.02 The application of the income tax law [1] to a trust will invariably involve treating the income arising to:

(a) the settlor himself (ignoring the trust),

(b) the trustees of the trust (with a right to recover any tax paid from the beneficiaries), or

(c) the beneficiaries of the trust.

References
1   ITA 1967 ss 208, 209, 210 and 213.

Revenue Commissioners

10.03 The Revenue Commissioners may question the validity of a trust in various ways:

(*a*)   Are the trustees exercising more power than has been properly granted to them by the settlor (in the deed of trust)?

(*b*)   Is the trust void on grounds of perpetuity (see 3.29)?

(*c*)   Is the trust voidable because there are no beneficiaries (see 5.01)?

(*d*)   Are the beneficiaries receiving or claiming more than what has been properly granted to them by the settlor (in the deed of trust)?

Personal representatives

10.04 The expression "trustee" includes the duties of the office of personal representative of a deceased person.[1]

Personal representatives are the representatives of a deceased person in regard to his real and personal estate and they hold the estate as trustees for beneficiaries of the estate ie the persons who are entitled to it by law.[2]

The personal representative only becomes trustee for the person entitled by law to the estate of a deceased when he is in a position to distribute the assets of the estate.[3] A trustee is, nevertheless, deemed in law to be the heir and assignee of a deceased person "within the meaning of all trusts and powers".[4]

Thus a deceased person's personal representative acts as his trustee, standing in the place of the deceased, for example, in relation to an interest in the estate of another deceased person. A personal representative can therefore be liable to income tax on the income arising to the estate of a deceased person from the estate of another deceased person, even where it is not vested in him for his own benefit.[5] The income is deemed to be part of the aggregate income of the estate of the first deceased person.

References
1   Trustee Act 1893 s 50.
2   Succession Act 1965 s 10(3).
3   *F M Moloney, Inspector of Taxes v Allied Irish Banks Ltd* HC [16 February 1985]. Keane J. followed the decision in the Scottish case of *Reid's Trustees v CIR*. 14 TC 451.
4   Succession Act 1965 s 10(2).
5   ITA 1967 s 454(1).

Body of persons

10.05 For income tax purposes the trustees of a trust are a "body of persons" which means "any body politic, corporate or collegiate, and any company, fraternity, fellowship and society of persons, whether corporate or not corporate".[1]

Such bodies of persons are chargeable to income tax in the same manner as any individual is chargeable.[2] Income tax on business and investment income, other than distributions of Irish companies, is chargeable under Schedule D.[3] Irish residents are chargeable on all income arising irrespective of source, while the charge on non-residents is confined to Irish income.[4] Distributions made by Irish companies are chargeable under Schedule F.[5]

References
1   ITA 1967 s 1.
2   ITA 1967 s 207.
3   ITA 1967 s 105.
4   ITA 1967 s 52.
5   CTA 1976 s 83(1).

Residence of a trust

Introduction

10.06 There is no simple rule that can decide where a trust is resident, since the trust is not an entity, but usually a document (deed of trust) whose provisions are administered by trustees. A trust does not therefore "reside" in the sense that an individual does, but in the context of this chapter "residence" of a trust refers to the State where the tax laws apply to the trust. Furthermore, the concept of a trust (involving a settlor, a transfer of property, trustees and beneficiaries) while recognised by former British colonies (including the United States) is not recognised for example, in France, Germany.

Ireland-UK Double Taxation Agreement

10.07 While the 1926 Double Taxation Agreement between this country and the United Kingdom was unique in the scope of the mutual exemptions granted it did not provide any specific rules to determine the residence of a trust. As a result, the Revenue authorities in both countries agreed to divide the residence of a trust under the Agreement by reference to the "forum of administration".

In effect this was a "place of management" test. If that test did not resolve the matter, the residence of the majority of the trustees was used to decide where the trust was resident. If both these tests failed, the trust was regarded as resident in the jurisdiction in which the settlor was domiciled.

The later 1976 Double Taxation Convention between the two countries follows the wording of the 1977 OECD Model Convention.[1] This Ireland-UK Double Taxation Convention provides that a person other than an individual (for example, a company) who is resident in both States under the respective domestic laws, is deemed for the purposes of the Convention to be resident only in the State where the company is effectively managed.[2]

The Revenue authorities of the two countries have agreed the following tests to determine the residence of a trust:

(*a*)   Where all the trustees are individuals and resident in one State only, that State is to be the place of effective management.

(*b*)   If (*a*) fails to resolve the matter then the trust is resident in:
   (i)   the State where the individual who controls the trust's activities resides; or
   (ii) the State where the majority of the meetings of the trustees are held.

(*c*)   Where a professional body is acting as trustee either alone or in conjunction with individuals, the place where its business is carried on (including a branch of a bank subsidiary of the other State) is to be regarded as the place of effective management (and therefore of residence).

References
1   Published by the OECD, 2 Andre-Pascal, Paris. The wording of the Model Convention had been agreed over a number of earlier years and its proposed wording was imported into the 1976 Convention.
2   Ireland-UK Double Taxation Convention 1976 art 4(3).

Residence of trustees

10.08 There have been a number of recent developments in the United Kingdom concerning the residence of trusts. As trustees are a body of persons it was held [1] that a trust was only to be regarded as resident in the United Kingdom if *all* the trustees are resident there. Amending legislation[2] was passed to provide that a trust is to be resident in the United Kingdom if any of the trustees and the settlor was ordinarily resident or domiciled in the United Kingdom at the time the funds were provided, directly or indirectly, or at the date of death (in the case of a will).

Because there is no equivalent Irish law the test of residence used in practice is in effect "place of management" test under the 1976 Ireland-UK Double Taxation Convention.

References
1   *Dawson v CIR* [1989] 2 WLR 858.
2   F(No 2)A 1989 s 110.

Beneficiaries

Introduction

10.09 Income tax on income arising to a trust is generally payable by the trustees unless a beneficiary has a vested interest in the income arising. As discussed at 5.06, a beneficiary's interest in property may be:

(*a*)   vested,

(*b*)   vested liable to be divested,

(*c*)   contingent, or

(*d*)   discretionary.

Vested interest

Vested interest in possession

This is also called a fixed interest. It describes a present right to property or income and it applies to both absolute and limited interests.

Vested interest in expectancy

This arises where there is no present entitlement to an interest in property or income but a certain future right to the interest exists.

Example

A, by his will, provided that his widow, at her option, was to take either her statutory legal right[1] or a life interest in all his property with remainder over to his children C and D equally. The widow did not opt for her statutory right. In the circumstances she had a vested life interest in possession of her late husband's estate. Both C and D had vested interests in expectancy during their mother's life. However, even if either child predeceased the mother that children's share would not be lost but would form part of the child's estate on the death of the mother.

References
1   Succession Act 1965 s 111.

Vested liable to be divested

Such an interest gives a present right to property or income which can be removed on the happening of a future event.

Example

A by his will leaves a holiday home worth £50,000 to his wife B, for life, or until she remarries, upon the happening of which event, the property is to pass to A's son C.

Contingent interest

A contingent interest is an interest which depends upon the happening of some future event.

'n government securities to his nephew B. In the meantime, the income o be accumulated contingent[1] upon B reaching the age of 18.

.erences
1   ITA 1967 s 154.

Discretionary interest

A discretionary interest is an interest which comes into possession at the discretion of some other person.

Example

A leaves £50,000 worth of government securities in a discretionary trust. D (A's wife) and E (A's brother) the trustees of the discretionary trust have discretion to make allocations from the fund to E's son B, after B reaches the age of 18.

Note

Note the difference between a contingent interest and a discretionary interest. In the previous example, when B reaches the age of 18, he becomes absolutely entitled to the £50,000 in government securities in addition to any accumulated income.

In this example, when B reaches the age of 18, payment to him is at the discretion of D and E.

Minors

10.10 If an individual beneficiary who is under 18 years of age has a contingent interest in property (for example, contingent upon his reaching 18 years of age) and if the property is to pass to another person if the contingency is not fulfilled, then the minor's interest is vested in possession liable to be divested.[1]

Example

A leaves £50,000 worth of government securities to his nephew B contingent upon B reaching 18 years of age. If B dies before reaching 18 years of age, the securities are to pass to A's niece C, immediately. B's interest is vested, liable to be divested.

In a UK case, where the income on a gift was to be accumulated and the gift was to pass to the beneficiary contingent upon the beneficiary reaching 21 years of age (or marrying, if earlier) it was held that the beneficiary had a vested interest in the income. Consequently the beneficiary was liable to be taxed on income as it arose.[2]

In Ireland the rule that a minor's contingent interest is vested and liable to be divested does not apply to personal as distinct from real property.[3]

The issue was further clarified in a case where a settlement provided for the accumulation of capital and income on a number of separate funds until the attainment of specified ages by beneficiaries with a gift over to the other beneficiaries on an earlier death. The Revenue had claimed that the interest of each beneficiary was vested liable to be divested

In so far as real estate is concerned the issue whether a devise of settlement has created a vested or contingent interest is always difficult to decide because of the rule of construction said to have been established in *Phibbs v Ackers* (9 CI and Fin 583) but the property settled in this case consisted of shares and debentures and so the meaning of the settlement is to be determined by the words used in the context and not by artificial rules derived from medieval social conditions (see *Murphy v Murphy* [1951] IR 308).[4]

References

1   This is known as the rule in *Phibbs v Acker* [1842] 9 Cl & Fin. The basis for the rule was that in respect of real property there must at all times be an interest in possession.
2   Rowlatt J in *Gascoigne v CIR* [1927] KB 594; 13 TC 573. The ruling was upheld by the House of Lords in *CIR v Pakenham and Others* 1928 AC 252; 13 TC 573.
3   *Murphy v Murphy* [1951] IR 308. Recent English decisions even where personal property was involved have followed the rule in *Phibbs v Ackers*. See *In Re Kilpatrick's Policies Trusts* [1946] 1 WLR 248.
4   Kenny J in *Revenue Commissioners v Royal Trust Co (Ireland) Ltd*, unreported, HC, 8 November 1971, (1971) No 149 sp. The judge's decision did not discuss the implications of accumulated income of persons not of full age arising from real property.

Liability of trustees

10.11 If the trustees of a trust are assessed to income tax on the income of the trust no deduction is allowed for management expenses.[1]

Furthermore, as trustees are collectively a separate body of persons from the individuals or other persons acting as trustees they are not entitled to claim the personal allowances and reliefs available to individuals or the management expenses allowable to investment companies.[2]

However income received by an individual in a fiduciary or representative capacity, is taxable at the standard rate (27% for 1994-95).[3]

References

1   *Aiken v MacDonald Trustees* 3 TC 306.
2   *CIR v Countess of Longford* [1928] AC 252; 13 TC 573. See also 10.13 (guardians or committee of incapacitated persons).
3   FA 1974 s 3(2).

Liability of beneficiaries

Introduction

10.12 Where a trustee has authorised the receipt of profit from trust property by a person entitled thereto directly or by his agent and furnishes particulars of the beneficiary and the amount of the distribution to the Revenue Commissioners he is not required to do any other act for the assessment of the beneficiary.[1]

If a beneficiary receives income from trust property directly (ie where the income does not pass through the hands of the trustees), and the trustees give details of the beneficiary's name, the amount of the distribution etc to the Revenue Commissioners, then the beneficiary (not the trustee) is liable to income tax on the income arising.

Thus a foreign resident beneficiary who was directly entitled to interest on UK Government securities (not taxable in the hands of a foreign resident) was regarded as the assessable person (not the trustees) in the leading UK case[2] in this matter.

In practice if the trustees furnish a return of trust income with full particulars of distributions made to the Irish resident beneficiaries who are directly entitled to the income arising the beneficiaries will be directly assessed to tax. In the case of a non-resident beneficiary, a formal appointment of an interest is necessary[1] and income arising constitutes an annual payment from which tax is deductible[3] unless the income is exempt in the hands of a non-resident (for example, income arising on government securities).[4]

Trustees should consider carefully whether to have trust income paid directly to the beneficiaries as under general trust law trustees are accountable to beneficiaries for the administration of a trust and a beneficiary may look for a statement of the allocation of trust property.[5]

If for example, an annuity is a charge on income of a trust the trustees must deduct tax on payment and account for the deduction to the Revenue Commissioners.[3] This can be overcome in practice if all the beneficiaries agree to set aside the income from specified property to pay the annuity.

References
1   ITA 1967 s 213.
2   *Williams v Singer* [1921] AC 165; 7 TC 387.
3   ITA 1967 ss 433, 434.
4   ITA 1967 s 474.
5   *Chaine-Nickson v Bank of Ireland* [1946] IR 393.

Incapacitated persons

10.13 Trustees, guardians etc of incapacitated persons are charged to tax in the same manner as the incapacitated person would be if he were not incapacitated. This means that personal allowances and reliefs to which the incapacitated person is entitled can be claimed by the appointed persons. However such trustees etc can also be charged to tax at rates higher than the standard rate.[1]

References
1   ITA 1967 ss 208, 209.

Foreign trusts

10.14 As discussed in 10.12, where (in the case of an Irish resident trust) a beneficiary is paid income directly, and the trustees have supplied his name etc to the Revenue, the beneficiary (not the trustee) is liable to the income tax arising. This is known as the "look through" principle: the trustees are ignore.

If the trust is a foreign trust (all trustees are non-resident) the matter is more complex. In the case of a US trust, the "look through" principle was applied on the basis that US law governing the trust was similar to English law.[1] Later, it was held that the same beneficiary was only entitled to a payment from the trust and not to a specific share of the trust income. Accordingly the "look through" principle was not to be applied and therefore only the income remitted to the UK was to be charged.[2]

Depending on whether the charge to tax is on income arising or remittances, it may be more beneficial to have the "look through" principle applied as there may be exemptions or tax credits available under double taxation agreements with the State of residence of the governing settlement.

References
1   [1927] AC 844; 11 TC 749.
2   *Garland v Archer-Shee* [1931] AC 212; 15 TC 693.

Income arising in the State

10.15 The trustees of an Irish resident trust are not liable to Irish income tax on trust income which arises abroad (other than in the United Kingdom) payable to a non-resident beneficiary (including a resident of the United Kingdom).[1]

The trustees of a foreign trust that has Irish sourced income are liable to Irish income tax on such income.[2] However, that persons who are not ordinarily resident in the State are exempt from Irish income tax on interest arising from Irish Government and semi-State securities.[3]

References
1   *Williams v Singer* [1921] AC 165; 7 TC 387; ITA 1967 Sch 6.
2   ITA 1967 s 52(1).
3   ITA 1967 s 474.

Income arising abroad

10.16 Irish residents who are domiciled abroad, and Irish citizens who are not ordinarily resident in the State, are only liable to Irish income tax on income remitted into the State (the remittance basis). The remittance basis does not apply to UK sourced income or Sch E (employment) income.[1]

References
1   ITA 1967 s 76(2)-(3). See Butterworth Ireland Tax Guide at 4.01.

Tax credits on company distributions

10.17 Only Irish resident companies or persons resident in the State are entitled to tax credit relief in respect of distributions made by Irish resident companies.[1]

However, double taxation agreements negotiated since the enactment of the Corporation Tax Act 1976 provide partial tax credit relief to foreign resident investors in Irish resident companies. Full tax credit relief is also given to non-resident individuals who qualify for a proportion of the personal allowances and reliefs available to resident individuals against their taxable income.[2]

References
1   CTA 1976 s 88.
2   CTA 1976 s 160, ITA 1967 s 153.

Payments by trustees

Income and capital payments

10.18 Distributions by trustees are governed by the terms of the deed of trust. While trusts can be created orally or by informal transfers such trusts may be impossible to enforce.

A typical trust document may provide for one or more of the following kinds of payments from the trustees to the beneficiaries:

(*a*)   payment of income only,

(*b*)   payment of income with recourse to capital,

(*c*)   discretionary payments,

(*d*)   payments from accumulated income which pass as capital on the happening of a contingency.

Where the deed of trust provides for continuing or annual payments out of income with a recourse to capital all such payments are regarded as being of an income nature with tax deductible at source on payment.[1]

Nevertheless, in certain circumstances, exceptional large payments may still qualify as capital, and thus avoid deduction of tax at source. Thus where trustees exercised discretion in paying the substantial nursing home fees of an aged beneficiary, who was entitled to maintenance and support out of the trust funds, the exceptional payments were regarded as being of an emergency nature and should be classed as capital.

References
1 *Brodie's Trustees v CIR* TC 432; *Jackson's Trustees v CIR* 25 TC 13.
2 *Stevenson v Wishart and Others* [1987] 2 All ER 428; 59 TC 740.

Winding up of trust

10.19 Under the rules of equity where all the beneficiaries of a trust have interests in possession and are of full age they are entitled, although the trust period may not be exhausted and irrespective of the wishes of the trustees, to seek a winding up of the trust.[1] If such beneficiaries opt not to wind up the trust, each is chargeable directly to income tax on his appropriate share of income as it arises to the trust.[2]

References
1 *Saunders v Vautier* [1841] Cr & Ph 240. See 5.03.
2 *Hamilton-Russell's Executors v CIR.* [1943] 1 All ER 474; 25 TC 200.

Remuneration of trustees

10.20 Where a trust deed provides for remuneration to be payable to trustees, such remuneration is regarded as an annual payment subject to taxation at source.[1] If, however, under the terms of a trust a professional body is entitled to payment for work done any such payment should be made gross and is to be regarded as taxable income in the hands of the recipient.

References
1 *Baxendale v Murphy* 9 TC 76.

Discretionary payments to beneficiaries

10.21 Payments made on a discretionary basis by trustees to the beneficiaries that are not paid from accumulated income are to be regarded as the income of the beneficiary in the year of receipt.[1]

References
1 *Drummond v Collins* 6 TC 525.

10.22 The recipient of a payment made from a trust may not be beneficially entitled to such payments. Thus, where a life tenant of Slane Castle was entitled to an annual sum to be used for the maintenance and upkeep of the Castle it was held that the sum payable was on capital account as the life tenant received such payments as a trustee and not beneficially.[1]

References
1   *Marchioness of Conyngham v Revenue Commissioners* 1 ITC 259.

Accumulated income

10.23 Many deeds of trust include a term which provides that the trustees must accumulate the income on behalf of the beneficiaries.

Example

A leaves £50,000 in government securities to his nephew B. In the meantime, the income on the securities is to be accumulated contingent [1] upon B reaching the age of 18.

When the income can be said to have been accumulated is not clear. It can be important, for example, when determining the entitlement of persons to a payment of tax credit under the 1976 Ireland-United Kingdom Double Taxation Convention.[2] It appears that there is an accumulation of income when there is evidence to support it.

It should not be assumed that all undistributed income arising in a tax year or accounting period is automatically accumulated.

If no beneficiary is absolutely entitled in possession, the trustees may require time to decide what distributions to make. It is likely that income can be regarded as having been accumulated when trust accounts are prepared, or an income tax return is lodged. It may be significant that 18 months must elapse after the end of a tax year before a surcharge is imposed on undistributed income of certain trusts.[3]

References
1   ITA 1967 s 154.
2   Articles 11 and 20 (SI 319/1976).
3   FA 1976 s 13.

Trust management expenses

Introduction

10.24 Where trustees of a trust are chargeable to income tax they are liable to tax on the gross income without any deduction for management expenses (see 10.11).

The amount available for the beneficiaries is accordingly reduced both by the tax liability of the trustees and also by any other management expenses. The cost of acquiring or disposing of property is clearly capital expenditure. On the other hand, a professional trustee's authorised expenses are revenue expenses. Capital expenditure does not reduce the size of income for distribution. Although the trustees pay tax on gross income, only the tax applicable to the net distributed income is available to beneficiaries either by way of a credit or by repayment. [1] This restriction can be overcome by providing in the governing deed that all the trust expenses are to be funded out of capital.

The personal liabilities of beneficiaries are not "management expenses" of the trustees. Such problems mainly arise in respect of limited interests in land or buildings. Thus it has been held that payments of rates, taxes, ground rent, insurance and energy costs by the trustees in respect of a life tenant's interest were on behalf of the life tenant (and were not management expenses) [2].

References

1   *CIR v Lord Hamilton of Dalzell* 10 TC 406; *Murray v CIR* 11 TC 133; *MacFarlane v CIR* 14 TC 532. In the MacFarlane case the implications of the decision in *Baker v Archer-Shee* (11 TC 749) were considered not to overrule the effect of the two earlier quoted decisions.
2   *Lindus and Hortin v CIR* 17 TC 442: see also *Lord Tollemache v CIR* 11 TC 279.

Computation

10.25 Where a beneficiary with a vested interest in property is chargeable directly to income tax on income as it arises there is no adjustment for trust management expenses. Similarly, where trustees arrange to have payments of income made directly to beneficiaries whose names they have reported to the Revenue [1] there is no adjustment to the management expenses.

References

1   ITA 1967 s 213.

Example

A, in 1990-91, under a testamentary disposition had a life interest in leased property producing a gross rental of £2,000. The benefit was charged with an annuity of £200. The management expenses of the trustees were bank charges of £10 and collection costs of £50. Rates and insurance on the premises amounting to £400 were paid by the trustees .

	£	£
Charge on trustees		
Gross rent (Case V)		2,000
Tax chargeable (2,000 @ 30%)		600
		1,400
Less annuity (net after tax)	140	
Management expenses	60	200
		1,200
Deduct payments made on behalf of life tenant		400

Available for distribution	800
Charge on life tenant	
Net income receivable	800
Payments made by trustees on life tenant's behalf	400
	1,200
Gross income (1,200 grossed @ 30%)	1,714
Expenses allowable (ITA 1967 s 81(5))	400
Chargeable income	1,314
Tax credit available (1,714 - 1,200)	514
Annuitant	
Chargeable income (140 grossed @ 30%)	200
Tax credit available	60

Example

The 1990-91 income of an Irish trust was as follows:

Source	Net	Tax/tax credit
	£	£
Irish dividends (manufacturing company)	360	40
Irish deposit interest (subject to DIRT)	140	60
Irish National Loan interest	200	-

The trustees had purchased, with the consent of the beneficiaries, the Irish Government stock to meet an annuity liability to a UK resident. The remaining funds were held in trust for an Irish resident life interest holder. Trust management expenses amount to £60.

Charges on trustees

No direct charge to income tax. The national loan interest is not chargeable as it was beneficially receivable by a person not ordinarily resident in the State in accordance with the provisions in ITA 1967 s 474.

The arrangement in this matter constitutes a severed portion of the trust property. The other income arising is franked and not chargeable further in the hands of the trustee. The income available for distribution to the life tenant is calculated as follows:

Source	Net	Tax/tax credit
	£	£
	500	100
Management expenses	60	12
60 x (100/500)		
	440	88
	528	

Notes

1. Under CTA 1976 s 83(1), the sum chargeable under Schedule F is the amount of the distribution plus the tax credit.

2. The amount chargeable on the life tenant, £528, is liable, where appropriate, to the higher (but not the standard) rate of tax.

3. Even if there had been no separate identifiable fund to pay the annuity due to the UK resident the same exemption could also have been achieved if the trustees formally

authorised that the National Loan interest be paid directly to the annuitant under ITA 1967 s 213. Ireland-UK Double Taxation Convention 1976 article 12(1) [1] provides that Irish sourced interest arising to a UK resident is chargeable only in the UK.

References
1   SI No 319/1976.

Example

The following was the income of an Irish resident discretionary trust for 1990-91 as disclosed in the trust's return of income for 1991-92.

Source	Net	Irish tax
	£	£
UK dividends (after payment of credit relief by the UK)	170	30*
UK loan interest	1,000	300*
US common stock dividend	425	0*
(15% credit allowed on encashment)		
	1,595	330

* Figures after adjustment for tax credit relief allowable. The US dividends were subject to a non-refundable 15% withholding tax at source.

The management expenses of the trust were £75. The trust distributed £1,000 to a single Irish resident member of the qualifying class and accumulated the balance.

	£	£
Management expenses		
330 x (75/1,595)	75	15

Amount available for distribution

Source	Net	Irish tax
	£	£
	1,595	330
Management expenses	75	15
	1,520	315

Liability of trustees		
UK dividends as declared (ITA 1967 Sch 6 Pt I)	200	
UK loan interest	1,000	
US common stock dividends (net 425 grossed up at	607	
trustees effective rate 30%)		
	1,807	
Tax chargeable @ 30%		542
Less		
Tax credit allowable		
UK dividends (15% max)	30	
US dividends (607-425)	182	212
		330

Position of beneficiary
Share of Irish tax
315 x (1,000/1,520)   207

Distribution (£1,000) plus tax (£207) amounts to £1,207.

Notes
1. Tax is chargeable on the beneficiary on a sum of £1,207 at the higher rates of tax if relevant.
2. No further tax credit is due on the share of the UK dividends taken by the beneficiary as the full relief allowable has already been granted to the trustees. Indeed technically if a beneficiary's personal effective rate of tax chargeable as determined in accordance with ITA 1967 Sch 10 para 5 is less than the rate of credit allowed to the trustees (15%) a claw-back of relief is required calculated on the principles set out in the following example but such adjustments are ignored in practice.
3. A further allowance of tax credit may arise in respect of the US Common Stock dividends where the personal effective income tax rate of the beneficiary exceeds the standard 30% rate. The figure available for relief is as follows:

$$425 \text{ (net dividend)} \times (1,000/1,520) = 280 \text{ (A)}$$

This figure (A) is grossed up at the beneficiary's personal effective rate of tax to arrive at a revised gross on which tax is chargeable (B). The amount of further tax credit allowable is (B)-(A) subject to a maximum of the combined rates of US withholding tax and the underlying rate of tax suffered by the paying company.

Repayment of UK Tax (Ireland-UK Double Taxation Convention 1976 articles 11 and 12).
Tax credit payable (article 11)

	Net	*Irish Tax*
	£	£
Distribution	150	50
Restriction (article 11(2))		<u>30</u>
Amount available for payment by UK Revenue		20
Allocation of payment		
Beneficiary 20 x (1,000 x 1,595)		12.54
Trustee 20 x (520/1,595)		6.52

Repayment on loan interest (article 12)

	Net	*Irish tax*
	£	£
Amount	750	250
Beneficiary 250 x (1,000/1,595)		156.74
Trustee 250 x (520/1,595)		81.50

The United Kingdom side has, effectively, confined the proportionate repayment entitlements to tax on income arising after deducting the management expenses figures applicable.

Anti-avoidance

Introduction

10.26 For tax years to 1972-73 inclusive, one of the principal advantages of having income accrue in trust was that such income was only taxed at the standard rate, thus avoiding sur-tax.[1]

Up to the income tax year 1972-73 where income of a trust was accumulated for the benefit of a person contingent on that person attaining a certain age or marrying earlier, the person could, when the accumulated income vested in him, claim personal allowances and reliefs against the trust income for all years since the settlement was made.[2] Normal statutory time limits for claims did not apply. In the absence of this relief the accumulations would have passed to the beneficiary as capital.

For 1973-74 and later years, the income arising to a trust is taxed at the standard rate,[3] and for 1976-77 and later tax years, a 20% surcharge applies to any trust income that is undistributed within 18 months after the tax year.[4]

References
1   *CIR. v Countess of Longford* 13 TC 573.
2   ITA 1967 s 154.
3   FA 1974 s 3.
4   FA 1976 s 13.

Offshore companies

10.27 Apart from a question of secrecy of the effect of transactions, a trust provided a safe haven for family property to be protected and distributed as needed. Despite the rules against perpetuities and accumulations the period of a private trust can extend over a hundred years under present Irish law (see 3.29).[1]

In more recent times companies registered in so called tax havens have become more popular than trusts as a means of preserving and protecting property. Some countries which have double taxation agreements with Ireland have lower tax rates, especially in relation to personal property or choses in action. Such companies provide a perpetual legal entity separate from the individual settlors. The rights to the property are embodied in the company's shares which can be transferred with relative ease. In addition the absence of records available for public scrutiny may facilitate the transfer of property without the intervention of trustees.

10.28 In addition to low rates of tax and other charges in the country of registration, foreign companies may benefit from exemption from tax of dividends received from external sources if the shareholding is substantial.

References

1 Under the Perpetuities and Accumulations Act 1964, which applies in England and Wales, the maximum perpetuity period of settlement, whether inter vivos or testamentary, is eighty years. This rule is not, as in Irish circumstances, applied on a theoretical basis by reference to the position existing at the date of the settlement, but considered in the light of emerging facts.

Surcharge on undistributed trust income

10.29 The 20% surcharge is chargeable on the trustee in respect of income arising in a tax year in excess of any management expenses applicable where the income:[1]

(*a*)   is accumulated (irrespective of whether this is done under express provisions in the governing documentation or at the discretion of the trustees);

(*b*)   is not regarded as the income of any person other than the trustees for income tax purposes; and

(*c*)   is not distributed or paid away on behalf of any beneficiary within the tax year or 18 months after the end of that year.

In essence, the surcharge applies to contingent (see 5.09) or discretionary trusts (see 5.14) where there is no vested interest in possession (see 5.07) of income when it arises.

The surcharge does not apply to bodies established for charitable purposes only or approved superannuation funds or schemes.

Since the introduction of self-assessment on a current year basis the surcharge is to be treated as income tax chargeable in the year of assessment for which it is so charged.[2]

Example

The income of an Irish resident discretionary trust for 1988-89 was £2,000, which was all accumulated subject to the payment of £100 management expenses. No distributions or payments on behalf of any of the class of beneficiaries were made before 5 October 1990.

1988-89 (self assessment)

	£	£
Trust income (preceding year basis)		2,000
Income tax @ 35%		700
		1,300
Management expenses		100
Accumulated income		1,200
1990-91		
Accumulated income (1,200) grossed at 1989-90 standard rate (35%)		1,846
Surcharge @ 20%		369
Net income available for distribution by trustees (1,200-369)		831
Position of beneficiaries when distribution made		
1988-89 1,279 less tax @ 35%		448
Net		831

Note

The effects of the surcharge are disregarded in the hands of beneficiaries if and when distributions out of the accumulation are made. The charge is imposed on the trustees and in the circumstances there can be no separate charge made on beneficiaries in respect of the same transaction because Schedules to the Income Tax Act are mutually exclusive.[3]

On the other hand no repayment in respect of the surcharge may allowed to beneficiaries.[4]

References
1   FA 1976 s 13.
2   FA 1990 s 8 amending FA 1976 s 13(2).
3   *Salisbury House Estate v Fry* [1930] AC 432; 15 TC 266.
4   FA 1976 s 13(2).

Transfer of assets abroad

10.30 In 1974 measures were introduced to counter tax avoidance by the transfer of assets abroad by Irish residents.[1] They do not apply where either:

(*a*)   the purpose or one of the purposes of the transfer or associated operations was not the avoidance of tax; or

(*b*)   the transfer and any associated operations were bona fide commercial transactions.

10.31 Thus, the formation of an offshore company, or a foreign trust, followed by the transfer of assets to such a body from an Irish resident, to avoid tax, could run foul of this legislation.

References
1   FA 1974 ss 57 and 58. The latter section deals with administrative matters relating to the charge under s 57. See Judge: *Irish Income Tax* at 17.2

10.32 In effect, if an Irish resident has power to enjoy income (or receive a capital sum) from a foreign asset (which he has transferred abroad), he may be liable to Irish income tax on the income (or the capital sum) under Sch D Case IV, even where the income (or capital) is not remitted into Ireland.

Example

On 1 July 1976 A, an Irish resident individual transfers £100,000 to a Swiss bank account in the name of A Trust, a UK trust, over which A has discretionary power. The income is to be accumulated; the purpose of the transaction is to avoid tax.
On 1 July 1990 the account contains £250,000.
Since A has power to enjoy the income for tax years 1976-77 to 1990-91, he is liable to income tax on the notional annual interest, which totals £150,000.

Note
The Waiver of Certain Tax Interest And Penalties Act 1993 (incentive amnesty) would allow A to clear his tax liability on a once off basis at £150,000 x 15% = £22,750, provided the £250,000 was returned to Ireland. The amnesty expired in January 1994.

10.33 The transfer of assets abroad rules also apply to transactions under which income becomes payable to persons resident or domiciled outside the State. "Persons" in this context include both companies and bodies of persons. "Company" is defined as any body corporate or unincorporated association.[1]

A body corporate which is incorporated outside the State is treated as resident outside the State whether or not it is so resident.[2] In normal circumstances the residence of a company for Irish tax purposes is determined by reference to the place of effective management.[3]

References
1   FA 1974 s 57(8),
2   FA 1974 s 57(7). The UK Finance (No 2) Act 1990 s 66 provides that, in similar circumstances, a company is to be treated as resident outside the UK when foreign resident status arises under double taxation treaties.
3   This test is used to determine the residence of persons other than individuals under the OECD Model Tax Convention 1977, art 4(3). However, individual tax treaties need to be examined as they do not all follow the Model (for example, Japan).

General anti-avoidance

10.34 In 1989 general anti-avoidance legislation[1] was introduced which allows the Revenue to deal with any "tax advantage" which arises in respect of reliefs or exemptions resulting from transactions.

The Revenue Commissioners are given power to re characterise for tax purposes the nature of any payment or other relief which, in their opinion, is a "tax avoidance transaction".[2] A "tax avoidance transaction" is one which:

(*a*)   gives rise to a tax advantage; and

(*b*)   was not undertaken or arranged primarily for purposes other than to obtain a tax advantage.

The Commissioners must also give relief for any double taxation which arises as a consequence of any adjustment they make.[3]

References
1   FA 1989 s 86, following the Supreme Court decision in *MacDermott v McGrath,*   1988   ILRM 847; ITR December 1987 (HC) and July 1988 (SC). See Judge: *Irish Income Tax* at 17.3.
2   FA 1989 s 86(5)(*b*)(iii).
3   FA 1989 s 86(5)(*c*).

Foreign trusts

10.35 In a case taken to the House of Lords in 1949 that body decided that where two Vestey brothers had transferred property abroad to be held as capital and accumulated income for the benefit of children and remoter issue of the settlors who had, however, retained power over the nature of the investments to be made under the settlement, the income arising was *not* that of the settlors for income tax purposes.[1]

In 1979 the House of Lords, having examined two cases also involving the Vestey family, decided that the Commissioners of Inland Revenue had no power to assess the accumulated income of a foreign resident discretionary trust on any of the class of beneficiaries who were resident in the United Kingdom.[2]

References

1   *Vestey's Executors and Vestey v CIR* [1949] 1 All ER 1108; 31 TC 1.
2   *Vestey v CIR (No 1)*; *Vestey v. CIR (No 2)* [1979] WLR 915; 1979 3 All ER 976; 54 TC 503; see also *Pratt v CIR* 57 TC 1.

Interpretation

10.36 The Irish courts will interpret tax law provisions according to its ordinary or natural meanings in the absence of any special meanings or definitions in the legislation. Furthermore, the courts will not add to or delete from the expressed statutory wording to achieve objectives which might be considered desirable. It appears therefore that the persuasive effect of the English decisions cited above will be to confine the effect of the transfer of assets abroad legislation to settlors, and spouses of settlors.

The transfer of assets abroad legislation also applies to the enjoyment, by an individual ordinarily resident in the State, of income and certain capital receipts received by a person resident or domiciled out of the State when:

(*a*)   at sometime, irrespective of the form in which they are received, the receipts ensure for the benefit of the individual;

(*b*)   the receipts increase the value of the assets held by the individual or for his benefit;

(*c*)   the receipts are received by the individual or there is an entitlement to a receipt by the individual;

(*d*)   the receipts arise to the individual following the exercise of a power of appointment, revocation or any other power under a discretionary trust; and

(*e*)   the individual can exercise direct or indirect control over the application of the receipts.

References

1   *Kieran v de Brún* ITL 117; *MacDermott v McGrath* [1988] ILTR 847; [1987] ITR 406 (HC) and [1988] ITR 131 (SC).
2   FA 1974 s 57(5).

Offshore funds

Introduction

10.37 The general provisions to curb tax avoidance by the transfer of assets abroad have been supplemented by detailed measures ("the offshore funds legislation")[1] designed to curtail activities by resident (or ordinarily resident) Irish taxpayers which result in the conversion of income receipts from foreign invested capital into tax-free capital gains receipts.

The method mostly used was to establish, usually in areas with low tax charges and lax controls on investments, a trust company which accumulated (rolled up) the income arising on its investments. When the company was later wound up the proceeds, including the accumulated income, were distributable to shareholders (who were not the settlors) as capital free from any Irish capital gains tax charge. The provisions apply from 6 April 1990.[2]

References
1   FA 1990 Pt 1 Ch VII, and Schs 5-6.
2   FA 1990 s 66(8). See Judge: *Irish Income Tax* at 17.4.

Material interest

10.38 A material interest in an offshore fund is defined as a material interest in any of the following:
- (*a*)   a company resident outside the State;
- (*b*)   a unit trust scheme, of which the trustees are non-resident; and
- (*c*)   any other arrangements creating rights of co-ownership including those recognised by foreign jurisdictions.[1]

10.39 A material interest is one which an investor could reasonably expect to be able to realise within a period of seven years.[2]

From 6 April 1990 onwards, where such an interest exists in a non-distributing offshore fund, any undistributed income element included in any consideration received by an Irish resident or ordinary resident on a disposal of trust property is to be chargeable as income without any indexation.[3] While the meaning given to a disposal in taxing gains in offshore funds is generally the same as for capital gains tax purposes there are two important exceptions:
- (*a*)   a death constitutes a disposal of an interest in an offshore fund;[4] and
- (*b*)   exchanges of share or debentures in non-distributing offshore funds are to be regarded as disposals.[5]

References
1   FA 1990 s 65(1).
2   FA 1990 s 65(2).
3   FA 1990 s 67(2) and (3) applying CGTA 1975 s 4.
4   FA 1990 s 63(3).
5   FA 1990 s 63(5).

Distributing fund

10.40 The offshore funds legislation does not apply to an offshore fund which qualifies as a distributing fund. To qualify, a distributing fund must distribute, either directly or through an equalisation fund, at least 85% of the income and profits arising.[1]

An offshore fund must be certified as qualifying by the Revenue Commissioners for each separate account period.[2] Except in special circumstances where investments are made by a distributing offshore fund in another offshore fund,[3] the Commissioners may not certify a fund as a distributing one for an account period where;[4]

(*a*)   more than 5% of the assets of the fund consist of interests in other non-distributing offshore funds;

(*b*)   more than 10% of the assets are invested in a single company; or

(*c*)   there are differing classes of interests in the fund with separate distribution benefits.

References
1   FA 1990 Sch 5 paras (1) and (4).
2   FA 1990 s 66 and Sch 5.
3   FA 1990 Sch 5 Pt II.
4   FA 1990 s 66(3), (4), (5) and (7).

Charities

10.41 A charity (within the definition in ITA 1967 s 334) is exempt from tax on an offshore income gain arising from a disposal made by a non-qualifying offshore fund.[1]

References
1   FA 1990 s 67(5).

Offshore gains

10.42 Where offshore gains accrue to a company resident abroad which if it had been an Irish resident would have been regarded as a close company (controlled by five or fewer participators[1]) any distributions made out of the proceeds of the disposal to a shareholder who:

(*a*)   is resident or ordinarily resident in the State;

(*b*)   if an individual is domiciled in the State;

are to be treated as income within the charge to Schedule D Case IV in respect of the appropriate share of any rolled up income included in a disposal.[2]

References
1   CTA 1976 s 94(1).
2   FA 1990 ss 67(1) and 68 (1).

Accumulated income

10.43 Where the earlier accumulated income of an offshore fund subsequently becomes chargeable to income tax under Schedule D Case IV one half-share of the profits is to be disregarded to the extent that the accumulations are profits from dealing in commodities through future or option contracts.[1] The excluded share is subject to a capital gains tax charge in the normal way.

References
1   FA 1990 Sch 5, para 4.

Tax credit

10.44 Provisions have been included in the offshore funds legislation to avoid a double charge to tax on the same property.[1] When determining any capital gains tax charge leviable on a disposal a deduction is to be made for any offshore gain chargeable as income.

References
1   FA 1990 s 69.

Double taxation relief

Deduction

10.45 Where foreign income is chargeable in full to Irish income tax a *deduction* for any foreign tax suffered is allowable from the Schedule D Case III charge.[1]

No such deduction is available when the charge on an individual is by reference to remitted income, as it is considered that all such remittances are made after satisfying all external liabilities.

References
1   ITA 1967 s 76(1).

Credit for foreign tax

10.46 A *credit* for foreign tax is only given by Irish tax legislation when there is an appropriate double taxation treaty in operation. Otherwise a deduction for foreign tax is given (see 10.43). A limited measure of unilateral tax credit may be claimed for dividends on interest arising from reinvestment of profits which qualified for export sales relief or Shannon relief.[1]

The wording of the OECD Model Double Taxation Convention 1977, article 21, paragraph 1, has given rise to differing views on the effect of double tax relief arrangements on trust income:

> 1. Items of income of a resident of a Contracting State, wherever arising, not dealt with in the foregoing articles of this Convention shall be taxable only in that State.

No guidelines are set out as to the nature of the income which it is intended to cover. The United Kingdom has entered a reservation against the wording in order to preserve a right to tax trust income paid by UK residents to non-residents. Ireland has not followed the UK in this matter.

Double tax agreements do not create a charge for Irish income tax purposes but provide for exemption or relief from an existing charge under Irish tax law.

In the first instance, the nature of any income payment is examined under the appropriate charging sections and if there is no charge or an exemption applies, that is the end of the matter. The existence of a relevant foreign double tax agreement does not change the nature of a payment under Irish tax law.[1] Claims for relief by beneficiaries of trusts are examined by applying the "look through" principle (see 10.14) to the items of income making up the payments from the trust.

In such circumstances the need for a specific reference to trust income in an Other Income Article in a double taxation convention appears unnecessary, as the earlier articles relating to the separate and distinct categories of income have covered the matter. Such references have, however, been included in the formal arrangements in force with both Sweden[2] and the United Kingdom.[3]

References
1   This view finds support from the decisions of both the High and Supreme Courts in *Asahi Synthetic Fibres (Ireland) Ltd v Murphy* [1985] IR 509 (HC) and [1986] IR 777 (SC) where it was held that a distribution under Irish tax law was not to be reclassified as an interest payment in accordance with the provisions of the 1974 Ireland/Japan Double Taxation Agreement (SI 259/1974).
2   SI 348/1987.
3   SI 319/1976.

Chapter 11

Special categories of private trusts

Maintenance agreements

Introduction

11.01 Historically trusts have been used to preserve property within the extended family circle and, accordingly, it is not surprising that transfers of assets and income between spouses and by them to their children and/or remoter issues have figured prominently in tax law.

Payments to spouses

11.02 Where a husband transfers property to a wife, child (or to an individual for whom he is acting in loco parentis) there is a presumption that he has advanced the property with effect that the transferee becomes immediately entitled in possession.[1]

References

1   See 3.13-3.15 and *Equity and the Law of Trusts in the Republic of Ireland* Keane J (Butterworths) at 12.3-12.6. *Family Law in the Republic of Ireland* Shatter (Wolfhound Press), 505-508 and 514-516.

Payments to or for children

11.03-04 In 1939 the UK Court of Appeal[1] held, in divorce proceedings, that where under a court order payments were to be made to a spouse for the benefit of children of marriage while they were under 21 years of age and unmarried, any such payments were to be regarded as the income of the receiving spouse and not that of the children.

In a 1951 UK Court of Appeal case[2] again concerned with divorce proceedings, it was decided that where a husband was required to pay annual sums to his former wife in trust for the children the wife was a trustee and the beneficial ownership of the sums vested in the children.

These decisions were in practice followed by the Irish Revenue. Thus where income for the support of dependent children was taken by a spouse directly and not a trustee or guardian the spouse was personally liable for income tax in respect of that income.

However in the light of a High Court decision delivered on 9 November 1988[3] which has been accepted by the Revenue without further appeal, it is now doubtful if this principle is applicable in Ireland. That case concerned pension payments payable to a widow of a Garda Síochána dependent on the circumstances of her children. The relevant regulations read:

> (1) a children's contributory pension will be paid to the member's widow if the eligible children are in her care, ... In all cases, the pension is to be applied for the benefit of the children for whom it is granted.

> (6) ...., where the deceased leaves a widow and a widow's contributory pension is not granted to her, or is granted but ceases to be paid before her death, a children's contributory pension shall not be payable as respects any period comprised within the time in respect of which no widow's contributory pension is payable, unless the Minister in his absolute discretion directs that a children's contributory pension shall be payable, ...

The inspector claimed that the widow was liable to income tax on the children's contributory pension entitlements (para (6)). The judge rejected this argument and held that such payments were the personal income of the children.

While the regulations provided specifically that payments were to be applied for the benefit of the qualifying children, the tenor of the decision appears to indicate that the principle underlying the decision would have been accepted by the Judge even if this specific requirement was absent.

References
1   *Stevens v Tirard* [1939] 4 All ER 186; 23 TC 321.
2   *Yates v Starkey* [1951] 1 All ER 732; 32 TC 38.
3   *O'Coindealbháin v O'Carroll* [1989] IR 229.

Taxation of maintenance payments

Maintenance agreements made before 8 June 1983

11.05 Before 8 June 1983, general maintenance and other similar payments receivable by a spouse under a deed of separation, a court order or a foreign divorce decree created many practical difficulties for tax purposes. Whether Irish tax was to be deducted at source when making maintenance payments depended on whether the payment was regarded as an annual payment within ITA 1967 s 433.

In general, if the law governing the maintenance agreement was Irish, the payer was obliged to deduct Irish tax irrespective of his own residence status. Otherwise payment was to be made in full. [1] The matter was further complicated by a High Court decision [2] and the passing of family law legislation [3] which established that maintenance payments payable under Irish court orders were not be regarded as annual payments from which tax was deductible on payment.

This meant that such payments were regarded as applications of income in the hands of the payer and, accordingly, no deduction was allowable for the payments in arriving at net statutory income, in contrast to maintenance payments which were not governed by a court order. Furthermore, maintenance payments governed by foreign law were deductible from any foreign income chargeable on the payer under Schedule D Case III. However, where there was no foreign income the income constituting the maintenance payment was effectively taxed twice by the two different countries concerned.

References

1   Following UK decisions in *Stakes v Bennett* [1953] 2 All ER 313; 34 TC 337, and *Keiner v Keiner* [1952] 1 All ER 643; 34 TC 346.
2   *Brolly v Brolly* [1939] IR 562.
3   Family Law (Maintenance of Spouses and Children Act) 1976 s 24.

Maintenance agreements made on or after 8 June 1983

Maintenance agreements entered into on or after 8 June 1983 are governed by simpler procedures. Two spouses may opt, by agreement, that the newer simpler procedures may apply to an arrangement entered into before 8 June 1983. The new procedures do not refer to the family home, or indeed to the law applicable to maintenance arrangements.

In essence, as regards maintenance payments made to (or for the benefit of) a spouse:

(*a*)   tax need not be deducted from the payment,

(*b*)   the payment is regarded as income in the hands of the recipient spouse,

(*c*)   the paying spouse is entitled to deduct the entire payment from his total income when calculating taxable income.

As regards maintenance payments made to (or for the benefit of) a child of the marriage:

(*a*)   tax need not be deducted from the payment,

(*b*)   the payment is *not* regarded as income in the hands of the child,

(*c*)   the paying spouse is *not* entitled to deduct the payment when calculating his taxable income.

Dispositions and settlements

Introduction

11.06 The term "disposition" is frequently used in Irish law to denote an agreement by which property is transferred. The term is very broadly defined for capital acquisitions tax purposes, in order to capture any method (including any omission or failure to act) by which property is transferred.[1]

For income tax purposes, as regards:

(*a*)   revocable dispositions,

(*b*)   dispositions for short periods,

(*c*)   dispositions in favour of children,

the term is defined as including "any trust, covenant, agreement or arrangement".[1]

References
1   ITA 1967 s 442.

Revocable dispositions

11.07 A disposition which purports to transfer a right to receive income, while reserving a power which allows the disponer to revoke the disposition, is not recognised as a valid transfer of income for income tax purposes. In effect, if the disponer is entitled to receive or enjoy the benefits of the whole or part of any income from the transferred interest, by howsoever means, without the consent of any other person the transfer is invalid for income tax purposes.[1] Any other person does not include a spouse of the settlor except where the spouses are separated.

Example

A, a wealthy individual creates a settlement under the terms of which B, A's former spouse is to enjoy the income arising from £50,000 worth of government securities (approximately £4,000 per annum). The settlement contains a clause which allows A to revoke the settlement at any time.
The income (£4,000 per annum) purportedly settled by A on B, is regarded as A's income for income tax purposes.

The disposition is invalid for income tax purposes if the disponer can revoke it "by means of the exercise of any power of appointment, power of revocation or otherwise howsoever". The phrase is to be given its ordinary meaning which includes any lawful means of effecting the transfer.[2]

It would appear that any power of revocation must be explicitly included in the terms of a disposition if the income is to be deemed that of the settlor. In a

UK case a disponer who had absolute control of a company's operations through a 70% shareholding covenanted to pay dividend income from the company's profits to his sisters. The indirect control which the disponer could exercise over the amount due under the disposition by determining the amount of the company's distributions was disregarded by the court.[3]

The corresponding provisions in UK law have been examined by the courts on several occasions.[4] In one such case, it was held that a disposition made by a widow which could benefit a future spouse was revocable.[5] The UK courts have also held in the context of revocable dispositions, that the term "spouse" does not to include a widow or widower.[6]

References
1   ITA 1967 s 438.
2   *Hughes v Smith* [1933] IR 253; 1 ITC 418.
3   *CIR v Wolfson* [1949] All ER 865; 31 TC 166.
4   ICTA 1988 s 673.
5   *CIR v Tennant* 24 TC 215.
6   *Vestey's Executors v CIR* 1 All ER 1109; 31 TC 1.

Dispositions of income for short periods

11.08 Dispositions for short periods, commonly known as deeds of covenant,[1] allow income which is, in effect, gifted to be recognised as income of the recipient and not of the disponer. This applies even where the transfer is not "for valuable and sufficient consideration".[2] For a deed of covenant to be valid, the income being transferred must:

(*a*)   arise from capital of which the disponer has divested himself in favour of, or for the benefit of, another person; or

(*b*)   be payable to an individual for his own use, or for the benefit of a named individual, for a period which exceeds or may exceed six years;

(*c*)   be payable to a trust fund governed by Irish law and administered in the State for the sole purpose of teaching the natural sciences in any university, college or school in the State, and be payable for a period which exceeds or may exceed three years.[3]

Income dispositions which do not meet the above conditions will be regarded as income of the disponer even if there is no power of revocation.

A disposition within (*b*) is also ineffective if the disposition is made by a parent in favour of his child while the child is under 18 years of age and unmarried. In such cases the income continues to be treated as income of the parent.[4]

After a child reaches 18 years of age or marries a parent may make a tax effective disposition but the total amount of such dispositions which will be tax effective is restricted to 5% of the parent's total or statutory income. [5] This restriction also applies to descendants – children, adopted children, stepchildren, illegitimate children or grandchildren of a settlor who are not permanently incapacitated by mental or physical infirmity.

Total or statutory income for income tax purposes excludes all income payments which are regarded as the income of another person. This means that the 5% restriction is applied after deducting superannuation contributions, mortgage interest on main residence and charges which include dispositions such as deeds of covenant.

In practice, therefore, to determine how much a parent can give to an adult descendant all other relevant payments are first deducted from his income and the fraction $5/105$ of the remainder is calculated. The resulting sum is the maximum tax effective disposition for all descendants.

References

1   ITA 1967 s 439.
2   *CIR v Plummer* 3 All ER 775; 54 TC 1. The House of Lords decided in this case that a settlement must involve an element of bounty.
3   ITA 1967 s 439(2)(*a*). The section also permits allowable payments to be made directly to the institutions shown for the same limited purpose. The institutions would be entitled to repayment of tax deducted as charitable bodies as they would be exempt from income tax (advancement of education: see 7.06 et seq).
4   ITA 1967 ss 440, 443.
5   ITA 1967 s 439(1A).

Example

A, a widower, had earnings of £14,000 in 1990-91. He paid £400 medical insurance in 1989-90. His mortgage interest payments on his residence in 1990-91 were £2,000. A had committed himself to pay £600 to each of three grandchildren under dispositions which satisfied the conditions for relief. The eldest grandchild only was over 18 years of age.

Calculation of restriction

	£	£
Total earnings	14,000	
Deductions:		
Mortgage interest (maximum relief)	1,600	
	12,400	
Restriction £12,400 x (5/105) =		590

Note
The revised amount allowable under ITA 1967 s 439(1) in respect of the disposition payable to the oldest grandchild is £590.

Example

The total incomes of a husband and wife who have opted for joint assessment under ITA 1967 s 194 amounted to £10,000. The husband A whose separate income amounted to

£8,000 had made a "seven year covenant" in favour of his grandson C in an annual sum of £300. The wife B had made a similar disposition for the same amount in favour of a grand-daughter D. The income and commitments of both spouses are aggregated to determine the measure of any restriction applicable. Both grandchildren are over 18 years of age.

Amount recognised as effective under ITA 1967 s 439(1A):

$$£10,000 \times (5/100) = £500$$

Each of the covenanted payments is restricted to:

$$£300 \times (5/6) = £250$$

Example

A widower with a total income of £12,000 settles £300 on each of three grandchildren aged over 18 under "seven year covenants".
Restriction applicable under section 439 (1A):

$$£12,000 \times (5/100) = £600$$

Amount allowable under each covenant:

$$£600 \times (300/900) = £200$$

Note
The sums shown as payable under the deeds of covenant included in both examples are, apart from any income tax consideration involved, valid contracts enforceable by or on behalf of the payee.
There is an initial commitment by the payer to remit the full sum due. The payer is then obliged to deduct tax at the standard rate (ITA 1967 s 433).
The subsequent 5% restriction (ITA 1967 s 439(1A) if applicable is a matter to be settled between the payer and the beneficiary (or his trustee or guardian) taking into consideration, where necessary, any increased liability of the settlor arising from the disallowance of relief.

Effective period of a covenant

11.09 Principles arrived at by the UK courts after considering the similar (but not identical)[1] UK legislation should be taken into consideration when drawing up a short term disposition of income (deed of covenant).

The effective period of a deed is to be calculated from the due date of the first payment until the due date of the last payment. To ensure that a disposition covers a period which is six years or longer the deed should state that the annual payments are to be made for a minimum period of seven years.[2]

There must also be an element of constancy in the annual payments made under a deed of covenant. An arrangement to pay part of a disponer's income for a period which *could* exceed six years would not qualify for relief on the grounds of uncertainty as to the amounts which would be payable to the disponer.[3]

The provisions of a disposition designed to qualify for the relief allowable should preferably be governed by Irish law given that a foreign disposition may not be recognised by the English courts.[4]

References
1   ICTA 1988 s 671.
2   *CIR v Trustees of St Luke's Hostel* 15 TC 682.
3   *D'Ambrumenil v CIR* [1940] 2 All ER 71; 23 TC 440. In that case it was decided that a further disposition seeking to extend the period of the earlier disposition was to be looked at separately.
4   *CIR v Countess of Kenmare* [1957] 3 All ER 33; 37 TC 383. *Becker v Wright* [1966] 1 All ER 563; 42 TC 591.

Settlements on children

Settlement for a period less than the life of the child

11.10 There are two provisions in Irish income tax law whose effect is to treat income settled on children by a parent as income of the parent.

The first provision[1] applies only to dispositions for the benefit of a child made directly or indirectly by a parent for a period which is less than the life of the child. It applies even where the settlor is non-resident.

The second provision[2] applies to every settlement, no matter where or when it was made or entered into, but it does not apply to income arising in any tax year in which the settlor is non-resident. Both sections apply to income of a settlement which is paid while the child is an infant (under 18 years of age) and unmarried.

In the UK a covenant by a father to pay annual sums to a child of his during their joint lives provided that the settlor could exercise a power of revocation with the consent of any of five named persons.[3] The court held that, despite the power of revocation, the interest transferred was not limited to a period less than the life of the child. This decision was based on the fact that the power was discretionary and not obligatory.[4]

References
1   ITA 1967 s 440.
2   ITA 1967 s 443.
3   *Wiggins v Watson's Trustees* [1933] ALL ER 504; 17 TC 741.
4   See also *E G v MacSamhrain* [1958] IR 217. This case concerned an appointment of income to a child by his mother out of income she had from a life interest in a settlement by her father. The High Court held that the deed of appointment was a settlement by the mother and the income was taxable as hers. ITA 1967 s 443 applied to settlement. ITA 1967 s 440(2) says that s 440 does apply to any settlement to which s 443. applies.

Deduction of tax

11.11 If income settled on a child (under a valid settlement for a period less than the life of the child) is regarded as income of the disponer, the disponer is entitled to recover the additional tax payable from the trustee or other person to whom the income is actually payable.[1]

The disponer must also pay over the benefit of any relief which he receives to the trustee or other person to whom the income is payable. In such circumstances the trustee or other person receiving the amount payable under a qualifying disposition is to refund the additional tax chargeable on the settlor, calculated as being referable to the highest part of the income of the settlor.

Example

A, by a short period disposition, dated 30 September 1984, covenanted to pay his mother as trustee for his incapacitated brother B an annual payment of £800, less income tax, for a period of six years, the first payment of which was due on 6 April 1984, payable in arrears on the signing of the disposition. Subsequent payments were to be made annually on 6 April.

As the last payment was due and payable on 6 April 1989, the effective period of the disposition is less than six years and while enforceable by the trustee is not within the relief available under ITA 1967 s 439(1). There is a continuing obligation on the disponer to pay the annual amount due under the covenant less income tax at the standard rate under ITA 1967 s 433.

	£	£
Total income of A for 1989-1990	10,000	
Annuity charge	800	@ 32%
256		
	9,200	
Deemed income (ITA 1967 s 439(1))	800	
	10,000	
Personal allowances and reliefs	3,500	
	6,500	
Tax chargeable		
£6,100 @ 32%		1,952
£400 @ 48%		192
		2,144
Amount applicable under ITA 1967 s 441		
(Annuity payment 800)		
£400 @ 48%		192
£400 @ 32%		128
		320
Amount retained on payment		256
Refundable by trustee		64

References
1 ITA 1967 ss 440, 441.

Other settlements on children

11.12 The more general anti-avoidance legislation has been designed to disregard for income tax purposes the effect of any settlements of property or income wheresoever or whensoever made[1] by a parent to a child or for the benefit of such a child who is either under the age of 18 years or unmarried at the time at the time of any relevant payment.[2] The term "settlement" is very broadly defined to include any method of transferring income or property to a child. The term "child" includes a stepchild, an adopted child and an illegitimate child.[3]

The exercise of a power of appointment by a parent in favour of a minor child has been held to constitute a "settlement".[4]

In England where two brothers had made cross settlements of income in favour of each other's minor children the combined effect of both settlements was regarded as an "arrangement" within the corresponding UK legislation.[5]

References

1   ITA 1967 s 447.
2   ITA 1967 s 443(2).
3   ITA 1967 s 443(1). The age restriction was reduced from 21 to 18 by FA 1986 s 112.
4   *E G v MacSamhrain* [1958] IR 288; 3 ITC 217.
5   *CIR v Clarkson-Webb* 17 TC 451.

When a parent settlor dies[1] or is not resident in the State the anti-avoidance legislation does not apply.[2]

Where income under a settlement made by a parent is not currently payable to or for the benefit of a child of that person but could become payable in the future on the satisfaction of a condition (or the happening of a contingency) the income is to be regarded as part of the parent settlor's income.[3]

Nominal payments not exceeding £60 in a year made by a parent under a settlement towards the support of a permanently incapacitated child are not treated as income of the settlor.[4]

References

1   ITA 1967 s 443(1).
2   ITA 1967 s 443(3). This provision can cause problems in an Ireland-United Kingdom context. The corresponding United Kingdom legislation is contained in ICTA 1988 s 662(1). If the parent and child are resident in the different countries there may be a charge on both residents resulting in double taxation which is not relieved by the Ireland-United Kingdom Double Taxation Convention 1976. Under the old 1926 agreement concessional relief was allowed by both countries to overcome this problem but there appears to be no similar approach under the present arrangement.
3   ITA 1967 s 443(1) (proviso).
4   ITA 1967 S 443(4).

Irrevocable instruments

11.13 The anti-avoidance legislation which deems income transferred to a child of a settlor to be the income of the settlor does not apply to income accumulated under an irrevocable trust.[1] Where, however, payments are made to or for a child, any such payments are to be treated in the first instance as coming out of undistributed income.

Example

A, an Irish resident, transferred investments valued £10,000 to trustees by way of a settlement in April 1987 to pay at their discretion the capital and the income arising thereon to or for the benefit of his daughter until she attained the age of 25 or on earlier marriage when she was to take an absolute interest in the settlement funds including unappointed income. The trustees advanced the beneficiary £2,000 in April 1989 to take swimming instruction in the United States. She was at that time aged 17 and unmarried.

	Gross	*Tax*	*Net*
	£	£	£
Income of trust			
1987-1988	1,000	350	650
1988-1989	1,200	384	816
		734	1,466
Distribution April 1989			
Income	1,466		
Capital	534		
	2,000		

Position of beneficiary:
There is no charge to tax. There is no relief available. The part of the distribution made by the trustees which is paid out of all income arising since its inception is deemed to be income of the parent under ITA 1967 s 443.

The tax position of the parent settlor is:
Deemed income chargeable to tax under ITA 1967 s 443

1987-1988	1,000
1988-1989	1,200

Any additional charge arising to the parent on this income for higher rate tax charges is recoverable from the trustees (ITA 1976 s 446).

References
1   ITA 1967 s 444.

11.14 The term "irrevocable instrument" is defined negatively.[1] An instrument (ie a deed) is *not* to be regarded as irrevocable if it provides for any of the following:

(*a*)   payment (or the application) of a benefit in favour of the settlor during the life of the child;

(*b*)   payment during the life of the settlor to any spouse of the settlor or for his or her own benefit during the life of the child;

(*c*)   termination of the instrument by the act or the default of any person;

(*d*)   payment of an penalty by the settlor where there is a failure by him to comply with the provisions of the instrument.

In other words, if the settlor is capable of recovering any benefit from the child (to whom the income has been transferred) the transfer will not be regarded as irrevocable. On the other hand, if a deed provides that:

(*a*)   payments under (*a*) and (*b*) above may be made following the bankruptcy of the child or where an assignment of or a charge on the capital or income (including accumulations) has been made by the child;

(*b*)   the trust may be ended on condition that the distribution of the trust property is confined to the child or that child's spouse or children.

11.15 As discussed at 11.11, if income settled on a child (under a valid settlement for a period less than the life of the child) is regarded as income of the disponer, the disponer is entitled to recover the additional tax payable from the trustee or other person to whom the income is actually payable. [1] Similar provisions apply for the purposes of settlements on children generally.[2]

A settlor who becomes liable to tax on the income of a settlement is entitled to recover the tax from a trustee or the other person to whom the income was paid. On the other hand if the settlor obtains any allowance or relief from tax he must pay the benefit to the trustee or other person to whom the income is payable.

References

1   ITA 1967 Pt XXVIII Ch I, ss 440, 441.

2   ITA 1967 Pt XXVIII Ch II, s 446.

Transfer of interest in trade to a child

11.16 Where an individual who is a sole trader or in partnership admits, by any means, direct or indirect, a minor child as a partner the transfer thereby of an interest in the trade is to constitute a settlement.[1]

The share of profits of the minor child or children must therefore be treated as income of the parent. However the parent may deduct from the amount on which he is taxed as a result of this provision the amount of salary which would be paid to the child if he were an employee. This notional salary is deemed to be income of the child taxable under Schedule E. This legislation was introduced following a case where a café proprietor successfully argued in the Supreme Court that his (minor) children were "partners" in the business, and thus entitled to their own share of the profits etc.[2]

References

1   ITA 1967 s 448.

2   *O'Dwyer v Cafolla & Co* [1949] IR 210; 2 ITC 374.

Pension arrangements

Retirement benefit schemes

11.17 It is public policy to encourage the provision of benefits for the elderly, the incapacitated and the deprived. The State, through social welfare legislation, pays old age contributory pensions to persons aged 66 or more, and similar payments are made on a non-contributory basis subject to a means test.

The income tax code with its special reliefs for life assurance, [1] dependent relatives, incapacitated children and special age allowances has also been used for this purpose.

In addition, the State encourages individuals to fund their own pensions by granting tax relief for pension contributions. There are two main kinds of pension relief:

(*a*)   occupational pension schemes for employees and their dependants, and

(*b*)   retirement annuities for both the self-employed and employees who do not enjoy the benefit of a sponsored scheme.

References
1   Relief withdrawn by FA 1992 s 4 for 1992-93 and later tax years.

Occupational pension schemes

Relevant benefits

11.18 Pension schemes for employees[1] must be approved by the Revenue Commissioners. They will approve schemes that pay pension benefits ("relevant benefits"):

> any pension, lump sum, gratuity or other like benefits given or to be given on retirement or on death, or in anticipation of retirement, or in connection with past service after retirement or death, or to be given on or in anticipation of or in connection with any change in the nature of the service of the employee in question, except that it does not include any benefit which is to be afforded solely by reason of the death of disability of a person from an accident arising out of or in the course of his office or employment and for no other reason.[2]

While there are special provisions for statutory schemes[3] and the Revenue Commissioners have power to approve an occupational pension scheme in unusual circumstances, a scheme must normally be established under an irrevocable trust[4] and managed by an administrator (that is, a trustee) resident in the State.[5]

References
1 FA 1972 Pt I Ch II. Earlier legislation in ITA 1967 Pt IXX Ch II ceased to be effective after 5 April 1980.
2 FA 1972 s 13(1).
3 FA 1972 s 17.
4 FA 1972 s 16(1).
4 FA 1972 ss 13(1) and 15(2)(c). Where an administrator cannot be traced the employer is responsible for the discharge of duties.

Conditions for approval

11.19 An occupational pension scheme must satisfy the following conditions if it is to receive official approval:

(*a*)   its objects must be limited solely to providing pension benefits for an employee or his dependants;

(*b*)   the employer must both recognise and make contributions to the scheme;

(*c*)   all qualifying employees must be advised of the essential features of the scheme; and

(*d*)   it must be related to a business activity in the State.

11.20 In addition, the following restrictions are imposed on the scale of benefits payable by an approved occupational pension scheme:[1]

(*a*)   where a pension is involved it must not be paid earlier than the age of 60 (or 55 if the employee is a woman) and not later than the age of 70 or on earlier incapacity, in a sum not exceeding a one sixtieth share of the employee's final remuneration for each year of service subject to a maximum of a two thirds share;

(*b*)   a widow of an employee can only qualify for a maximum two-thirds proportion of the benefits applicable to her late husband's entitlements;

(*c*)   a lump sum payable to a widow or other dependant is not to exceed four times the average of the annual remuneration of the employee for the last three years of service; and

(*d*)   where a lump sum is taken by an employee on retirement in consideration of future pension payments the maximum is to be a half of the remuneration applicable to the last three years of service.

If a pension scheme does not meet all of these conditions, the Revenue Commissioners may nevertheless approve the scheme.

References
1 ITA 1972 s 15(3).

Tax treatment

11.21 The income of a trust or company whose sole activity is the operation of an approved occupational pension scheme is not chargeable to income tax or capital gains tax. Such a body is also exempt from deposit interest retention tax at source.[1]

Employee contributions to such a scheme are deductible in arriving at taxable income subject to a maximum deduction of 15% of annual remuneration.[2] Employers are authorised to deduct PAYE from the net emoluments after approved pension contributions.[3] In certain circumstances exceptional payments in excess of the annual 15% contribution limit may be deductible.[4] Contributions may be refunded to an employee but such refunds are chargeable to income tax at a special rate of 25%, as regards refund applications made on or after 29 January 1992.[5]

The pension that is eventually paid to the contributing employee is liable to income tax under Schedule E.[6]

References
1   FA 1992 s 22.
2   FA 1972 s 15(5).
3   Income Tax (Employments) Regulations 1960 Pt IX as inserted by Income Tax (Employments) Regulations 1972 (SI 260/1972).
4   FA 1972 s 15(5).
5   FA 1972 s 21.
6   FA 1972 s 20.

Pension law

11.22 While a trust established for occupational pension schemes must be a valid trust (see Chapter 3) it must also comply with the requirements of the Pensions Act 1990.

This Act is intended to:

(*a*)   establish standards for occupational pension schemes;

(*b*)   provide a regulatory framework for their operation; and

(*c*)   ensure equal treatment for members in accordance with European Union law.[1]

The provisions concerning trustees provide that:

(*a*)   an occupational pension scheme must be registered with the statutory "An Bord Pinsean - The Pension Board";

(*b*)   contributions to a scheme are to be properly invested and benefits paid as they become due;

(*c*)   proper financial records of members and of activities are to be kept; and

(*d*)   the High Court may order the replacement of trustees on the application of the statutory Board if it considers that such action is necessary in the interest of members.

The Board is also entitled to appoint trustees to a scheme where there are no existing trustees or the trustees cannot be traced.[2]

References
1   Directive 86/378/EEC.
2   Pensions Act 1990 Pt VI.

Retirement annuities

11.23 Retirement annuity schemes are, in effect, pension schemes for the self-employed, and employees where the employer does not operate a sponsored scheme. Normally, annuities of this class are contracted for by individuals with life assurance companies but such schemes may be administered by Revenue approved trusts [1] that are:

(*a*)   established under Irish law and administered in the State;

(*b*)   for the benefit of individuals engaged in or connected with a particular occupation for the purpose of providing retirement benefits for them, with or without subsidiary benefits for dependants; and

(*c*)   established irrevocably by a body of persons, company, or persons representing the majority of the individuals so engaged in the State.

References
1   FA 1967 s 235(4), (5).

Retirement annuity contracts

11.24 A retirement annuity contract made with a life assurance company carrying on business in the State must also be approved by the Revenue Commissioners. The contract may not provide for payment:

(*a*)   of any additional sums other than the annuity during the life of an individual;

(*b*)   which commences before the age 60 or after 70;

(*c*)   of any sums other than the return of premiums with any applicable interest where the participant dies before the qualifying time;

(*d*) to a widow or widower of an individual greater than the amount payable to the individual; or

(*e*) of an annuity other than for the life of the participant.[1]

The Revenue Commissioners may mitigate the effect of these restrictions when considering approval of a retirement annuity containing one or more of the following provisions:

(*a*) an annuity to a dependant other than the widow or widower of the individual;

(*b*) payment before the age of 60 on the permanent incapacity of the individual;

(*c*) payment either after 50 or 70 where this is customary in the occupation being exercised by the individual;

(*d*) payment for a period certain not exceeding 10 years notwithstanding the earlier death of the individual.[2]

A provision for an early termination of the contract on marriage or otherwise may not prevent an annuity contract from being regarded as a qualifying contract. This also applies where there may be an assignment by way of a will of a retirement annuity payable for a period certain, or an entitlement to have unexpired rights included as part of the individual's estate.

References
1   ITA 1967 s 235(2).
2   ITA 1967 s 235(3).

Tax treatment

11.25 A trust approved by the Revenue Commissioners for payment of retirement annuities, enjoys the exemption from income and capital gains taxes available to approved occupational pension schemes (see 11.21).

11.26 Contributions to such approved trusts are allowable as income tax deductions subject to a limit of 15% of net relevant earnings.[1] Where benefits are confined to a surviving spouse a reduced 5% maximum applies.[2] "Relevant earnings" are defined as:

(*a*) remuneration arising from an employment other than a pensionable employment;

(*b*) income from property attached to or connected with an employment as in (*a*);

(*c*) income chargeable under Schedule D in respect of trading or professional profits whether applicable to an individual or a partner in such undertakings; or (*d*)   earned income, as distinct from investment or rental income, arising from companies but excluding such income paid to proprietary directors or employees.[3]

In all circumstances a married woman's relieved earnings are to be determined independently of her husband's earnings.[4]

Before 31 January in the year following the tax year an individual may elect to have qualifying premiums treated as paid in that tax year and not in the year in which they were paid.[5]

References
1   ITA 1967 s 236(1)(*a*).
2   ITA 1967 ss 235(*a*) and 236(1)(*b*).
3   ITA 1967 s 235(7).
4   ITA 1967 s 235(6).
5   ITA 1967 s 236(11) as substituted by FA 1990 s 27.

Profit-sharing schemes

Anti-avoidance

11.27 Export sales relieved dividends, and Shannon company dividends paid directly or indirectly, to or for the benefit of employees in lieu of remuneration[1] are chargeable to income tax under Schedule E on the employee.[2]

References
1   FA 1974 s 54.
2   See FA 1992 s 35. The general exemption available on these dividends did not apply to income arising after 5 April 1990. FA 1992 reduces the relief allowable on such undistributed export sales relieved dividends by prescribing that the average dividend is to be excluded for 1991-92. A one-third share is to be taxable in 1992-93, two-thirds in 1993-94 and the full amount thereafter.

Approved profit-sharing schemes

Deduction for employee

11.28 For 1982-83 and later tax years bona fide profit-sharing schemes for employees allow both the company and the employees significant tax relief.[1]

11.29 To obtain the approval of the Revenue Commissioners a profit-sharing scheme must be established under a deed of trust which is administered by Irish resident trustees and:

(*a*)   must use the money paid to the trustees by a company to acquire fully paid up ordinary shares in the company (or a controlling company) and which are not subject to any special restrictions;[2]

(*b*)   must oblige the trustees to distribute the shares acquired among qualifying employees of the company up to a maximum value of £2,000 for any individual employee for 1992-93 and later tax years (previously £5,000); [3]

(*c*)   requires that the shares are either:
   (i)   quoted on a recognised stock exchange;
   (ii) shares in a company which is not under the control of another company; or
   (iii) shares in a company which is under the control of a company whose shares are quoted on a recognised stock exchange and which is neither a close company[4] or a foreign company that would not be a close company if it were resident in Ireland.

References
1   FA 1982 Pt I Ch IX and Sch 3. The relief has been restricted for 1991-92 and later tax years (FA 1992 s 17).
2   FA 1982 Sch 3 Pt 2 paras 5 and 7.
3   If in the year 1991-92 shares to a value of less than £2,000 were appropriated to an employee an additional amount may be allocated to him in 1992-93 to bring the value to £2,000. The additional shares will be deemed to have been allocated on 5 April 1992. For 1982-83 and 1983-84 the limit was £1,000.
4   CTA 1976 s 94.

Deduction for company

11.30 Sums transferred by a company to trustees of an approved profit-sharing scheme are deductible in calculating the company's corporation tax liability provided the trustees acquire qualifying shares in respect of the payment within nine months after the end of the accounting period in which the payment was made.[1]

Similar relief is available for payments made by a company towards the administration of a trust scheme.

References
1   FA 1982 s 58.

Shares

11.31 The shares held by an approved profit-sharing scheme must be allocated among full-time employees "on similar terms".[1] In other words, the share cannot be allocated only to directors or managers. Nevertheless different allocations may be made by reference to levels of remuneration or the length of service.[2]

When shares are allocated by the trustees but remain within the trust they become vested in possession of the employees for tax purposes but no charge to income tax (or benefit in kind) arises on the allocation.

If after five years from the date of allocation of shares by the trustees ("the release date") they are then transferred from the trust to the employee there is no tax charge.[3]

Shares must be retained in the trust for a minimum of two years after allocation[4] ("the period of retention").

Sales of shares by employees after that time but before the minimum five year release date attract income tax liability on the full amount of the market value or sale price up to the fourth anniversary of the allocation. A 25% discount is allowed for disposals made in year five.

If an employee dies before the release date, his personal representative will not be liable to tax on disposing of the shares.[5] When employees who reach pensionable age or who cease to be employees or directors due to either disability or redundancy dispose of shares before the release date a discount of 50% of the market value or sale price is given for income tax purposes.[6]

References
1   FA 1982 Sch 3, para 2(1).
2   FA 1982 Sch 3, para 2(2).
3   FA 1982 s 52(7).
4   FA 1982 s 52(5).
5   FA 1982 s 53(1).
6   FA 1982 s 52(8).

Income from the shares

11.32 Any income which arises after the allocation of shares by trustees to individual employees but which is still retained within the trust is chargeable on the employee as being beneficially entitled in possession. The employee is also liable to income tax (or capital gains tax, as appropriate) in respect of any proceeds occurring on the disposal of rights to bonus shares attached to his allocated shares while they are still held within the trust.[1]

Trustees' tax

11.33 The trustees are liable to income tax under Schedule D Case III in respect of any income arising on sums transferred by companies before the transfer of shares for allocation among the employees.

The trustees are also chargeable to income tax under Schedule D Case IV for the tax due on disposals of shares before the release date.[2]

References
1   FA 1982 ss 53(5) and 54(3).
2   FA 1982 s 57.

Unit linked investments

Introduction

11.34 Many financial institutions have in recent times introduced tax-based schemes in order to compete for and attract funds. In the corporate area there are the well known "Section 84" loans. These are loans whose interest rate partly (usually only to a very small degree) depends on the results of the company. This results in the interest being regarded as a distribution. A distribution received by an Irish company from another Irish company is regarded as franked income and is not subject to corporation tax in the hands of the recipient company, companies which are either exempt from tax or paying at a low rate have no use for an interest deduction. Such a company can pass a tax benefit to another company (the bank) by way of a distribution ("section 84" loan) in return for a lower interest rate.

The other main tax reliefs are the "Business Expansion Scheme" (see 11.52) and the scheme for Investment and Research and Development (see 11.58). Tax advantages can also be obtained from interest and currency swaps.

On the level of the individual investor there are unit linked investments. In practice, there are two kinds of unit linked investment. Firstly, there are unit linked funds promoted by life assurance companies and forming part of the property and assets of such companies. Secondly, there are collective investments in transferable securities (including trusts) sponsored by independent legal entities.

Unit linked funds

11.35 These funds are a modern variation of "with profits" policies formerly contracted by life assurance companies. While investment in such funds can be made by way of annual payments (for example, a mortgage or educational endowment policy) they are usually made by single lump sum payments.

The company provides life cover to the investor for a specific capital sum payable on death and also provides for the allocation of part of its own investment income in favour of the life assured by reference to a share expressed in terms of units based on the amount invested.

The return on the investment is related to the performance of the securities backing the value of the units. While income and capital gains are accumulated during the investment period the overall market value of units at any particular time may increase or decrease in response to market conditions.

A life assurance company remains the beneficial owner of the stocks backing the unit linked investments and it is liable to corporation tax on the income receipts and capital gains tax on disposals.[1]

References

1   Prior to 1 January 1993, CTA 1976 s 36 provided that investment income reserved for policy holders was chargeable at 35%. After that date, the standard rate of income tax is applied.

Advantages of unit linked funds

11.36 Investments in unit linked funds have a number of advantages:

(*a*)   a taxpayer is relieved from income tax at the higher rates on the rolled up share of income applicable to the units held;

(*b*)   facilities usually exist for transferring investments to other funds of the life assurance company without any penalty; and

(*c*)   funds can be withdrawn and capital realised on demand or within a short period on giving due notice to the company.

Life assurance relief for income tax purposes was available on sums invested in tax years to 1991-92.[1]

Disadvantages of unit linked funds

The disadvantages of unit linked funds are:

(*a*)   funds are generally concerned with capital growth rather than income performance, accordingly, they are not suitable where an income supplement is desired on investments;

(*b*)   investments need to be held for the medium to longer term (more than three years);

(*c*)   an investor who is exempt from income tax or capital gains tax is not entitled to reclaim the underlying tax paid by the life assurance company on his units; and

(*d*)   the annual exemption available to individuals for capital gains tax [2] cannot be imported by the life assurance company to offset its capital gains tax liability.

There is a Government levy on all such investments. Furthermore, commission payable to an insurance agent may decrease the income available for distribution.

There is a penalty charge on investing in an existing fund as the management company may charge up to 5% when selling units (the offer price) as compared with the market value of units (the bid price). Accordingly, a deficit of up to 15% of the invested capital may need to be re-couped before any profit arises.

References
1   FA 1992 s 4.
2   CGTA 1975 s 16.

Undertakings for collective investment in transferable securities (UCITS)

Introduction

11.37 The legislation governing Irish unit trusts [1] has been substantially amended in recent years, in order to bring the Irish law into line with EC law [2] designed to protect investors in such funds.

References
1   Unit Trust Act 1972 as amended by Unit Trust Act 1990 which became law on 26 December 1990. This Act provides governing rules for trusts outside the terms of the EC Directives (see below).
2   Council Directive 86/611/EEC of 20 December 1985 and Council Directive 88/220/EEC of 22 March 1988.

Unit Trust Act 1990

11.38 This Act transferred the supervision of authorised unit trusts from the Minister of Industry and Commerce to the Central Bank of Ireland.[1] Trusts registered under the Unit Trust Act 1972 are entitled to be included in the register of authorised trusts which the Central Bank is obliged to keep.[2]

A unit trust scheme must meet the following requirements before it can be registered by the Central Bank:

(*a*)   the competency and probity of the management and trustee companies to carry out their functions must be established;

(*b*)   both the management and trustee companies, apart from being incorporated in Ireland or another European Union Member State, must have adequate financial resources; and

(*c*)   there must be a trust deed which provides for the independent functions exercisable by the management and trustee companies.

References
1   Unit Trusts Act 1990 ss 3-8.
2   Unit Trusts Act 1990 s 4.

Unauthorised trusts

11.39 Only authorised trusts are allowed to operate in Ireland or seek the participation of the public as unit holders.[1] Unauthorised trusts may not solicit funds from the public or advertise for funds without the Central Bank's approval.[2]

Unauthorised trusts may not:

(*a*) raise loans to buy securities;

(*b*) loan scheme monies to buy units; or

(*c*) mortgage scheme property.

The Unit Trust Act 1990 does not apply to private unit trusts.

References

1   Unit Trust Act 1990 ss 9 and 10.
2   These prohibitions do not apply where entry into a unit trust is conditional on the taking out of a policy on a human life (Unit Trust Act 1990 s 9(2)) or to a company incorporated under the Companies Acts or by statute or charter, or to building societies or industrial and provident societies (Unit Trust Act 1990 s 9(1)(*b*)).

Council Directive 86/611/EEC

11.40 The trust is not a feature of continental law and, accordingly, the separate equitable interests created by such bodies are not recognised as effective outside the United Kingdom and Ireland. This has meant that on the European main-land the property, assets or income of holding or fiduciary bodies is regarded as vested in the beneficiaries concerned on the "look through" principle (see 10.12).

As this Directive permitted UCITS from any of the member States to operate in other EC States, the Irish tax system was amended to take account of the changes.

11.41 The general control of UCITS operating in the State after 18 April 1989 has been vested in the Central Bank of Ireland.[1] UCITS are undertakings:

(*a*) the sole object of which is the collective investment in transferable securities or funds raised from the public and operating on the principle of risk-spreading; and

(*b*) the units of which are, at the request of the holder, redeemable out of the undertaking's assets.

The undertakings may be constituted as:

(*a*) unit trusts;

(*b*) investment companies with fixed capital; or

(*c*) investment companies with variable capital where:
  (i) the shares have no par value; and
  (ii) the net assets at all times must be equal to the paid up share capital.

These rules do not apply to private trusts or to UCITS promoting the sale of the units outside the EEC.[2]

11.42 Investments made by UCITS are to be restricted to securities where there is a regulated market open to the public.[3] An investment company may acquire real and personal property for its business.[4] However:

(*a*) a UCITS may not acquire precious metals or certificates representing them; and

(*b*) a limit of 10% of assets is imposed on UCITS[5] for investment in transferable debt instruments.

References
1   SI 78/1989.
2   SI 78/1989 para 3(5) and annex C.
3   Para 45.
4   Para 46.
5   Unit Trust Act 1990 s 2. Registered unit trusts coming within the provisions of Unit Trust Act 1990 are not to be considered as UCITS covered by the 1989 Statutory Regulations.

Tax treatment to 1988-89

11.43-44 The taxation of unit trusts for years up to 1988-89 was straightforward. A unit trust[1] was chargeable to income tax as a body of persons (the trustees).[2] Capital gains were also chargeable on the trustees as a single and continuing body of persons.[3] This is still the case for private unit trusts. An Irish resident unit trust registered under the Unit Trust Act 1972 s 3 which satisfied certain conditions was entitled to be charged to capital gains tax at half of the normal rates.

11.45 The Irish tax treatment of unit trust income and capital gains as outlined in the last paragraph was out of line with that of other EC States where, in accordance with the "look through" principle, a unit holder was treated as entitled to any income or capital gains referable to the proportionate share of the overall trust fund.

Provisions introduced in 1989,[4] covering the taxation of collective investment undertakings have broadly reconciled the Irish tax treatment with the European law except as regards private unit trusts.

The undertakings covered by the new legislation are:

(*a*) an authorised unit trust within the meaning of the Unit Trust Act 1990;

(*b*)   a UCITS authorised by the Central Bank of Ireland; and

(*c*)   an authorised company [5] operating as an investment company selling its shares to the public.

References
1   ITA 1967 s 1.
2   ITA 1967 s 105.
3   CGTA 1975 s 31.
4   FA 1989 s 19.
5   CA 1990 Pt XIII.

Tax treatment for 1989-90 and later years

11.46 The new taxation system introduced by FA 1989 provides that the unit holder (not the trustees of the collective investment undertaking, as heretofore) is to be chargeable to tax on the income and capital gains distributed to him by the undertakings.[1]

However, a withholding tax at the standard rate income tax in force at the time of payment is to be retained by the paying agent on all the relevant payments (which may include capital gains)[2] made to unit holders.

In addition, the trustees or managers must pay tax at the standard rate of income tax on all undistributed income (but not capital gains) available for payment to unit holders at the end of an accounting period. These advance payments are available for set off purposes against the withholding tax charge arising when the relevant income is distributed at a later date.

References
1   FA 1989 s 18(3).
2   FA 1989 s 18(1). A deduction is allowed for management expenses: FA 1989 s 18(5)(*a*).

11.47 A collective investment undertaking is exempt from the surcharge on accumulated income of cumulative or discretionary trusts (see 10.29).

11.48 Undertakings operating within the Custom House Dock or Shannon Free Airport areas and having non-residents as unit holders are exempt from the tax charges imposed on paying agents in respect of distributions and undistributed income.

Additionally, a non-resident unit holder in other collective investment undertakings is entitled to a refund of any tax withheld on distributions of income and capital gains.[2]

References
1   FA 1976 s 13 and FA 1989 s 18(8).
2   FA 1989 s 18(6)(*a*)(i).

11.49 An Irish resident unit holder receiving distributions from a collective investment undertaking is regarded for 1989-90 and later tax years as having a vested interest in possession of the income or capital gains included in the distribution. This means that the general tax rates in force apply to the gross distribution with a credit for the withholding tax retained.[1]

There is a problem where Irish or UK company distributions are received by a collective investment undertaking. The undertaking itself cannot claim relief from any tax credit attached to these distributions. The paying agents can only deduct withholding tax or the charge on undistributed income on the income which is actually received by the undertaking. An Irish resident unit holder is entitled to a proportionate share of any tax credit attached to an Irish company distribution received by the undertaking. Such a holder is entitled to offset this tax credit share against the payment received.

In the case of UK source distributions the holder is entitled on a claim to the UK Revenue under art 11(2) of the Ireland-UK Double Taxation Agreement 1976 to payment of a restricted tax credit .[2]

In such circumstances the trustees or managers may need to issue supplementary vouchers to investors to show the amount of tax credit available. The respective Revenue authorities may require paying agents or other management of collective investment undertakings to supply full details of all distributions involved.

References
1   FA 1989 s 18(6)(*a*)(ii).
2   SI 319/1976.

Advantages of collective investment undertakings

11.50 Investments in collective investment undertakings, as distinct from unit linked funds (see 11.36), have a number of advantages:

(*a*)   an exempt taxpayer is entitled to repayment of any withholding tax suffered;

(*b*)   the annual capital gains tax exemption available to individuals may be used to claim relief against any withholding tax charge imposed on the proceeds of disposals by the undertaking which is included in a distribution; and

(*c*)   the full relaxation of exchange controls (1 January 1993) allows investors complete freedom to invest internationally.

Disadvantages of collective investment undertakings

11.51 Against these advantages the following should be taken into consideration:

(*a*)   income tax is chargeable, depending on personal circumstances, at the higher rates on resident individuals in respect of distributions, with a credit for any withholding tax suffered; and

(*b*)   there is no freedom to transfer funds without incurring disposal and repurchasing charges.

Unit trusts are not regarded as collective investment undertakings in transferable securities (UCITS) within FA 1989 s 18 where admission to a unit holder depends upon the taking out a life assurance policy.[1]

Such excluded funds may qualify as UCITS if not later than 1 November 1992 capital gains tax at one-half of the normal rate applicable is paid on the notional gain arising on a notional disposal of assets.[2]

References
1   FA 1990 s 35.
2   FA 1992 s 36.

Relief for investment in corporate trades

Business Expansion Scheme

Qualifying activities

11.52 Since 1984, individuals may obtain tax relief by investing either directly or indirectly (through a designated investment fund) in Irish incorporated and resident companies operating a trade consisting wholly or mainly of:

(*a*)   the manufacture of goods;

(*b*)   the provision of services grant aided for employment purposes by the Industrial Development Authority;

(*c*)   activities in respect of sea-going Irish resident vessel;[1]

(*d*)   the propagation and cloning of plants;[2]

(*e*)   the construction and leasing of an advanced factory;[3]

(*f*)   tourist traffic undertakings;[4] and

(*g*)   the export of goods by Special Trading Houses.[5]

References
1   Applies after 31 December 1986 - FA 1987 s 28(4) as amended by FA 1988 s 40(2).
2   Applies after 5 April 1988 - FA 1988 s 7.
3   Applies after 29 May 1990 - FA 1990 s 10(4).
4   Applies after 5 April 1987 - FA 1987 s 11.
5   FA 1987 s 29. The meaning of Special Trading House is given in FA 1980 s 39 (ICC2) inserted by FA 1987 s 31.

Shares

11.53 Shares acquired in a business expansion scheme company must normally be held by the investor for five years after issue to qualify for the relief allowable and, additionally, they must be fully paid-up new ordinary shares of a company not quoted on a stock exchange at the time of their issue or within the following three year period.[1] Qualifying shares may not carry any special privilege rights which are not available to other shareholders of the same class during the five year "locked-in" period.[2]

References
1   FA 1984 s 15(2), applying s 12(7)(*b*).
2   FA 1984 s 12(2).

Disposal of shares

11.54 The consequences of a disposal of qualifying shares before the end of the period of five years after issue are as follows:

(*a*)   where the disposal is on an arm's length basis the amount of the overall relief allowable is to be reduced by the consideration received;

(*b*)   where the disposal is by way of a gift or involves a transfer of interest for preferential consideration all the relief allowed earlier is to be withdrawn; and

(*c*)   disposals between a husband and wife living together are not penalised or subjected to a claw-back.[1]

Furthermore, where an option is given or an agreement made whereby the individual investor holding shares otherwise qualifying for relief can dispose of his holding during the restricted five year period at a price which does not reflect the market value of the shares relief is not to be allowed.[2]

References
1   FA 1984 s 17.
2   FA 1984 s 17(2)(*a*) inserted by FA 1989 s 9 as respects shares issued after 11 April 1989.

Investment limits

11.55 A minimum investment of £200 is required from an individual when a direct application for shares is involved. This restriction does not apply to indirect investments made through designated investment funds.

    A maximum annual deduction of £25,000 is allowed against the total income of an individual for investments in a qualifying scheme.[1] A husband

and wife living together and assessed jointly can claim for separate measures of relief provided they each have the necessary income. Unused relief, due to a deficiency in chargeable income, can be carried forward to later years up to 1992-93.[2]

While there was no overall quantitative limitation for allowable expenditure on qualifying shares under the original legislation as regards shares issued on or after 29 January 1991, a £75,000 lifetime limit applied to each individual for 1984-85 and later tax years.[3] This lifetime limit does not apply to issues after 23 February 1994.[4]

Under the original legislation there was no limit on the amount which a company was entitled to raise under the business expansion scheme. From 12 April 1989 to 29 January 1991 a company limit of £2.5 million was imposed. After 29 January 1991 the company limit was reduced to £0.5 million. This limit was increased to £1 million as regards shares issued on or after 6 May 1993.[5] There are provisions to prevent the use of splitting devices to circumvent the limit.[6]

References
1 FA 1984 s 13(1).
2 FA 1984 s 12(11) as substituted by FA 1991 s 14.
3 FA 1984 s 13(2) as amended by FA 1991 s 15.
4 FA 1993 s 25(*c*).
5 FA 1993 s 25(*d*).
6 FA 1984 s 13A as amended by FA 1991 ss 15 and 17.

Designated investment funds

11.56 Subject to the general conditions and restrictions applicable to direct investment an individual may invest in corporate trades through a designated fund.[1] Qualifying funds must be established under irrevocable trusts for the sole purpose of enabling individuals to invest in eligible companies carrying on activities set out in 11.52.

11.57 A qualifying fund must be approved by the Revenue Commissioners who require to be satisfied that:[2]

(*a*)   subscribed funds will be invested without undue delay in companies which are eligible to participate in the business expansion schemes (see 11.52);

(*b*)   the benefits arising from all the operations of the fund are to be held for the fund participants;

(*c*)   the rate of the management charge is set out in the governing trust deed;

(*d*) annual audited accounts will be prepared and submitted to them;

(*e*) the fund is a closed fund and the date of closing precedes the date of the first investment (the European Communities (Undertakings for Collective Investment in Transferable Securities) Regulations 1989 do not apply to a closed fund);[3]

(*f*) companies in which shares are acquired by a fund are not connected with the fund managers, trustees or associated of such persons; and

(*g*) investors are not allowed to have shares (in any company in which the fund has invested) transferred to their names until five years have elapsed from the date of the issue of the shares to the fund.

References
1   FA 1984 s 27.
2   FA 1986 s 27(3) and (5).
3   Pt II para 3(5)(*a*).

Research and development companies

11.58 Since 1986, individuals may also obtain relief by investing in ordinary shares of Irish resident research and development companies. Subscriptions up to £25,000 annually may be set off against total income for income tax purposes.

However, all such investment must be made directly and there is no provision for the establishment or intervention of a trust or management body to operate a fund on behalf of a group of investors.

References
1   FA 1986 Pt I Ch III ss 17-30.

Chapter 12

Charitable and other exemptions

Exemption from income tax

Income received then applied for charitable purposes

12.01 A body of persons established for charitable purposes is exempt from income tax:

   (*a*)   under Schedule C in respect of any interest, annuities or dividends;

   (*b*)   under Schedule D in respect of any yearly interest or other annual payment;

   (*c*)   under Schedule F in respect of any distributions;

provided the income is spent for charitable purposes.[1]

References
1   ITA 1967 s 333.

Investment income

12.02 The scope of the relief is limited and does not extend to foreign investment income, interest arising on deposit receipts or other short term loan investments, building society interest or rents other than rents receivable by hospitals, schools or almshouses.[1]

However, in practice, such receipts are not charged to income tax if they are applied for charitable purposes. The 1921 decision not to allow charity exemption on rents from lettings on external property received by the Rotunda Hospital Dublin was based on a restriction of relief under the Income Tax Act 1918 which confined the relief on rental income to Schedule A. The present legislation provides for a Schedule D exemption.[2]

The tax credit attached to Irish dividend payments may be paid to bodies exempt from tax.[3] The surcharge on accumulated income of a trust does not apply to charitable bodies.[4] A charitable body is exempted from the deposit interest retention tax charge (DIRT).[5]

References
1   ITA 1967 s 333(1).
2   *Cowan v Governors of Rotunda Hospital* [1921] AC 1; 7 TC 517.
3   CTA 1976 s 88(3) and (4).
4   FA 1986 s 13.
5   FA 1986 s 38.

12.03 The tax exemptions apply to a trust established for charitable purposes only where there is no possibility of funds being appointed for non-charitable purposes.[1]

The universal application of this principle has been eroded somewhat by a recent English decision[2] which disallowed the part of the income of a charitable body used to fund non-charitable educational purposes.

While it is essential that income must be expended for charitable purposes, such expenditure may be deferred provided that the deferment is for a particular purpose.[3]

References
1   *R v Special Commissioners (ex parte Rank's Executors)* 8 TC 286.
2   *CIR v Educational Grants Association Ltd* [1967] 2 All ER 893; 44 TC 93.
3   *General Nursing Council of Scotland v CIR*, 14 TC 645. The Council established by statute to provide a scheme for the registration of nurses was refused charitable exemption by the English Courts.

Charitable purposes

12.04 For taxation purposes the terms "charity", "charitable object" and "charitable purposes" all take their meanings from broader legal precedents.[1]

A charity is by its nature a body of persons and can be established by incorporation under the Companies Acts, by statute, charter, decree, trust or will. This flexibility has led to the legal difficulties in determining clear and consistent demarcation limits for charitable bodies and activities. However, the exemptions from income tax charges enjoyed by charitable bodies have helped considerably in the development and interpretation of the meaning of both "charitable purposes" and "charitable objects", mainly by the English courts, arising from challenges which have been entered against official refusal of tax exemption claims. The following have come to be regarded as charitable purposes:[2]

(*a*)   the relief of poverty (see 7.01),

(*b*)   the advancement of education (see 7.06),

(*c*)   the advancement of religion (7.16),

(*d*)   the benefit of the public (7.29).

References
1 See 1.17 and Chapter 7.
2 Lord MacNaghten in *Special Commissioners of Income Tax v Pemsel* 3 TC 53 applying principles established in *Morice v Durham* [1804] 9 Ves 399.

Relief of poverty

12.05 The relief of poverty is regarded as a good charitable purpose (see 7.01)

Advancement of education

12.06 The advancement of education is regarded as a good charitable purpose (see 7.06 et seq).

Scholarships

12.07 A trust set up solely for the advancement of education by the provision of scholarships open for public competition qualifies as a charitable body.

Additionally, scholarship payments received by an individual receiving full-time education at a university, college, school or other educational establishment are not regarded as income for tax purposes.[1]

References
1 ITA 1967 s 353. See also *Wicks v Firth* 56 TC 318.

Although payments to teaching colleges would not normally be deductible against business profits for income or corporation tax purposes, payment to certain approved colleges, to teach or undertake to teach research in:

(*a*) industrial relations;

(*b*) marketing; or

(*c*) any other subject approved by the Minister for Finance to an Irish university or the other third level educational bodies operating in the State;

may be deducted as an expense in computing business profits.[1]

References
1 FA 1973 s 21.

Education in the arts

Although payments to educational bodies would not normally be deductible against business profits for income or corporation tax purposes, payments to certain approved colleges for education in architecture, art and design, music, theatre, film etc may be deducted as an expense in computing business profits. The maximum deduction is £10,000 in any tax year.[1]

References
1 FA 1984 s 32.

Advancement of religion

12.08 The advancement of religion is regarded as a good charitable purpose (see 7.16 et seq).

Gifts for the general public benefit

Sport and recreation

12.09 The promotion of recreational facilities (even for the public benefit) is not generally regarded by the Revenue as a charitable activity. This was also the general position in England until 1978.[1]

There is no corresponding Irish legislation although the income received by bodies of persons established for the sole purpose of promoting athletic or amateur games or sport are exempt from income tax.[2] For tax years 1983-84 inclusive, a body of persons established for sporting purposes qualified for tax exemption on income applied for those purposes even where it was not specified that the body should continue to exist for those purposes. Thus, in a case[3] where a club consisted of two trustees and four other individuals who were either employees or members of the families of the trustees and the sports club's activities were funded by income on loans provided by the trustees the club's income was held to be exempt from income tax.

For 1984-85 and later tax years, a sports club must be an "approved body of persons". The Revenue Commissioners may serve notice in writing on a club that it does not qualify as an approved body of persons. Consequently sporting bodies formed to provide a tax advantage are excluded from the relief.

Although payments to Cospóir (the National Sports Council) would not normally be deductible against business profits for income or corporation tax purposes, persons making such payments are granted a special tax deduction. The maximum deduction is £10,000 in any tax year.[4]

References
1 *Baddeley v CIR* [1955] AC 572, Recreational Charities Act 1978.
2 ITA 1967 s 349. CTA 1976 s 11(1) applies the exemption for corporation tax purposes.
3 *O'Reilly and Ors v Revenue Commissioners* [1984] ILRM 406.
4 FA 1986 s 8.

Gifts to the State

12.10 A gift of money made to the Minister for Finance for any purpose for (or towards the cost of) which public monies are provided, if accepted by the Minister, may be set off against the income of the person making the gift.[1]

References
1   ITA 1967 s 547 which is applied for corporation tax purposes by CTA 1976 Sch 2 para 27.

Thalidomide children

12.11 Payments made to or on behalf of handicapped thalidomide children by either the Minister for Health or the special German foundation established for such purposes are exempt from income tax in the hands of the beneficial recipients but the income must nevertheless be declared in the recipient's income tax return. The exemption applies also to investment income derived from such payments.[1]

References
1   FA 1973 s 19.

Haemophilia HIV Trust

12.12 Income consisting of payments made to a beneficiary under the Haemophilia Trust is to be disregarded for all purpose of the Income Tax Acts.[1]

References
1   FA 1990 s 7.

The Great Book of Ireland

12.13 The application of the proceeds of the unique manuscript volume referred to as "The Great Book of Ireland" to two specific companies is also disregarded for all purposes of the Income Tax Acts.[1]

References
1   FA 1991 s 13.

Amateur societies

12.14 Amateur societies established for various purposes have been held to be charitable (see 7.37). A society for the promotion of agriculture was regarded by the UK courts [1] to be exempt as a charitable body from tax on its investment income. This decision is followed for Irish tax purposes. In fact, the exemption available has been extended to cover the profits arising from a show or exhibition held by such a society.[2]

References

1   *CIR v Yorkshire Agricultural Society* [1928] 1 KB 149; 13 TC 58.
2   The meaning of "agricultural society" is set out in ITA 1967 s 348(2). FA 1978 s 17 as amended by FA 1992 s 48 deals with exemptions allowable to agricultural societies for corporation tax purposes.

Charity that also carries on a trade

Introduction

12.15 A charitable body that also carries on a trade may be exempt from tax on its trading profits. Chargeable profits from quarrying or mining land are exempt if the lands out of which such profits arise are both owned *and* occupied by the charity.[1]

Otherwise, trading profits are only exempt from tax where:

(*a*)   the profits are applied solely to the purposes of the charity; and

(*b*)   (i)   the trade is carried on as part of the charity's primary activity, or

         (ii)   the work in connection with the trade is mainly carried on by the beneficiaries of the charity (in the case of a charitable trust).[2]

The relief ((*b*)(i)) allowed to charities carrying on a trade as part of the charity's primary activity has applied for 1955-56 and later tax years.[3] However, for 1974-75 and later tax years, if the trade carried on by the charity is farming, that farming trade need not be carried on as part of the charity's primary activity.[4] This means that if the profits of the farming trade are applied for the purposes of the charity ((*a*) above), no income tax liability will arise.

References

1   The activities covered by the exemption are set out in ITA 1967 s 53(*b*) in the rules applicable to Case I, Schedule D
2   ITA 1967 s 334.
3   FA 1955 s 3.
4   ITA 1967 s 334(2A) inserted by FA 1981 s 11.

Fee-paying schools (and hospitals)

12.16 Fee-paying schools or general hospitals that take in paying students (or patients) are regarded as charitable bodies for income tax purposes and the additional fee income is exempt from tax if it is applied towards the primary charitable activity.[1] For tax years to 1954-55 inclusive, such additional trading income of a charitable body was liable to income tax.[2]

Certain religious communities supply goods (for example, communion wafers) used in religious services. Such communities may depend on the receipts from such activities for the maintenance and support of members. The UK courts have held that school fees receivable by nuns were exempt on the basis that the nuns were the beneficiaries of the charity.[3]

The income tax relief for charitable trading bodies does not apply to activities such as general book publishing or acting as a travel agency.

It may be possible to have a separate company carry on the trading activity. Any religious person employed could take a salary up to the amount of the single exemption limit and, additionally, payment of the tax credit attached to any distributions of profits could be reclaimed by the controlling charitable body.

References
1   ITA 1967 s 334(1)(*c*); FA 1955 s 3.
2   *Davis v Superioress, Mater Misericordiae Hospital* [1933] IR 480 and 503; 2 ITC 1. The hospital authority was held liable to tax on fee income from private patients who were cared for in a separate annexe. It is not clear whether private nursing homes run by religious institutions would be taxed on the basis of this decision, or exempt on the basis that the profits were applied for charitable purposes (ITA 1967 s 334(1)(*c*)).
3   *Convent of the Blessed Sacrament, Brighton v CIR* 18 TC 76.

Religious communities

12.17 Because the income tax treatment of trades carried on by religious communities differed from the tax treatment of other businesses in that the religious did not receive any personal income, the Revenue Commissioners introduced an alternative tax treatment of such bodies, called Community Concession, in the 1930s. The concessionary treatment involved:

(*a*)   a disallowance of any debits in the financial accounts for all sums included for the maintenance of the community;

(*b*)   a deduction in determining the chargeable profit of:
   (i)   the single personal allowance for each member of the community participating in the trading activity; and
   (ii)   an agreed maintenance charge for other members of the community not within (i).

If a member of a community within (*b*)(i) had personal income (for example, a teacher's or nurse's salary) the maintenance allowance due was restricted.

The fact that a religious community's trading income will now generally be regarded as exempt, provided the profits are applied for the purposes of the charity, has made the operation of Community Concession redundant in practice.

Human rights organisations

12.18 A body of persons having consultative status with the United Nations Organisation or the Council of Europe which:

(*a*)   has as its sole or main object the promotion of the Universal Declaration of Human Rights and/or the implementation of the European Convention of Human Rights and Fundamental Freedoms; and

(*b*)   is precluded from making any direct or indirect payments or transfers to members other than for valuable and sufficient consideration;

is to be treated as a body established for charitable purposes.[1]

References
1   FA 1973 s 20.

Part 5

Corporation tax

Chapter 13

The provisions governing trusts

Introduction

13.01 This chapter sets out brief summaries of the corporation tax provisions dealing with trusts. The application of these provisions is then explained in Chapter 14.

Corporation Tax Act 1976

Income received by a company

Section 1(2)

13.02 Income received by a company acting in a trustee capacity is liable to income tax (not corporation tax).

Section 6(2)

13.03 Income received by a company as a beneficiary of a trust is liable to corporation tax.

Trustee of a non-resident company

Section 8(4)

13.04 Income tax assessments on a non-resident individual may be made and charged on a trustee, guardian, committee or agent of such a person (ITA 1967 s 200). Similarly, corporation tax assessments on a non-resident company may be made and charged on the trustee, guardian or agent of such person.

Income tax exemptions

Section 11(6)

13.05 Exemptions allowable for income tax apply in like manner for corporation tax (see *Butterworth Ireland Tax Guide* 1993-94 at 13.27 et seq).

195

Company reconstructions

Section 20(11)

13.06 Where a company ceases to trade, and another company takes over the business, the trade will not be treated as having ceased and recommenced, provided at least 75% of the trade belongs to the same persons.

If the trade in question belongs to a person as trustee (other than for charitable or public purposes) the trade is deemed to belong to the person entitled to the trust income. This may be the beneficiary, if the beneficiary is absolutely entitled to the income.

Pension fund trustees

Section 50

13.07 The pension business of a life assurance company is to include contracts made with trustees of officially approved pension funds (see 11.17 et seq).

Lower rate of tax

Section 79

13.08 For accounting periods ending before 1 April 1989, a lower 35% corporation tax rate applied to profits of a company formed for the advancement of religion or education if the company was prohibited from distributing any part of its profits to members. This lower rate does not apply for profits of accounting periods ending on or after 1 April 1989 (FA 1988 s 33(2)).

Tax credit

Section 88(5)

13.09 If a person other than the recipient of a distribution is liable to tax on the distribution income, that person is also entitled to the tax credit attaching to the distribution. This means that if the trustees of a trust (resident in the State) are liable to tax on distribution income, they are also entitled to the tax credits attaching to the distribution. If the beneficiaries are liable to tax on the distribution income, they are entitled to the tax credits.

Close companies

Section 94(6)

13.10 If shares are held on trust for an approved pension fund (see 11.17 et seq) the shareholders are regarded as the beneficial owners, and the company will not be regarded as a close company.

Section 98

13.11 Where a close company makes a loan to a participator (a shareholder or "stakeholder" in the company) the amount of the advance is treated as a payment upon which income tax (at the standard rate) was liable to be withheld. This means the company will have an income tax liability on such loans. If the total of all loans made to the borrower is less than £15,000, the borrower works full time for the company, and the borrower does not have a material interest in the company, the company will not have an income tax charge.

These provisions also apply to a loan made to a company acting as trustee.

Section 99

Where a loan to a participator (which was treated as a payment upon which income tax was liable to be withheld - see previous paragraph) is written off, that amount is treated as income (after deduction of tax) of the recipient. Neither the individual nor the company is entitled to repayment of the income tax withheld.

If the (written-off) loan was made to a person who has died, or to trustees of a trust which has ceased, the beneficiary is regarded as having received the income, and is liable to income tax accordingly.

Section 103

13.12 A "participator" in a company includes:
   (a)   a shareholder or person entitled to vote in the company,
   (b)   a loan creditor of the company,
   (c)   a person entitled to share in company distributions,
   (d)   any person who can ensure that the company's income or assets are applied for his benefit.
This definition does not exclude a trustee of a trust.
   An "associate of a participator" includes:
   (a)   a relative (husband, wife, ancestor, lineal descendant, brother or sister) or partner of a participator,
   (b)   a trustee of a trust where the participator (or his relative, as above) was the settlor,
   (c)   any person having an interest in a trust which that participator also has an interested in - this does not apply to:
        (i)   approved pension scheme trusts (see 11.17 et seq),
        (ii)   a trust for the benefit of employees and the individual does not (or cannot with relatives etc) own more than 5% of the company's ordinary shares,

     (iii) charitable trusts (see Chapter 7) which may arise on the failure of other trusts (see 6.16).

Section 104

13.13 Any person (including a trustee of a trust) in whose name company shares are registered, must, when requested to do so by an inspector of taxes:

    (*a*)   state whether he is the beneficial owner of the shares, or

    (*b*)   if he is not the beneficial owner, give the name and address of the person who is the beneficial owner.

A provider of loan capital to a company must, when requested, provide equivalent information. The inspector may also request the company (including a trustee company) to provide him with details of bearer securities issued, the names and addresses of the persons to whom they were issued and any other information necessary to trace the present owners of the shares.

Connected persons

Section 157

13.14 This section sets out detailed rules which determine when persons are regarded as "connected" for the purposes of corporation tax.

    A person is regarded as "connected" with:

    (*a*)   a spouse (husband or wife),

    (*b*)   a relative (brother, sister, ancestor or lineal descendant),

    (*c*)   a relative's spouse,

    (*d*)   a spouse's relative,

    (*e*)   a settlor of a trust of which he is a trustee (and any person connected with that settlor and any company connected with that settlement),

    (*f*)   a partner, a partner's spouse, and a partner's relative.

A company is "connected" with a person if that person (or that person together with "connected " persons) controls the company. Two companies are "connected" if they are both controlled by the same person or "connected" persons.

    Even where two persons are not "connected" by any of the above rules, if, by acting together they can control a company then, as regards that company, they are deemed to be connected, and they are also deemed to be connected with any person who acts with them to exercise control of the company.

    A company is regarded as connected with a settlement in an accounting period if:

    (*a*)   it is a close company (or would be a close company if resident in the State), (*b*) its participators (see s 103 above) then include the trustees of, or a beneficiary under the settlement.

Finance Act 1982

Profit-sharing schemes

Sections 50-58

13.15 These sections provide administrative rules whereby company employees who participate in a bona fide profit-sharing scheme may legitimately avoid tax on share allocations up to a maximum of £2,000 for 1992-93 and later tax years.

The scheme must have a governing trust instrument, and the body of persons administering the scheme ("the trustees") must be resident in the State.

In computing its profits for corporation tax purposes, a company is entitled to deduct payments made to the trustees of an approved profit-sharing scheme.

Finance Act 1988

Foreign unit trusts

Section 36

13.16 A company carrying on "foreign unit trust business" in the Custom House Docks area which consists of the management of one or more unit trusts, registered under the Unit Trust Act 1990, and in respect of which all the unit holders are non-resident is chargeable to corporation tax on its profits at the 10% rate.

Finance Act 1989

Collective investment undertakings

Section 18

13.17 This section changes the basis of the charge to be applied on income arising to registered unit trusts and Undertakings for Collective Investment in Transferable Securities (UCITS) approved under EEC Regulations.

In effect, the unit holder is to be the person chargeable to tax. Previously the trustees as the persons initially receiving the income were the persons chargeable (ITA 1967 s 105). However, payments of income made to Irish resident unit holders are to be subject to deduction of income tax at the standard rate.

Finance Act 1990

Trust for Community Initiatives

Section 45

13.18 Payments made between 20 April 1990 and 31 March 1992 (period extended by FA 1991 s 39) by a company to the Trust for Community Initiatives, a company licensed under the Companies Act 1963 s 24, are deductible either as a trading or management expense in computing taxable profits of the paying company.

The Enterprise Trust Ltd

Section 56

13.19 Payments made by a company between 1 April 1992 and 31 March 1994 to the Enterprise Trust Limited, a company set up to implement a community response to long-term unemployment, are deductible in computing the company's taxable profits.

Chapter 14

Tax liabilities of trustees

Trustee companies

Liability to income tax

14.01 Income received by a company acting in a trustee (fiduciary) capacity is liable to income tax (not corporation tax).[1] This means that a company which carries on a trade, and also acts in a fiduciary capacity may have a corporation tax liability (on its trading income) and an income tax liability (in respect of income received in a fiduciary capacity).

Income received by a company in a fiduciary capacity is only liable to income tax at the standard rate.[2]

References
1   CTA 1976 s 1(2).
2   FA 1974 s 3.

Exemption from income tax

14.02 Income tax exemptions apply in like manner for corporation tax.[1]

References
1   CTA 1976 s 11(6). See *Butterworth Ireland Tax Guide 1993-94* at 13.27 et seq.

Reduced rate of corporation tax

14.03 For accounting periods ending before 1 April 1989, a lower 35% corporation tax rate applied to profits of a company formed for the advancement of religion or education if the company was prohibited from distributing any part of its profits to members.[1] This lower rate does not apply for profits of accounting periods ending on or after 1 April 1989.[2]

References
1   CTA 1976 s 79.
2   FA 1988 s 33(2).

Surcharge on undistributed investment income

14.04 This section is related to FA 1974 s 3, which provided that the income arising to trustees of a trust (in their fiduciary capacity) would be taxed only at the standard rate. This gave rise to tax avoidance in that if income was accumulated in a trust, it would not be taxed at more than the standard rate. There was therefore an incentive for high rate taxpayers to divert income into such trust, and allow the income to accumulate, knowing it would not be taxed at more than the standard rate.

This section, by imposing a 20% surcharge on income of a trust (that is not distributed to the beneficiaries within 18 months of the end of the income tax year in which it arises) removes the incentive to accumulate income in a trust. No repayment of or credit for the surcharge is available to beneficiaries when the income is distributed at a later date.

Bodies established for charitable purposes only and approved superannuation funds are specifically excluded from the effects of the surcharge.

Income accumulated by the trustees of an approved profit sharing scheme within FA 1982 Pt I Ch IX (see below) is not subject to the surcharge.

A trustee company within the charge to income tax may therefore be subject to the surcharge.

Close companies

Loans

14.05 A "close company" is a company that is controlled by five or fewer "participators" (CTA 1976 s 94).

A "participator" in a company includes:

(*a*)   a shareholder or person entitled to vote in the company,

(*b*)   a loan creditor of the company,

(*c*)   a person entitled to share in company distributions,

(*d*)   any person who can ensure that the company's income or assets are applied for his benefit.

This definition does not exclude a trustee of a trust.

An "associate of a participator" includes:

(*a*)   a relative (husband, wife, ancestor, lineal descendant, brother or sister) or partner of a participator,

(*b*)   a trustee of a trust where the participator (or his relative, as above) was the settlor,

(*c*)   any person having an interest in a trust which that participator also has an interested in - this does not apply to:

(i)   approved pension scheme trusts (see 11.17 et seq),
(ii) a trust for the benefit of employees and the individual does not (or cannot with relatives etc) own more than 5% of the company's ordinary shares,
(iii) charitable trusts (see Chapter 7) which may arise on the failure of other trusts (see 6.16).

Where a close company makes a loan to a participator (a shareholder or "stakeholder" in the company) the amount of the advance is treated as a payment upon which income tax (at the standard rate) was liable to be withheld. This means the company will have an income tax liability on such loans. If the total of all loans made to the borrower is less than £15,000, the borrower works full time for the company, and the borrower does not have a material interest in the company, the company will not have an income tax charge.

These provisions also apply to a loan made to a company acting as trustee (CTA 1976 s 98).

Where a loan to a participator (which was treated as a payment upon which income tax was liable to be withheld - see previous paragraph) is written off, that amount is treated as income (after deduction of tax) of the recipient. Neither the individual nor the company is entitled to repayment of the income tax withheld.

If the (written-off) loan was made to a person who has died, or to trustees of a trust which has ceased, the beneficiary is regarded as having received the income, and is liable to income tax accordingly (CTA 1976 s 99).

Unless the memorandum and articles impose the necessary restrictions if a trustee company is regarded as a participator in a close company and if, as a participator, it receives a loan which is subsequently written-off while the trust is still in existence the company that forgives the loan will be liable to income tax.[1]

References
1   The forgiving of the debt under CTA 1976 s 98 is regarded as being an annual payment which after deduction of tax at the standard rate (recoverable by the Revenue in accordance with the charging provisions of CTA 1976 s 151) consists of the amount of the debt.

Companies established for charitable purposes

14.06 As regards trusts established for charitable purposes (hospital, school etc - see Chapter 7), income from property vested in the trustees and income from interest and dividends (Schedules C, D, F) is exempt from income tax (ITA 1967 s 333).

A trustee company which does not trade is also entitled to these exempions (CTA 1976 s 11(6)).

Every person (including a trustee of a trust) who receives income belonging to any other person chargeable to tax thereon or who would be so chargeable if resident in the State, must deliver particulars of the person to whom the profits are payable when so required by an inspector of taxes. Since 28 May 1992, this information must be submitted to the inspector without an official request.

A trustee company which trades is entitled to equivalent exemptions (CTA 1976 s 11(6)).

Part 6

Capital gains tax

Chapter 15

The provisions governing trusts

Introduction

15.01 This chapter sets out brief summaries of the capital gains tax provisions dealing with trusts. The application of these provisions is then explained in Chapter 16.

Capital Gains Tax Act 1975

Definitions

Section 2

15.02 This section sets out definitions of words and terms frequently used in the capital gains tax legislation.

The term "body of persons", as for income tax purposes, means any body politic, corporate or collegiate, and any company, fraternity, fellowship and society of persons, whether corporate or not corporate. The trustees of a trust are therefore a "body of persons" (ITA 1967 s 1).

The term "charity", as for income tax purposes, means any body of persons or trust established for charitable purposes only (ITA 1967 s 334).

The term "legatee" includes any person taking property under a will, under intestacy, or by survivorship, whether the person takes the property beneficially or as trustee. In other words, a trustee of a trust may be a "legatee" for capital gains tax purposes.

The term "personal representative", as for income tax purposes, means the executor of a deceased person's estate, and any person having equivalent functions under the law of another country (ITA 1967 s 450(2)).

The terms "resident" and "ordinarily resident" have the same meaning as they have for income tax purposes (see 10.06-10.08).

The terms "settlor" and "settlement" are defined as for income tax purposes. "Settlement" broadly means any method of transferring property and includes any disposition, trust, covenant, agreement, arrangement and any transfer of property (or money) or right to property (or money). A "settlor" includes any person who, directly or indirectly, provides the funds of a settlement (ITA 1967 s 96(3)(*h*)).

"Settled property" means property held in trust other than:

(*a*) property held in trust where the beneficiary is absolutely entitled to take the property - CGTA 1975 s 8(3),

(*b*) property held by a trustee in bankruptcy (or under a deed or arrangement).

Rate of tax

Section 3

15.03 Chargeable gains accruing on disposals made on or after 6 April 1992 (in 1992-93 and later tax years) are taxed at 40%, irrespective of the length of time for which the asset was held.

Chargeable gains accruing on disposals made in prior tax years were taxed at various rates, depending on the length of time for which the asset was held:

Tax year in which disposal occurs

Asset held for:	*1990-91 to 1991-92*	*1986-87 to 1989-90*	*1982-83 to 1985-86*
Less than 1 year	50%	60%	60%
1-3 years	50%	50%	50%
3-6 years	35%	35%	40%
Over 6 years	40%	30%	40%
Authority:	FA 1990 s 82	FA 1986 s 6	FA 1982 s 30

Persons chargeable

Section 4

15.04 A person resident or ordinarily resident in the State for a tax year is liable to capital gains tax on all (world-wide) chargeable gains accruing to him in that tax year.

A person who is not resident in the State is only liable to capital gains tax on disposals of land or minerals (or mineral rights) in the State, or assets of a branch in the State. These provisions also apply to disposals of shares etc deriving their value from land or minerals (or mineral rights) in the State

Nominees

Section 8

15.05 Where assets are held by a person as nominee (or trustee) for another person, and that other person is absolutely entitled to those assets, the "bare trust" is ignored. Any gain arising on the asset's disposal is regarded as accruing to the person who owns the asset ie the person for whom the nominee is acting.

Assets passing on death

Section 14

15.06 The personal representatives of a deceased person are regarded, for capital gains tax purposes as taking that person's assets at market value at the date of death. No disposal arises on the passing of the assets to the personal representatives, except in the case of certain units in (non-qualifying) offshore funds. Where a deceased person owned such units at the time of his death, he is deemed to have disposed of them at market value and the chargeable amount is liable to income tax (FA 1990 s 63(3)).

Settled property

Section 15

15.07 The trustees of a trust are regarded as a single and continuing "body of persons" (see s 1 above), as distinct from the individuals who, from time to time, may act as trustees. That body of persons is regarded as resident (and ordinarily resident) in the State unless:

(*a*) a majority of the trustees reside outside the State, and

(*b*) the trust is administered outside the State.

Nevertheless, in relation to a trust where the settled property was provided by a person not domiciled, resident or ordinarily resident in the State, a person carrying on a trust management business (for example, a bank trustee department) will be regarded as not resident (s 15(1)).

A gift of property, by way of settlement, is a disposal of that property for capital gains tax purposes. This applies even where the gift is revocable, and even where the transferor retains some (reversionary) interest in the settled property (s 15(2)).

If a beneficiary of a trust becomes absolutely entitled to trust assets, the trustee is regarded as having disposed of such assets to the beneficiary at that time (which is not necessarily the time of the transfer of the assets) giving rise to a chargeable gain (s 15(3)).

"Absolutely entitled" means having the exclusive right to direct how the asset shall be dealt with (s 15(10)). If this result is a loss, and the trustee cannot offset the loss against chargeable gains accruing in that tax year, the beneficiary is given the chargeable loss (for offset against his chargeable gains) (s 15(8)).

If a beneficiary of a trust becomes absolutely entitled to trust assets, on the death of a person having a life interest, the trustee is treated as having disposed of the assets and having immediately re-acquired them. In such circumstances, no chargeable gain accrues on the disposal, and the assets are treated as re-acquired at the market value at the date of the death (s 15(4)).

If a person's life interest in trust assets (including annuity income) ceases, and the assets *remain* trust assets (settled property), the assets are treated as having been disposed of by the trustee, and having been immediately reacquired by the trustee at market value (s 15(5), (7)).

Where a beneficiary has become absolutely entitled to trust assets, and the trustee is treated as having disposed of the assets (and having reacquired them at market value), and any capital gains tax assessed on the trustee remains unpaid six months after the due date, the beneficiary may (within two years of the due date) be assessed in respect of that tax (s 15(9)).

Annual allowance

Section 16

15.08 For 1992-93 and later tax years, an individual is entitled to an annual allowance of £1,000 (previously £2,000) against chargeable gains.

If a person dies, his personal representative can use this annual allowance, in respect of gains accruing prior to the person's death.

Pension funds

Section 21

15.09 Capital gains arising to approved pension funds which qualify for an income tax exemption (see 11.17) are not to be treated as chargeable gains.

Charities

Section 22

15.10 If a capital gain arises to a charity and the proceeds of the disposal are charitable purposes (see Chapter 7) no chargeable gain will arise.

Life interest

Section 24

15.11 Where a person disposes of his future interest (in settled property) before coming into possession of that interest, no chargeable gain will arise.

Principal private residence

Section 25

15.12 A disposal, by an individual, of a principal private residence will generally give rise to no chargeable gain. A trustee of a settlement is entitled to equivalent relief if the house was occupied (by the beneficiary) as a principal private residence.

Unit trusts

Section 31

15.13 Although a gain arising to a trustee is attributable to a beneficiary where that beneficiary is absolutely entitled to the trust asset giving rise to the gain (s 15), gains accruing to a unit trust are charged on the trustees of the trust, even though the beneficiaries (the unit holders) of such a trust are generally absolutely entitled to the trust assets (the units).

If all the units are held by persons who, if they disposed of the units would be exempt from capital gains tax in respect of any gain arising, (for example a pension fund), then the trustees will not be liable to tax in respect of any chargeable gains attributable to them.

Connected persons

Section 33

15.14 This section sets out detailed rules which determine when persons are "connected" for capital gains tax purposes. A person is "connected" with:

(*a*)   a spouse (husband or wife),

(*b*)   a relative (brother, sister, ancestor, lineal descendant, uncle, aunt, nephew, niece),

(*c*)   a relative's spouse,

(*d*)   a spouse's relative,

(*e*)   a settlor of a trust of which he is a trustee (and any person connected with that settlor and any company connected with that settlement),

(*f*)   a partner, a partner's spouse, and a partner's relative (other than as regards bona fide commercial disposals of partnership assets).

A company is "connected" with a person if that person (or that person together with "connected " persons) controls the company. Two companies are "connected" if they are both controlled by the same person or "connected" persons.

Even where two persons are not "connected" by any of the above rules, if, by acting together they can control a company then, as regards that company, they are deemed to be connected, and they are also deemed to be connected with any person who acts with them to exercise control of the company.

A company is regarded as connected with a settlement in an accounting period if:

(*a*)   it is a close company (or would be a close company if resident in the State), (*b*) its shareholders then include the trustees of, or a beneficiary under the settlement.

Non-resident company

Section 36

15.15 A chargeable gain accruing to a non-resident company (which if Irish resident would be a close company — a company controlled by five or fewer participators — see 13.12) is imputed (proportionately attributed) to the company's Irish resident shareholders as if the gain had accrued to them.

Non-resident trust

Section 37

15.16 A chargeable gain accruing to a non-resident trust (where all the trustees are non-resident) and the property in which was provided by an Irish resident (and Irish domiciled) settlor, is imputed (proportionately attributed) to the company's Irish resident (and Irish domiciled) beneficiaries.

Disposals to State and charities

Section 39

15.17 A chargeable gain does not arise on a disposal of an asset by way of a gift made to the State, to a charitable body or to certain national institutions and public bodies. If, however, the recipient of the gift subsequently disposes of the asset, the original exemption allowed is withdrawn.

Bankrupt persons

Section 40

15.18 Any disposals by a bankrupt person's assignee (or trustee), are attributable to the bankrupt person (not his assignee or trustee).

Section 42

15.19 Funds (including investments, stocks etc) held by a court accountant are deemed to be held as nominee for the funds' owners or trustees. This means that any gains accruing on such investments etc are attributable to the owners of the investments (not the court accountant).

Debts

Section 46

15.20 This section is concerned with the determination of capital gains or losses on the payment of debts. Payment of debts due by the original creditors, their personal representatives or legatees are to be disregarded for capital gains tax purposes. This also applies where a debt was incurred by trustees of a settlement and the liability is passed on to a beneficiary.

Market value

Section 49

15.21 "Market value" rules are used to provide a disposal value for assets when there is a likelihood that the full sale value will not be used to calculate the chargeable gain (or allowable loss), for example, where a person disposes of an asset to a "connected" person (see s 33).

"Market value" means the sale price the assets might reasonably be expected to fetch if sold in the open market. This value is not to be reduced on the assumption that placing the entire assets on the market at the same time will diminish the value.

Quoted shares, investments and unit holdings are valued at their officially recorded market price.

Computation rules

Schedule 1

15.22 This Schedule sets out the "computation rules" used to calculate the amount of a chargeable gain (or allowable loss). The general format of such a computation is:

	£	£
Disposal proceeds		x
Less costs of disposal		x
Net proceeds		x
Acquisition price	y	
add costs of acquisition	y	
Net cost	y	
Indexed costs (allowing for inflation)		z
Chargeable gain		z
Less annual allowance		z
Net gain		
Tax at appropriate rate(s)		

Where an asset (for example, a building) has had its value "enhanced" by further work, such enhancement expenditure is deductible (as indexed for inflation from the year in which the expenditure was incurred) in the same manner as acquisition costs.

As mentioned at 15.07, if a beneficiary of a trust becomes absolutely entitled to trust assets, the trustee is regarded as having disposed of such assets and having immediately reacquired the assets at market value (CGTA 1975 s 15(3)). Any costs of transferring the assets are deductible as a disposal cost (where the gain is charged on the trustee) or an acquisition cost (where the gain is charged on the beneficiary).

"Wasting assets" are assets having a predictable useful life of less than 50 years, for example, plant and machinery. Land or buildings are not wasting assets. A life interest in settled property is not a wasting asset unless the life tenant's life expectancy (calculated actuarially) is less than 50 years.

Collection of tax

Schedule 4

15.23 This Schedule deals with the general administration, assessment and collection of capital gains tax.

When requested in writing by an inspector of taxes, an Irish stockbroking firm (or agent) must provide:

(*a*)   the names of the buyer and seller of the shares (or units in a unit trust),

(*b*)   the number of shares (or units) traded,

(*c*)   the payment (or value of the consideration) (para 4(4)).

The Revenue Commissioners may request particulars of a settlement from any person who is a party to the settlement (settlor, trustees, beneficiaries - see 2.04). If a trust is non-resident (all the trustees are non-resident - see s 37 above) a person who acts as agent for a beneficiary of the trust may be required to give details to the Revenue Commissioners which will allow them to decide whether:

(*a*)   the trust is non-resident, or

(*b*)   any chargeable gains have accrued (paras 6-7).

A capital gains tax assessment may be made in the name of any one or more of the trustees of a settlement (para 12).

Finance Act 1991

Self-assessment

Section 45

15.24 This section extends the "self-assessment" procedure (that was introduced for income tax and corporation tax by FA 1988 s 9) to capital gains tax.

Chargeable gains accruing to an individual (or trustees of a trust) in 1990-91 and later tax years are subject to self-assessment. Chargeable gains accruing to a company in accounting periods ending after 30 September 1989 are also subject to self-assessment.

Finance Act 1992

Unit trusts

Section 36

15.25 FA 1990 s 35 excluded unit trusts (as defined by the Unit Trust Act 1990 s 1(1)) from qualifying as a collective investment undertaking within FA 1989 s 18 where effectively the admission of a unit holder was linked to that individual taking out a life assurance policy with a company which had control and ownership of the funds underlying the value of units. This section gives an option to the earlier excluded trusts to come within the section 18 provisions if not later than 1 November 1992 a notional disposal of assets is made and capital gains tax on the paper gains is paid at one-half of the normal rate applicable.

Anti-avoidance

Section 62

15.26 This is an anti-avoidance measure introduced to curb technical abuses of the principle that capital gains transactions should be considered by reference to market value figures. It provides that an arm's length valuation is only to apply where the same transaction gives rise to both an acquisition and a disposal for capital gains tax purposes. Previously a preferential acquisition of property, other than land or rights to land, and branch profits within CGTA 1975 s 4(2) accruing to a non-resident person who subsequently becomes an Irish resident and thereafter disposes of the property, could lead to substantial benefits by the substitution of the market value instead of the acquisition costs when determining the base for a capital gains tax charge.

Chapter 16

Liability on settled assets

Introduction

Assets

16.01 Capital gains tax, a tax on the "disposal" of "assets" was introduced in 1975 for 1974-75 and later tax years.[1]

The term "assets" covers all forms of property, whether situate in the State or not, including options, debts, currency, intangible assets and "any form of property created by the person disposing of it, or otherwise becoming owned without being acquired".[2]

Intangible, but quantifiable non-material rights, for example goodwill, are "assets" as are rights in leasehold property. In fact, the term "assets" has been so broadly defined that certain "non-chargeable assets" have, of necessity, also been defined. The disposal of such assets does not give rise to a chargeable gain (or allowable loss). The main non-chargeable assets are:

(*a*)   assets, the disposal of which gives rise to an income tax charge;[3]

(*b*)   tangible movable property (for example, an antique chair) worth less than £2,000;[4]

(*c*)   wasting assets (assets other than land, with a predictable useful life of less than 50 years);[5]

(*d*)   government stocks.[6]

References
1   CGTA 1975 s 3.
2   CGTA 1975 s 7(1).
3   CGTA 1975 Sch 1 para 2.
4   CGTA 1975 s 17.
5   CGTA 1975 s 18.
6   CGTA 1975 s 19.

Non-chargeable gains

16.02 In addition to the non-chargeable assets, certain gains are also exempt from capital gains tax:

(*a*)   the first £1,000 of gains accruing to an individual in any tax year (1992-93 and later tax years: previously £2,000);[1]

(*b*)   life assurance policy proceeds (gains arising to the beneficial owner);[2]

(*c*)   damages (compensation for injuries etc);[3]

(*d*)   betting gains (including lottery winnings);[4]

(*e*)   prize bond winnings;[5]

(*f*)   gain on disposal of private residence;[6]

(*g*)   disposal of business (where total consideration is less than £200,000)[7]

(*h*)   disposal of business to family member;[8]

(*i*)   disposal of business assets where proceeds are reinvested ("rollover relief");[9]

(*j*)   disposals by and to charities;[10]

(*k*)   disposals of woodland (forest trees);[11]

(*l*)   gains accruing to approved pension funds.[12]

References

1   CGTA 1975 s 16; FA 1992 s 59.
2   CGTA 1975 s 20.
3   CGTA 1975 s 24(1)(*c*).
4   CGTA 1975 s 24(2).
5   CGTA 1975 s 24(1)(*b*).
6   CGTA 1975 s 25. The trustees of settled property are entitled to the exemption on the disposal of a main residence of an individual where property disposed of was the only or main residence of an individual entitled to occupy it under the terms of the settlement. If the occupant of the residence was also the owner of another residence the trustee and the occupant jointly must satisfy the inspector of taxes on the status of the settled property.
7   CGTA 1975 s 26.
8   CGTA 1975 s 27.
9   CGTA 1975 ss 28-29.
10 CGTA 1975 ss 22, 39. A capital gain arising to a charitable body on the disposal of an asset and applied for charitable purposes is not to be a chargeable gain. If, however, the assets of the trust body cease to be held for such purposes (for example, there is a reversion of the property to the settlor or, other application after a specified period under a time clause) the trustees are regarded as having made a disposal of all the assets held at the time of the cesser. An arm's length disposal of an asset to a charity will give rise to no gain or no loss.
11 CGTA 1975 Sch 1 para 12.
12 CGTA 1975 s 21: see 11.17 et seq. Superannuation funds officially approved for income tax relief purposes are not chargeable to capital gains tax on the disposal of assets unless the income arising on the assets is taxable.

Disposal

16.03 Capital gains tax law does not define the term "disposal". The word therefore takes its ordinary meaning: the transfer of an interest in a right to an asset.[1]

However, a disposal also includes:

(*a*)   a part disposal of an asset and the term also covers circumstances where an interest or right in (or over) an asset is created by a disposal (for example, the granting of a lease by a freeholder of property);

(*b*)   a disposal of an asset by the owner where any capital sum is derived from the asset notwithstanding that no asset is acquired by the person paying the capital sum.[2]

Interests or rights acquired by way of security are disregarded when determining the consideration applicable to a disposal. In other words, if a house with an outstanding mortgage of £40,000 is sold for £80,000, the sale proceeds for capital gains tax purposes are £80,000 (not £80,000 less £40,000).[3]

A disposal of a security by the security holder (for example, a bank) in satisfaction of a debt is regarded as a disposal by the original owner.[4]

A gift of property, by way of settlement, is a disposal of that property for capital gains tax purposes. This applies even where the gift is revocable, and even where the transferor retains some (reversionary) interest in the settled property.[5]

References

1   *De Brún v Kiernan* TL 117.
2   CGTA 1975 s 8.
3   CGTA 1975 s 8(6).
4   CGTA 1975 s 8(5).
5   CGTA 1975 s 15(2).

Chargeable persons

Resident persons

16.04 A person (including a body of persons)[1] is chargeable to capital gains tax in respect of chargeable gains accruing to that person for each tax year in which that person was resident or ordinarily resident in the State.[2]

The terms "residence" and "ordinary residence" have the same meanings as used for income tax purposes but special rules apply for both personal representatives and trustees of a settlement.

Where a person is resident or ordinarily resident but not domiciled in the State the full gains accruing on Irish and United Kingdom assets are chargeable but other foreign gains are chargeable only to the extent that the proceeds are remitted to the State or applied to meet Irish secured liabilities. [3] As a remitted sum, by it nature, represents a net sum after expenses, no relief is allowable for losses arising on the disposal of other assets outside Ireland or the United Kingdom.[4]

References
1   CGTA 1975 s 2; ITA 1967 s 1.
2   CGTA 1975 s 4(1).
3   CGTA 1975 s 4(3), (4).
4   CGTA 1975 s 4(3)(c).

Non-resident persons

16.05 Where a person is neither resident nor ordinarily resident in the Irish Republic for a tax year liability for that year is confined to capital gains accruing, directly or indirectly, from "immovable property":

(*a*)   Irish land;

(*b*)   Irish sourced minerals or other rights, interests or assets in relation to mining or minerals or the searching for minerals;

(*c*)   shares deriving their value or the greater part of their value, directly or indirectly from the kinds of property mentioned in (*a*) or (*b*);

(*d*)   Irish based assets which at or before the time the chargeable gain accrued were used (or held or acquired) for the purposes of a trade operated through a branch or agency in the State;

(*e*)   a gain derived from the disposal of exploration rights in Irish territorial waters is regarded as accruing from a trade carried on within the jurisdiction.[1]

References
1   CGTA 1975 s 4(2), (6), (8).

Personal representatives

Continuing body of persons

16.06 The personal representatives of a deceased are to be treated as a single and continuing body of persons, distinct from the separate persons acting as the representatives, and that body is to be regarded as having the deceased's residence and ordinary residence.[1]

The terms "trust" and "trustee" include the duties incident to the office of personal representative of a deceased person.[2]

During the administration period the personal representatives are the sole owners of the entitlements of a deceased and stand directly in his place. They only become trustees for the beneficiaries when they are able to apportion estate property to meet specific charges or bequests or to distribute the residue on the completion of the administration.

References
1 CGTA 1975 s 14(3). But see CGTA 1975 s 36 concerning disposals by a non-resident company.
2 Trustee Act 1893 s 50; Succession Act 1965 s 10.

Death

16.07 The passing of a deceased person's assets to his personal representatives is not a disposal for capital gains tax purposes.[1] The value of such assets is taken to be their market value at the date of death.[2]

References
1 CGTA 1975 s 14(1).
2 CGTAA 1978 s 6.

Year of death

16.08 Where an individual has made chargeable gains on disposals in the tax year in which he dies any assessment on any such gains will normally be made on the personal representatives.[1]

In such circumstances, when calculating the chargeable gain, the personal representatives are entitled to deduct the individual's annual allowances (see 16.02, para (*a*)).

References
1 CGTA 1975 Sch 4 para 2(2).

Deed of family arrangement

16.09 Variations of the entitlements arising from a deceased's estate, whether under a will, intestacy or by way of rights under the Succession Act, made under a deed of family arrangement within two years of the date of death (or such longer periods as the Revenue Commissioners may allow, by notice in writing) are regarded as having been made by the deceased.[1] Thus the general relief that assets passing on a death do not constitute a disposal for capital gains tax purposes effectively extends to qualifying family settlements.

The two year time limit from the date of death to agree and verify the terms of a family arrangement should be adequate in normal circumstances. The discretion vested absolutely in the Revenue Commissioners, from which there is no independent right of review, may need to be exercised generously where difficulties arise (for example, foreign resident beneficiaries, title identification).

References
1   CGTA 1975 s 14(6).

Offshore funds

16.10 Prior to 5 April 1990, it was possible to avoid income tax on certain investment income as follows: if an individual bought units in an offshore fund, allowed the annual income to accumulate for several years, and then withdrew the accumulated capital and income at the end of the investment period, the "rolled up" income would be taxed as a single capital gain in the final year. If the final gain was below £2,000 (£4,000 for a married couple) no income tax or capital gains tax would arise. Even where the gain was greater than the annual allowance, it would generally be taxed at 35% (assets held 3-6 years) which was lower than the appropriate marginal income tax rate (56% in 1990).

The offshore funds legislation (FA 1990 Pt 1 Ch VII) counteracts such tax avoidance by treating a rolled up (unindexed) capital gain in a "non-qualifying offshore fund" as an income gain (in the appropriate tax years).

All offshore funds are automatically deemed to be "non-qualifying" funds unless the fund passes the distribution test, which enables it to be regarded as a qualifying fund.

If a deceased person had units in a non-qualifying offshore fund at the time of his death, he is deemed to have disposed of the units at the date of death. The resulting income tax liability will be a charge on the deceased person's estate.[1]

References
1   FA 1990 s 63(3).

Trustees

Introduction

16.11 Settled property in the general sense refers to disposals of property made by a settlor under a deed of settlement. However, for capital gains tax purposes the terms "settlement" and "settlor" are strictly defined, as for income tax purposes.

The term "settlement" includes any disposition, trust, covenant, agreement, or arrangement , and any transfer of money or other property or of any right to money or other property.

The term "settlor", in relation to a settlement, includes the person making the settlement, any person who "entered into" the settlement, any person who provides (or undertakes to provide) funds for the settlement, and any person who makes reciprocal settlement arrangements with another person.[1]

While "settled property" must consequently be interpreted in accordance with its income tax meaning, for capital gains tax purposes the term is separately defined to mean any property held in trust (other than property to which a beneficiary is absolutely entitled but does not include any property held by a trustee or assignee in bankruptcy or under a deed of arrangement).

The wording is thus broad enough to include will trusts and family settlement trusts drawn up for the disposal of á deceased's estate. However, as a trustee taking under a testamentary disposition or a deed of family arrangement covered by CGTA 1975 s 14(6) is technically regarded as a legatee[2] there is no capital gains tax charge on the creation of such a trust. The capital gains tax consequences for settled property are thus limited to the subsequent liabilities of trustees or the beneficiaries of the trust.

The term "legatee" includes any person taking property under a will, under intestacy, or by survivorship, whether the person takes the property beneficially or as trustee. In other words, a trustee of a trust may be a "legatee" for capital gains tax purposes.

References
1   CGTA 1975 s 2; ITA 1967 s 96(3)(*h*).
2   CGTA 1975 s 2.

Residence

16.12 The trustees of a trust are regarded as a single and continuing "body of persons" distinct from the individuals who, from time to time, may act as trustees. That body of persons is regarded as resident (and ordinarily resident) in the State unless:

(*a*)   a majority of the trustees reside outside the State, and

(*b*)   the trust is administered outside the State.

Nevertheless, in relation to a trust where the settled property was provided by a person not domiciled, resident or ordinarily resident in the State, a person carrying on a trust management business (for example, a bank trustee department) will be regarded as not resident.[1]

As a professional trustee is normally appointed in a sole capacity the relief provided enables a qualifying Irish resident to manage an overseas trust without incurring a liability to capital gains tax even where the general administration is carried out in Ireland. Where part of the property in a settlement is vested in one set of trustees and part in another set of trustees both sets of trustees are to be treated as constituting, and in so far as they act separately, as acting on behalf of a single body of trustees.[2]

Capital gains tax chargeable on the trustees of a settlement may be assessed and charged in the name of any one or more of the trustees. Tax owed by a trustee in his fiduciary capacity is separately assessed and is distinct from tax owed by that person in his capacity as an individual.[3]

References
1   CGTA 1975 s 15(1).
2   CGTA 1975 s 15(11).
3   CGTA 1975 s 8(3) and Sch 4 para 12.

Foreign trusts

16.13 A chargeable gain accruing to a non-resident trust (where all the trustees are non-resident) and the property in which was provided by an Irish domiciled settlor who is also resident in the State, is imputed (proportionately attributed) to the company's Irish resident (and Irish domiciled) beneficiaries.

In determining the chargeable amount no regard is had to any contingencies which could change the nature of the beneficiary's interest at a future time. The apportionment must be "just and reasonable between persons having interests in the settled property"[1]

Payments of capital gains tax liability made by the trustees of a non-resident settlement are not to be regarded as either chargeable to income tax or as creating a further capital gains tax charge.[2]

References
1   CGTA 1975 s 37(2).
2   CGTA 1975 s 37(5).

16.14 Capital losses arising to the trustees of a foreign trust may only be offset against capital gains arising to the trustees of that foreign trust. In other words, although capital gains arising to the trustees are attributable to the Irish resident beneficiaries, capital losses are not available to the beneficiaries.[1]

If an Irish resident beneficiary of a foreign trust has a capital gains tax liability because a chargeable gain has been proportionately attributed to him, and the trustees pay that tax on his behalf, the tax paid by the trustees is not regarded as a payment to the beneficiary for capital gains tax or income tax purposes. In other words, the tax paid will not, in the case of a foreign trust, be included as a payment made to the beneficiary for the purposes of calculating his interest in the settlement.[2]

The Revenue Commissioners may request particulars of a settlement, including a non-resident settlement, from any person who is a party to the settlement (settlor, trustees, beneficiaries: see 2.04).

If a trust is non-resident, a person who acts as agent for a beneficiary of the trust may be required to give details to the Revenue Commissioners which will allow them to decide whether:

(*a*)   the trust is non-resident, or

(*b*)   any chargeable gains have accrued.[3]

Beneficiaries who are restricted solely to an interest in income where the settlement was created before 28 February 1974 are excluded from the general charge applicable to beneficiaries of non-resident settlements. A beneficiary with a reversionary interest in the capital of a non-resident settlement made before that same date may postpone the imposition of capital gains tax otherwise chargeable until an interest in possession occurs or there is an earlier disposal of the interest in whole or in part unless he can by any means whatsoever obtain for himself the benefit at an earlier time.[4]

References
1   CGTA 1975 s 37(6).
2   CGTA 1975 s 37(5).
3   CGTA 1975 Sch 4 paras 6-7.
4   CGTA 1975 s 37(4).

Example

A non-domiciled foreign resident left his widow a life interest in his estate with remainder over to his children. The widow came back to live in Ireland permanently. A profit on the disposal of investments made by the trustees gave rise to an overall charge of £5,000 as determined under the capital gains tax legislation by reference to the base value as at date of death. The actuarial valuation of the widow's interest in the estate at the date of the disposal was considered to be a one-half share. She was, accordingly, chargeable to capital gains tax on a sum of £2,500.

Example

A, who had Irish domicile and was also permanently resident in the State, by his will created a settlement for the residue of his estate appointing a UK trustee company as the sole trustee. The residue consisted of various holding in non-Irish companies with a market value of £60,000 when transferred to the trust the income on which was payable to the widow for life but entitlement was to cease if she remarried, when the capital was to be divided equally between A's two children who were also named as taking in remainder on the death of the life tenant.

The three beneficiaries, who were all resident and domiciled in the State, survived the testator. All the stocks were sold for £76,000 on 31 March 1988 and the proceeds were invested in real property. Expenses incurred on the disposal were £1,000. The widow was aged 55 when the disposal was made and had not remarried. (All figures in £IR equivalents)

	£	£
Proceeds of disposal on 31 March 1988		76,000
Deduct cost of sale		1,000
		75,000
Market value at date of A's death	60,000	
Indexation of initial value (1.082)		64,920
Chargeable gain		10,080
Apportionment of gains		
Life tenant 10,080 x 0.7206	7,264	
(CATA 1976 Sch 1 Table A)		
Tax chargeable 7,264 @ 50%		3,632
Remaindermen's share Gross (10,000 - 7,264)		2,736
Tax chargeable 2,736 @ 50%		1,868

Notes
1. The market value of the contingency regarding the remarriage of the widow has been ignored.
2. As the apportionments refer to the liability of the trustees no annual allowance is due.
3. The liabilities arising are contingent on domicile and residence considerations. If any of the beneficiaries had a foreign domicile and was not resident or ordinarily resident in the State no Irish capital gains tax liability would arise on the relevant share.
4. As no mortality tables for the valuation of the market value of a life interest are included in the governing capital gains legislation the percentage figure has been taken from CATA 1976 Sch 1 Table A.

Foreign discretionary trusts

16.15 As mentioned in the preceding paragraph, a chargeable gain accruing to a foreign trust is proportionately attributed to the Irish resident beneficiaries. A chargeable gain attributable to a foreign *discretionary* trust is proportionately attributed to the Irish resident beneficiaries in a slightly different manner.[1] Each beneficiary's portion is calculated by reference to (the discretionary) payments made to him in the preceding five years.

The average annual payment over the five years is treated as an annuity, and the gain is attributed to the Irish resident beneficiaries in proportion to the size of each beneficiary's annuity.

References
1   CGTA 1975 s 37(3). In *Leedale v Lewis* [1982] 3 All ER 808, the UK House of Lords allowed a chargeable gain accruing to a foreign *discretionary* trust to be apportioned among the beneficiaries

under the rule in the equivalent of CGTA 1975 s 37(2), that is, in a manner "just and reasonable between persons having interests in the settled property". The court effectively ignored the special apportionment rules for foreign discretionary trusts in the equivalent provision to CGTA 1975 s 37(3). This matter has not yet been considered by the Irish Courts.

Beneficiaries

Beneficiary absolutely entitled against the trustees

16.16 If a beneficiary becomes absolutely entitled to trust assets (and the assets remain within the trust), the trustee is regarded as having disposed of such assets and having immediately reacquired the assets at market value.[1] "Absolutely entitled" means having the exclusive right to direct how the asset shall be dealt with. Unless the beneficiary is taking on the cesser of a priority life interest, where such a disposal is made, a charge to capital gains tax will arise on all gains not earlier accounted for by the trustees.[2]

If the deemed disposal by the trustee results in a loss, and the trustee cannot offset the loss against chargeable gains accruing in that tax year, the beneficiary is allocated the chargeable loss (for offset against his chargeable gains).[3]

Several cases have been considered by the English courts on the equivalent UK provisions regarding a release of trust funds where an appointment has been made out of settled property to further trusts with the original trustees retaining the management of the funds. While each case must be considered on the basis of its own relevant facts it appears that if there is an enabling power conferred on the trustees to create a further trust within the original trust structure no chargeable gain will arise.[4]

References
1 CGTA 1975 s 15(3).
2 CGTA 1975 s 15(10).
3 CGTA 1975 s 15(8).
4 *Hart (Inspector of Taxes) v Briscoe and others* [1978] 1 All ER 791; 52 TC 53; [1978] STC 89; *Bond (Inspector of Taxes) v Pickford* 57 TC 301; [1983] STC 517; *Swires (Inspector of Taxes) v Renton* [1991] Ch D; [1991] STC 490.

Life interest

16.17 The term "life interest", in relation to a settlement, includes a right to the income from settled property for life. The terms also includes a right to use settled property for life. The "life" need not necessarily be the life of the person having the life interest, for example, A might have the income from settled property while B is alive. A right which is at the discretion of a trustee cannot qualify as a life interest, nor can an annuity even where the annuity is charged on settled property unless appropriated by the trustees from a separate fund.[1]

References
1   CGTA 1975 s 15(12)(*a*).

Termination of life interest

16.18 If a beneficiary of a trust becomes absolutely entitled to trust assets, *on the death of a person having a life interest*, the trust is regarded as having disposed of the assets and having reacquired them at market value at the date of death. No chargeable gain arises on the deemed disposal.[1]

A "life interest" in these circumstances does not include an annuity charged on the trust property, or any right which is contingent on the exercise of discretion by the trustee (or any other person).[2]

References
1   CGTA 1975 s 15(4).
2   CGTA 1975 s 15(12)(*a*).

16.19 If a person's life interest in trust assets (including the ending of an annuity, other than an annuity charged on trust property, by the death of the annuitant), ceases, and the assets remain trust assets (settled property), the assets are treated as having been disposed of by the trustee, and having been immediately reacquired at market value.[1] The deemed disposal may give rise to a capital gains tax charge on any increase in the market value of the property which accrued between the time the prior life interest commenced and ceased. Where the life interest involved is a right to part of the income of settled property the capital gain is to be measured by reference to an interest in a corresponding part of the settled property of the appropriate separate property as necessary.

Example

A, by his will, bequeathed a life interest of his shareholding in a family controlled company to his widow B. He also left a life interest in rental income arising from real property to his brothers, C and D, equally or to the successor of both in the same interest with remainder over to a nephew, E. All four beneficiaries survived the testator. C died first.

Notes

1. The market value of any chargeable gain accruing on the successive life interest passing on C's death to D (a moiety of any increase in the value of the real property between the dates of death of A and C) is chargeable on the trustees. No annual allowance deduction is due but indexation relief on the value of the property taking A's date of death as the base value is allowable.

2. The widow's life interest in personal property is a separate trust for capital gains tax purposes and its value is accordingly ignored when ascertaining the market value of the interest passing as at C's date of death.

3. When E takes in remainder on the cesser of D's full life interest in the real property no chargeable gain will arise on his absolute interest.

References
1   CGTA 1975 s 15(5), (7).

Charge of tax on beneficiaries

16.20 Where a beneficiary has become absolutely entitled to trust assets, and the trustee is treated as having disposed of the assets (and having reacquired them at market value), and any capital gains tax assessed on the trustee remains unpaid six months after the due date, the beneficiary may (within two years of the due date) be assessed in respect of the tax.[1]

References
1   CGTA 1975 s 15(9).

Interest forgone

16.21 If a beneficiary forgoes an interest (including a life interest and a future interest) in the trust property no chargeable gain arises at that time. Whether a chargeable gain arises is only determinable when the relevant life interest (as provided in the governing deed) ceases.[1]

References
1   CGTA 1975 s 24(4).

Bankruptcy

16.22 Where property is held by a person as trustee or assignee in bankruptcy or under a deed of arrangement the trustee is the person chargeable to capital gains tax arising from any disposals of property made to third parties. Transactions involving the transfer of property between a bankrupt or arranging debtor and the acting trustee representative are ignored for capital gains tax purposes.[1]

Where a bankrupt or arranging debtor dies while his assets are still vested in a trustee the assets are regarded as being held by the trustee as a separate personal representative for these assets.[2] Accordingly, no capital gains tax arises on the death or in respect of any payments made by the deemed personal representative to legatees of the deceased.[3]

References
1   CGTA 1975 s 40(1).
2   CGTA 1975 s 40(2).
3   CGTA 1975 s 14(1), (4).

Nominee shareholders

16.23 A person in whose name any shares are registered must, when officially requested, state whether he is the beneficial owner of the shares and if he is not the beneficial owner he must supply the name and address of the person on whose behalf the shares are held.[1]

References
1 CGTA 1975 Sch 4 para 5.

Unit trusts

Introduction

16.24 Although a gain arising to a trustee is attributable to a beneficiary where that beneficiary is absolutely entitled to the trust asset giving rise to the gain, gains accruing to a unit trust are charged on the trustees of the trust, even though the beneficiaries (the unit holders) of such a trust are generally absolutely entitled to the trust assets (the units).[1]

If all the units are held by persons who, if they disposed of the units would be exempt from capital gains tax in respect of any gain arising (for example, a pension fund), then the trustees will not be liable to tax in respect of any chargeable gains attributable to them.[2]

References
1 CGTA 1975 s 31.
2 CGTA 1975 s 31(4), (6). The taxation of unit trusts and undertakings for collective investment in transferable securities is discussed at 11.34-11.51.

Broking firms

16.25 When requested in writing by an inspector of taxes, an Irish stockbroking firm must provide:

(*a*) the names of the buyer and seller of the shares (or units in a unit trust),

(*b*) the number of shares (or units) traded,

(*c*) the payment (or value of the consideration).[1]

References
1 CGTA 1975 Sch 4 para 4(4).

Rates of tax

16.26 Chargeable gains accruing on disposals made on or after 6 April 1992 (1992-93 and later tax years) are taxed at 40%, irrespective of the length of time for which the asset was held.

Chargeable gains accruing on disposals made in prior tax years were taxed at various rates, depending on the length of time for which the asset was held:

Tax year in which disposal occurs

Asset held for:	1990-91 to 1991-92	1986-87 to 1989-90	1982-83 to 1985-86
Less than 1 year	50%	60%	60%
1-3 years	50%	50%	50%
3-6 years	35%	35%	40%
Over 6 years	40%	30%	40%
Authority:	FA 1990 s 82	FA 1986 s 6	FA 1982 s 30

Computation of tax

16.27 A chargeable gain (or allowable loss) is calculated using the "computation rules". The general format of such a computation is:

	£	£
Disposal proceeds[7]		x
Less costs of disposal[1]		x
Net proceeds		x
Acquisition price	y	
Add costs of acquisition[1]	y	
Net cost	y	
Indexed costs[8] (allowing for inflation)[2]		z
Chargeable gain		z
Less annual allowance[3]		z
Net gain (allowable loss)[4]		
Tax at appropriate rate(s)		
Tax relief (if any)[5, 6]		

Notes
1. Expenditure incurred on the acquisition (for example, legal fees) subsequent enhancement, or disposal (for example, auctioneer fees) of an asset is deductible in computing the amount of the chargeable gain arising on the disposal of the asset, but expenditure that is deductible in computing income tax is not allowed (CGTA 1975 Sch 1 paras 3-4).
As mentioned at 15.06, if a beneficiary of a trust becomes absolutely entitled to trust assets, the trustee is regarded as having disposed of such assets and having immediately reacquired the assets at market value (CGTA 1975 s 15(3)). Any costs of transferring the assets are deductible as a disposal cost (where the gain is charged on the trustee) or an acquisition cost (where the gain is charged on the beneficiary) (CGTA 1975 Sch 1 para 3(5)).
2. For 1978-79 and later tax years allowable expenditure may be increased by reference to the All Items Consumer Price Index compiled by the Central Statistics Office at mid-

February immediately before the tax year of the disposal (indexation relief: CGTA 1978 s 3). The appropriate inflation adjustment multipliers may be found in annual regulations issued by the Revenue Commissioners, by way of statutory instrument.

The indexation relief does not apply to deductible expenditure which was incurred within twelve months before the time of the disposal (CGTAA 1978 s 3(1)(a) (proviso)). The relief does not operate to increase a gain or loss, or to convert a gain into a loss (CGTAA 1978 s 3(3)).

Indexation relief is not allowable on disposals of development land made on or after 28 January 1982 (FA 1982 s 38).

Where an asset, for example, a building has had its value "enhanced" by further work, such enhancement expenditure is also deductible (as indexed for inflation from the year in which the enhancement expenditure was incurred).

3. The annual allowance available to an individual (£1,000 for 1992-93 and later tax years; previously £2,000) is not available to trustees of a trust. It may be used by a beneficiary who is absolutely entitled to trust property - see 16.16 et seq (CGTA 1975 s 16(2)). A personal representative is also allowed to use the deceased individual's annual allowance against chargeable gains arising in the year of death (CGTA 1975 s 16(3)).

4. Generally, a capital loss may be directly offset against chargeable gains arising in the same tax year, provided the loss has not been allowed in any previous tax year (CGTA 1975 s 5(1)). A capital loss cannot be offset against chargeable gains arising in preceding tax years, unless the loss arises in the year of death of the disponer, in which case it may be offset against chargeable gains arising in the three tax years immediately preceding the year of death (CGTA 1975 ss 12(7) and 14(2)).

A loss arising from the disposal of a non-chargeable asset (see 16.01) is not an allowable loss (CGTA 1975 s 12(2)).

Losses arising on disposals of development land may only be set off against development land gains (FA 1982 s 40).

If, on a beneficiary becoming absolutely entitled to trust property, a deemed disposal by a trustee results in a loss, and the trustee cannot offset the loss against chargeable gains accruing in that tax year, the beneficiary is given the chargeable loss (for offset against his chargeable gains (CGTA 1975 s 15(8))).

5. Where, after 30 January 1975 capital gains and capital acquisitions tax are chargeable on the same event, any capital gains tax paid may be credited against the capital acquisitions tax charge (FA 1986 s 63). The credit is restricted to the lesser of the capital gains tax or the capital acquisitions tax charge (FA 1988 s 66).

6. Existing double taxation agreements between Ireland and other States for income taxes are to apply Irish capital gains tax and taxes of a similar nature imposed by the partner State. Nevertheless, some of Ireland's pre 1975 double taxation agreements that are still in force contain provisions concerning relief from capital gains or capital charges. These are with Belgium (Article 13), Cyprus (Article 12), Finland (Articles 13 and 23), Federal Republic of Germany (Article X and XX), Italy (Article 12), Japan (Article 14), Luxembourg (Articles 12 and 22), Netherlands (Articles 12 and 21), Norway (Articles 12 and 21) and Zambia (Article XI).

These agreements when approved by Dáil Éireann under ITA 1967 s 361(6) (or its statutory predecessor FA 1958) were directly limited in scope to income tax or corporation profits tax and can, accordingly, only apply to capital charge within the provisions of these and similar taxes. While it is accepted by the Revenue Commissioners that corporation tax does no more, in principle, than amalgamate the separate earlier charges for both income and corporation profits taxes on companies and is therefore a similar tax to these earlier charges for double taxation purpose nevertheless the determination of a capital gains of a company even though chargeable to corporation tax, when not arising on development land (ITA 1967 s 361 as extended by CGTA 1975 s 38), is governed by the provisions of the Capital Gains Tax Act (FA 1982 s 36(4)).

The wording in the Ireland/United States of America Double Taxation Convention 1949 (ITA 1967 Sch 8), includes in the signed document articles favouring residents of Ireland concerning gains from the disposal of United States capital assets (Article XIV) and the undistributed profits of an Irish controlled company arising in the United Stated (Article XVI). The United States Senate did not accept the inclusion of these two articles in the Convention as no reciprocal relief was available to residents of the United States under Irish law. The effect of the articles was therefore excluded when the other relieving measures under that Convention entered into force.

All the double taxation arrangements made by this country since 1976 covering income taxes also provide specially and separately (notwithstanding the differing methods and the scope of the charge in partner States) for general reciprocal relief from a double charge on capital gains on movable property, allocating a sole right of charge to the country of residence of the disponer. Immovable property is chargeable in the State where it is situated and also in the State of residence of the disponer if different, with the latter State allowing relief for the double charge. Such arrangements exist with the United Kingdom (SI 319/1976), Australia (SI 406/1983), Switzerland (SI 76/1984 by way of a Protocol to SI 240/1967), Sweden (SI 348/1987), Austria (SI 29/1988 by way of a Protocol to SI 250/1967), New Zealand (SI 30/1988), and the Republic of Korea (SI 290/1991).

The double tax charge is also eliminated for certain transport undertakings engaged in international traffic under agreements with Spain and the Soviet Union.

7. "Market value" rules are used to provide a disposal value for assets when there is a likelihood the full sales value will not be used to calculate the chargeable gain (or allowable loss), for example, where a person disposes of an asset to a "connected" person (CGTA 1975 s 33).

"Market value" means the sale price the assets might reasonably be expected to fetch if sold in the open market. This value is not to be reduced on the assumption that placing the entire assets on the market at the same time will diminish the value.

Quoted shares, investments and unit holdings are valued at their officially recorded market price (CGTA 1975 s 9).

8. While market value rules are generally used (see para 7 above) to provide a value for an acquired asset, this could have the effect of inflating the acquisition cost where an asset was bought at a discount, or for a preferential price. This would mean that when the asset was subsequently sold, a reduced chargeable gain would result because the base cost of the asset would be based on market value (net actual cost). FA 1992 s 62 ensures that this does not happen by providing that market value is to be used only when the same transaction gives rise to an acquisition and disposal for capital gains tax purposes.

Self-assessment

Introduction

16.28 The "self-assessment" procedure[1] (that was introduced for income tax and corporation tax by FA 1988 s 9) applies to chargeable gains accruing to an individual (or trustees of a trust) in 1990-91 and later tax years. Chargeable gains accruing to a company in accounting periods ending after 30 September 1989 are also subject to self-assessment.[2]

References
1 Introduced for income tax and corporation tax by FA 1988 Pt I Ch II.
2 FA 1991 Pt I Ch VI.

Payment of tax

16.29 A preliminary payment of capital gain tax must be made on or before 1 November in the tax year following the tax year in which the chargeable gains arise. This preliminary payment must amount to not less than 90% of the ultimate liability, if interest is to be avoided.[1] The return of capital gains is included with the income tax return, which must be lodged on or before 31 January in the year following the tax year.[2] Any balance of tax due must be paid with this return.

Example

Mr X, a single person, had the following chargeable gains and allowable losses (on disposal of quoted shares) in 1993-94:

	£
Chargeable gains	10,000
Allowable losses	(2,000)
Net	8,000
Less annual allowance	(1,000)
Net chargeable gains	7,000
Capital gains tax at 40%	2,800

Notes
1. Mr X must make a preliminary tax payment of £2,520 on or before 1 November 1994.
2. Mr X's return of chargeable gains for 1993-94 must be lodged on or before 31 January 1995. Any balance of tax owed (£2,800 - £2,520 = £280) must be paid on or before 31 January 1995 (the return date).

References
1 FA 1988 s 18(3).
2 FA 1988 s 9(1).

Part 7

Capital acquisitions tax

Chapter 17

The provisions governing trusts

Introduction

17.01 This chapter sets out brief summaries of the capital acquisitions tax provisions dealing with trusts. Detailed examples illustrating the general application of the law are contained in the companion volume to this work *Taxation of Estates: The Law in Ireland*. Cross-references are provided, where helpful, to the more general discussion in that work. The application of these provisions as regards trusts is then explained in Chapter 18.

Capital Acquisitions Tax Act 1976

Definitions

Section 2

17.02 This section sets out definitions of words and terms frequently used in the capital acquisitions tax legislation.

The term "absolute interest" in relation to property, includes the interest of a person who has a general power of appointment.

The term "benefit" includes any estate, interest, income or right.

The term "disposition" is used to describe any method by which property may be transferred from one person to another and includes:

237

(*a*)   a trust, covenant, agreement or arrangement whether made by a single operation or a series of operations, and

(*b*)   the exercise of a general power of appointment by a person in favour of another person.

A "general power of appointment" describes a power which is exercisable without restriction against settled property.

An "interest in expectancy" includes, apart from a reversion of a lease, an estate in remainder or reversion and every future interest.

A "limited interest" excludes a leasehold interest but otherwise extends to life interests.

"Property" includes rights and interests of any description.

"Real property" includes leasehold property.

A "special power of appointment" is a power restricted or qualified in its application.

Cross-references
Taxation of Estates Chapter 9.

Meaning of "on a death"

Section 3

17.03 The phrase "on a death" is carefully defined for capital acquisitions tax purposes. It usually means, in relation to a person coming into possession of property under the terms of a will (or intestacy) on the death of the person who made the will (or died intestate).

Example

A, by will dated 27 June 1992, left land worth £100,000 to his son B, absolutely.
A died on 24 November 1992.
B took an inheritance of £100,000 worth of land "on a death", ie on the death of A.

The phrase "on a death" can also mean after the cesser of an intervening life interest.

Example

A, by will dated 27 June 1992, left land worth £100,000 to his son B, for life, and then to C, B's brother, absolutely.
A died on 24 November 1992.
B took an inheritance consisting of a life interest in land worth £100,000 from A, on the death of A.
B died on 16 November 1993. The land was then worth £110,000.
C took an inheritance consisting of an absolute interest in land worth £110,000 from A, on the death of B.

Taxable gift

Section 6

17.04 Gift tax is charged on the taxable value of every taxable gift taken on or after 28 February 1974.

Generally, where the disponer had Irish domicile at the date of the disposition (deed of transfer of will etc), "taxable gift" means the whole of the gift.

In relation to a gift taken under a discretionary trust on or after 17 June 1993 if the disponer had Irish domicile at:

(*a*)   the date of the disposition,

(*b*)   the date of the gift, or

(*c*)   the date of his death (where the gift was taken after his death),

"taxable gift" means the whole of the gift. Gifts taken prior to 17 June 1993 were taxable gifts if the disponer had Irish domicile at the date of the disposition, or the trust (deed) was governed by Irish law.

Contingencies

Section 20

17.05 Where a benefit is taken in possession but is subject to a contingency which may result in the future cesser of the benefit (other than a power of revocation reserved to the disponer: see section 30) capital acquisitions tax liability is determined ignoring the contingency. If, however, the contingent event later intervenes to withdraw a benefit the earlier tax charge is recalculated on the basis that the donee or the successor had taken an interest confined to the period of the beneficial possession.

Valuation date

Section 21

17.06 The valuation date for a taxable gift is the date of the gift. The valuation date of a taxable inheritance consisting of trust property is the earliest date on which the trustees are entitled to retain the subject matter of the inheritance for the benefit of the successor or any person in the right of the successor or on his behalf.

The date of death of a disponer is the relevant valuation date where property is transferred because the transferor fails to exercise a power of revocation which he had reserved to himself.

Cross-references
Taxation of Estates 9.10.

Discretionary trusts

Section 22

17.07 A person who takes a benefit as a beneficiary of a discretionary trust, while the disponer (the person who provided the property comprised in the trust) is regarded as taking *a gift* from that disponer at the time he becomes entitled in possession to the property.

If the beneficiary takes the benefit under a discretionary trust:

(*a*)   created by a will,

(*b*)   within two years prior to the disponer's death, or

(*c*)   by a disposition that only becomes effective "on a death" (not necessarily that of the disponer)

then he is regarded as taking *an inheritance* from the disponer at the date of death.

Cross-references
Taxation of Estates 12.06.

Dealings with future interests

Section 23

17.08 The early release by a remainderman of an interest in property which has not yet come into possession due to the existence of a priority limited interest is regarded at the later time when the interest would have come into such possession under the governing disposition as constituting a gift or inheritance in the hands of the remainderman but any capital acquisitions tax charge due is primarily the liability of the person who has taken in possession.

It is that person whose personal circumstances are the ones considered in respect of any claim for the reduced market value applicable to agricultural property. Also, the gift or inheritance taken by the beneficial interest holder arising under the later disposition made by the remainderman gives rise to a separate and distinct charge. (See also FA 1985 s 62 which provides relief from a double charge to tax on the same property on the same event.)

Example

X, by will dated 12 June 1991, transfers land worth £100,000 to his son A for life, and then to B (X's other son) absolutely.
X died on 16 July 1993. On that date, the lands were worth £110,000.
A took an inheritance consisting of a life interest of lands worth £110,000 from X on 16 July 1993. B took nothing. His interest in the lands is a future interest, or remainder interest (also known as an interest in expectancy).

B may transfer his future interest to another person, for example Z (a stranger). If this happens, Z must pay B's tax (if any), when the interest comes into possession. Nevertheless, if **Z** is a "farmer" (CATA 1976 s 19), agricultural relief may be due.

The transfer of future interest, from B, to Z, may also constitute a taxable gift, which may give rise to a gift tax liability for Z.

Because tax cannot be charged twice on the same event, the tax charge on the benefit which is earlier in priority may be credited against the tax charge on the later benefit.

Cross-references
Taxation of Estates 15.03-15.06.

Release of limited interest

Section 24

17.09 Where a limited interest in possession has been released before the cesser of the limitation period as set out in the disposition which created that interest it is treated for capital acquisitions tax purposes as ceasing immediately before the release thus giving rise to a charge for both the relieved period of the limited interest and that which would have applied if the limited interest period had been fully exhausted. (See also FA 1985 s 61 which provides that property chargeable with tax more than once on the same event won't be included more than once (for that event) in any tax aggregate.)

Example

X, by will dated 12 June 1991 transfers land worth £200,000 to his son A for life, and then to B (X's other son) absolutely.
X died on 12 December 1991.
A is taxed on an inheritance consisting of a life interest in lands worth £200,000. On 27 August 1992, A assigned his life interest in the lands (then worth £220,000) to B.

A's death is "deemed" to have happened on 27 August 1992. On that date, B takes an inheritance of lands worth £220,000 from X.
A's tax is recalculated on the basis that he had an interest in the lands for the period 12 December 1991 to 27 August 1992 (see s 26 below).

Cross-references
Taxation of Estates 15.09.

Settlement of an interest not in possession

Section 25

17.10 This anti-avoidance provision provides that where a disponer makes a resettlement of property in which he had a future or contingent interest at the time of the resettlement the effects of the later disposition are disregarded for capital acquisition tax purposes when the interest in the property comes into the possession of that disponer under the terms which applied prior to the re-settlement.

Example

On 26 October 1992, by deed of trusts, A settled investments worth £1,000,000 on X (A's son) for life, and then to A (himself) absolutely.
Assume that on 1 July 1993, A wishes to transfer his remainder (future) interest in the investments to X absolutely.
The future interest is ignored. X is taxed on the value of gift consisting of an absolute interest taken on 26 October 1992.

Cross-references
Taxation of Estates 15.07.

Enlargement of interest

Section 26

17.11 Where a limited interest in possession has been enlarged by a taxable gift or a taxable inheritance to create an absolute interest in property (other than under a disposition which created the limited interest) a credit for the unexpired period of the limited interest is to be allocated when determining the capital acquisitions tax liability on the enlargement (see example after s 24).

Cross-references
Taxation of Estates 15.10, 15.13.

Dispositions involving powers of appointment

Section 27

17.12 In respect of the exercise (or the failure to exercise) a general power of appointment the disposition is that exercise (or failure to exercise) the power *not* the disposition which created the power. This means that the disposer is the holder of the general power. In contrast, where a special power of appointment is concerned the relevant disposer in such circumstances is to be the person who created the power.

Cross-references
Taxation of Estates 15.16.

Gift subject to power of revocation

Section 30

17.13 Where a gift of property has been made but is subject to a power of revocation by the disponer no transfer of beneficial possession is recognised for capital acquisition tax purposes until the power is released or ceases to be exercisable.

Cross-references
Taxation of Estates 10.11, 15.01.

Free use of property

Section 31

17.14 Where, other than for full consideration, a person obtains a benefit from property which he does not own (to which he is not entitled in possession) he is taxed on the annual open market value, as adjusted for any monetary consideration given, of the use, occupation or enjoyment of the property (as a gift or inheritance, as appropriate).

Cross-references
Taxation of Estates 10.13, 11.02, 12.11, 15.01.

Accountable person

Section 35

17.15 A trustee is a secondarily accountable person, but not primarily accountable (as for example a donee or successor) in respect of property or income therefrom which forms the subject of a gift or an inheritance arising from settled property.

Subsection (8) gives power to trustees to sell or mortgage property to pay any capital acquisitions tax due.

Cross-references
Taxation of Estates 20.04.

Returns

Section 36

17.16 Self-assessment became mandatory for capital acquisitions tax purposes with effect from 1 September 1989. This means that a beneficiary, as a primarily accountable person, must (within four months of the valuation date) submit a capital acquisitions tax return once the total value of benefits taken exceeds 80% of the appropriate threshold.

A trustee, as a secondarily accountable person may be called upon to pay outstanding tax if the primarily accountable person does not pay the tax.

Cross-references
Taxation of Estates 20.01.

Assessment of tax

Section 39

17.17 The Revenue Commissioners have retained the power to assess tax on any accountable person (including a trustee) or his authorised agent or on the personal representatives of a deceased accountable person.

Cross-references
Taxation of Estates 20.14.

Payment of tax by instalments

Section 43

17.18 A capital acquisitions tax liability on property, both real and personal, held under a life interest may be paid in five equal yearly instalments, the first of which is due twelve months from the date the tax becomes payable in the normal way. If the life tenant dies before the full instalment period has expired any instalments due after the date of death are cancelled and any tax overpaid is refunded with interest.

Cross-references
Taxation of Estates 16.06-16.07.

Tax to be a charge

Section 47

17.19 Unpaid capital acquisitions tax is to remain a charge on the property concerned (other than money or negotiable instruments) in priority to any burdens created by or on behalf of the donee or successor.

Where settled property comprised in a taxable gift or taxable inheritance is disposed of with the consent of the donee or successor or by such persons with the consent of another person the charge is transferred to the monies or investments arising from the exercise of such a consent.

Tax is not to remain a charge on property acquired by a purchaser or mortgagee for full consideration and their successors in title who have no notice of the charge. If, however, the purchaser or mortgagee had notice of the tax charge it ceases to be operative after the expiration of twelve years from the date of the respective gift or inheritance.

Cross-references
Taxation of Estates 16.12.

Receipts and certificates

Section 48

17.20 A secondarily accountable person, for example a trustee, is entitled to obtain a certificate of discharge from capital acquisitions tax.

Cross-references
Taxation of Estates 16.16.

Charities

Section 54

17.21 A gift or inheritance taken for public or charitable purposes and applied for such purposes anywhere in the world is exempt from tax. Gifts or inheritances taken for public or charitable purposes before 9 July 1987 were only exempt if the property was applied for charitable purposes within the State or Northern Ireland. A charitable body is entitled to the £10,000 class threshold (as indexed) where the body takes a gift or inheritance and the property is not applied for charitable purposes.

Exemption of certain securities

Section 57

17.22 Persons who are neither resident, ordinarily resident or domiciled in the State are exempt from income tax on income derived from government (and semi-State) securities (ITA 1967 Pt XXXII). Such persons are also exempt from capital gains tax arising on the disposal of such securities (CGTA 1975 s 19).

This section extends equivalent exemption from capital acquisitions tax for gifts or inheritances taken by persons who are neither resident, ordinarily resident or domiciled in the State. The capital acquisitions tax exemption however also includes unit trusts comprising government etc securities. To qualify for the exemption, securities comprised in gifts or inheritances taken on or after 13 April 1978 must, if the disponer was Irish resident or Irish domiciled, have been held by the disponer for three years before the date of the gift or inheritance.

Cross-references
Taxation of Estates 18.13-18.14.

Exemption of certain receipts

Section 58

17.23 Any normal or reasonable payments made by a disponer during his lifetime for the support, maintenance or education of his spouse, children or persons to whom he is in loco parentis or to a dependant relative for support or maintenance are ignored for capital acquisitions tax purposes.

Exemption where disposition made by donee or successor

Section 59

17.24 Tax is not chargeable on a gift or inheritance taken by a disponer under a self-made disposition.

Cross-references
Taxation of Estates 14.31 (Example 2), 15.07, 15.09, 18.01.

Schedule 1

17.25 This Schedule sets out the rules relating to the valuation of limited interests using the tables in Parts II and III of the Schedule.

Finance Act 1978

Exemption of certain securities

Section 40

17.26 This section provides that after 14 April 1978, securities issued by the State or semi-State bodies etc with a condition that they are to be exempt from capital taxation when held by a person who is not resident or domiciled in the State, will only qualify for relief in the hands of a donee or successor (who is thus non-resident and non-domiciled) if the disponer has held the securities for at least three years before the date of the disposition under which the gift or inheritance is taken. A similar restriction applies to units in a unit trust scheme (within the Unit Trust Act 1972) if the underlying investments of the scheme consist of such State or semi-State securities.

Finance Act 1980

Right to recovery by secondarily accountable persons

Section 84

17.27 CATA 1976 s 35(7) provided that a secondarily accountable person (for example, a trustee) could recover any tax he had paid from a primarily accountable person (for example, a beneficiary). This section by extending CATA 1976 s 35(7), restricts that right of recovery to primarily accountable persons who have taken an absolute interest in a benefit.

Finance Act 1981

Certain marriage settlements made before 1 April 1975

Section 46

17.28 This section, with retrospective effect to the introduction of capital acquisitions tax, provides that where, under a settlement made before 1 April 1975 by a grandparent of a donee or successor, the consideration involved was the marriage of the beneficiary's parents, a relevant gift or inheritance taken out of the settled property is to be dealt with as if the disponer grandparent were the parent of the grandchild.

Finance Act 1984

Discretionary trusts: 3% once-off charge

Sections 104-109

17.29 Sections 104-109 impose a once-off 3% charge on the chargeable value of discretionary trusts (including accumulation trusts) in existence on or after 25 January 1984. Exempt (see s 108) are:

(*a*) Trusts where any of the principal objects of the trust (spouse of disponer, child of disponer, or child or a deceased child of the disponer) are under 21 years of age. A 25 year age limit applies to trusts created before 30 January 1993. A liability arises once this condition ceases to be satisfied.

(*b*) Trusts created for public or charitable purposes in the State or Northern Ireland.

(*c*) Revenue approved pension scheme trusts.

(*d*) Trusts operative for the purposes of a units scheme within the meaning of the Unit Trust Act 1972.

(*e*) Trusts which came into existence to assist one or more incapacitated individuals.

(*f*) Trusts where the proceeds are used for the upkeep of an approved stately home or garden (see FA 1978 s 39).

The discretion of trustees under a discretionary trust to appoint the trust funds to beneficiaries is absolute: *In the matter of the Trustee Act 1893 s 36 and others*, HC, 24 July 1991.

The trustees of a discretionary trust are the persons primarily accountable for payment of the tax (s 107).

Charitable bodies

Section 110

17.30 As regards gifts or inheritances taken after 26 March 1984 CATA 1976 s 54 provides relief for gifts or inheritances to charitable bodies. Subs (3) of this section substituted CATA 1976 s 54(1) to provide that such bodies were to be entitled to the minimum threshold of £10,000 (FA 1984 s 111) as regards gifts or inheritances not applied in the State. FA 1987 s 50 subsequently introduced exemption for gifts or inheritances taken by such bodies but applied outside the State.

Certificates of discharge

Section 113

17.31 This section inserted CATA 1976 s 48(5)-(7). The need for these additional subsections arose following the introduction of aggregation of benefits taken from the same class, on or after 2 June 1982.

Persons who are not primarily liable for payment of tax may not be aware of aggregable taxable gifts or inheritances taken by a donee or successor. Such persons may obtain a certificate of discharge from capital acquisitions tax after two years from the date of the taxable gift or inheritance, provided that full returns of property (within the knowledge of the appropriate personal representative, trustee or other person concerned) have been submitted to the Revenue and the tax paid.

Finance Act 1985

Relief from double aggregation

Section 61

17.32 As regards gifts or inheritances taken on or after 2 June 1982, the same property, if chargeable to either gift tax or inheritance tax more than once on the same event, is not to be included more than once on one person for capital acquisitions tax charging purposes. This relief would apply for example on the release by a life tenant of his or her interest in favour of the remainderman under the original governing disposition (see CATA 1976 s 24 above).

Relief from double charge to tax

Section 62

17.33 This section, which inserted CATA 1976 s 34A, like the preceding section, relates to property passing from trusts. If tax is paid more than once on

the same event (for example, where a benefit in expectancy has been transferred at a earlier time before it came into possession) the net tax arising which
is earlier in priority is not to be *deducted* in arriving at the taxable value of the
later gift or inheritance but is to be allowed as a *credit* against any liability arising on the later benefit. The basis for the double charge applies to transactions
caught within the deeming provisions of CATA 1976 s 23.

Section 63

17.34 Where after 29 January 1985, a capital acquisitions tax charge and a
capital gains tax charge arise on the same event in relation to the same property,
no deduction is given for the capital gains tax liability in computing the taxable
value of the gift or inheritance. The liability is allowed by way of credit against
the capital acquisitions tax due. For events happening on or after 6 April 1988
the relief is confined to the lesser of the capital gains tax charge and the inheritance tax charge (FA 1988 s 66).

Exemption from 3% (once-off) discretionary trust charge

Section 65

17.35 With effect from 26 January 1984, this section, by inserting FA 1984
s 108(2), extends exemption from the 3% once-off discretionary trust charge to:

(*a*)   property comprised in a gift or inheritance taken by the State, and

(*b*)   an inheritance taken by a discretionary trust that represents free use
of property or a non-interest bearing loan.

Finance Act 1986

Discretionary trusts: 1% annual charge

Sections 102-109

17.36 Pt V, Ch I imposes a 1% annual charge on the value of property held
under discretionary trusts in existence on or after 25 January 1984 (discretionary trusts that are subject to the 3% once-off charge introduced by FA 1984
Pt V (ss 104-109)). The valuation date for the charge is 5 April each year. Discretionary trusts that are exempt (FA 1984 s 108) from the 3% once-off charge
are also exempt from the 1% annual charge.

The once-off 3% charge and the 1% annual charge cannot both be imposed in the same 12 months (s 103(4)).

The trustees are primarily accountable for the tax (s 104(*c*)) and they must
lodge returns and pay the tax on a self-assessment basis within three months
of the valuation date.

Real property and certain unquoted shares, may, by agreement with the
Revenue Commissioners, retain the same valuation for a three year period.

Finance Act 1987

Charities

Section 50

17.37 This section, by substituting CATA 1976 s 54(2) with effect from 9 July 1987, provides that gifts or inheritances taken by charities will be exempt from capital acquisitions tax, provided the gift or inheritance is applied for public or charitable purposes. Gifts or inheritances taken by charities prior to 9 July 1987 were required to be applied charitable etc purposes *in the State* (or Northern Ireland) in order to qualify for exemption.

Finance Act 1989

Self-assessment

Sections 74-79

17.38 A limited measure of self-assessment was introduced for the 1% annual discretionary tax charge imposed by FA 1986 Pt V Ch I.

This section, by substituting CATA 1976 s 36 introduced full self-assessment for capital acquisitions tax. Previously the person primarily accountable for the tax was obliged to furnish a return of chargeable property within three months of the valuation date. The new CATA 1976 s 36 widens the scope of self-assessment to cover all gifts and inheritances and also the once-off 3% discretionary trust charge, for valuation dates on or after 1 September 1989.

The primarily accountable person must furnish the return of chargeable property within four months of the valuation date, together with a computation of the tax arising, and a remittance for any tax due and/or an application for payment by instalments and/or an application to pay tax by transfer of government securities (CATA 1976 s 45). Instalment arrangements are not granted for personal property taken absolutely.

The self-assessment return must be submitted once the taxable value of a gift or inheritance exceeds 80% of the sum on which a tax liability would arise.

The Revenue Commissioners are empowered, as before, to require any accountable person to deliver a return or an additional return.

Collective investment undertakings

Section 85

17.39 Dispositions comprising the transfer of an in interest in a collective investment undertaking (of a unit trust nature) are exempt from capital acquisitions tax if the qualifying disposition is governed by foreign law and the donee or successor is not regarded as either domiciled or ordinarily resident in the State at the date of the disposition or in the date of the gift or inheritance.

Finance Act 1990

Pension schemes: anti-avoidance

Section 129

17.40 This is an anti-avoidance measure. It withdraws from 5 April 1990 the exemption from the 3% (once-off) and the 1% (annual) charges on discretionary trusts (imposed by FA 1984 Pt V Ch I and FA 1986 Pt V Ch I respectively) for pension schemes (within ITA 1967 s 235(9)) where the scheme includes arrangements that do not relate to the employment.

Finance Act 1992

Discretionary trusts

Section 224

17.41 The age of the youngest beneficiary (spouse, child or grandchild) applicable for an exclusion of the 3% charge on discretionary trusts (FA 1984 Pt V) following the death of the disponer has been reduced from 25 years to 21 years, for trusts created after 30 January 1993.

Section 225

17.42 The age of the youngest beneficiary (spouse, child or grandchild) applicable for an exclusion of the 1% annual charge on discretionary trusts (FA 1986 Pt V) following the death of the disponer has been reduced from 25 years to 21 years.

Finance Act 1993

Discretionary trusts

Section 131

17.43 This section substituted FA 1984 s 107(*a*) as regards inheritances taken on or after 24 February 1993. The 3% once-off discretionary trust charge is amended to take account of the new method of valuing shares in private companies.

Section 132

17.44 This section substituted FA 1986 s 104(*a*) as regards inheritances taken on or after 24 February 1993. The 1% annual discretionary trust charge is amended to take account of the new method of valuing shares in private companies.

Chapter 18

Trusts and trustees

Introduction

Gift tax and inheritance tax

18.01 Capital acquisitions tax is a tax on gratuitous benefits (property acquired for free) taken by an individual by way of gift or inheritance. The tax applies to benefits in possession. Therefore, if a person has not received a benefit, there can be no tax. Thus, a gift that is taken subject to a power of revocation is not a gift for capital acquisitions tax purposes because the recipient is not entitled in possession. The gift does not arise until the power of revocation is released by the disponer, or ceases to have effect.[1]

Nevertheless, a person who (while not being entitled in possession) has the free use of property is taxed on the annual value (as reduced by any consideration given) of the use of the property.[2]

There are two kinds of capital acquisitions tax: gift tax, and inheritance tax. Capital acquisitions tax replaced the old estate duties of legacy duty (personal property) and succession duty (real property).

Gift tax applies to gifts taken on or after 28 February 1974, and inheritance tax applies to inheritances taken on or after 1 April 1975.[3] In order to encourage lifetime transfers of property, gift tax is calculated as 75% of what the inheritance tax would have been.[4]

An inheritance is taken when a person (a successor) takes a benefit on a death (for example, by will) without full payment being made (for free or at reduced value). A gift is taken when a person (a donee) takes a benefit other than on a death (for example, by deed of transfer) without full payment being made (for free or at reduced value).[5]

The person who gives away the property (whether by way of gift or inheritance) is called the disponer. The method by which the property is given away is called the disposition. In the case of an inheritance, the disposition will usually be the will of the deceased person. In the case of a gift, the disposition will usually be the deed of transfer. However, for anti-avoidance purposes, the term "disposition" is very broadly defined; it can even include a failure to act, and circumstances where there is no documentation.[6]

The following exempt thresholds apply based on the relationship between the disponer and donee or successor.[7]

Class	Relationship the disponer bears to the donee or successor	Exempt threshold 1993	Benefits taken before 1 January 1990
		£	£
I	The spouse, child or minor child of a deceased child of the disponer	171,750	150,000
II	Lineal ancestor, lineal descendant (other than included in Class I), a brother, sister, nephew or niece of the disponer	22,900	20,000
III	Where the donee or successor does not on the date of the taxable gift or inheritance is taken to the disponer in a relationship of Class I or II	11,450	10,000

References

1   CATA 1976 s 30.
2   CATA 1976 s 31.
3   CATA 1976 ss 4, 10.
4   CATA 1976 Sch 2 para 6.
5   CATA 1976 ss 5, 11.
6   CATA 1976 s 2(1).
7   CATA 1976 Sch 2 para 1, FA 1990 s 128.

Aggregation

Before 2 June 1982

18.02 Before 2 June 1982 gifts or inheritances taken from the same disponer were aggregated. This meant that once the combined value of benefits taken, for example, from a mother, exceeded £150,000, the excess was taxable.

2 June 1982 to 25 March 1984

18.03 Benefits taken between these dates from the same class of disponer were aggregated. This meant that once the combined value of benefits taken, for example, from a parent, exceeded £150,000, the excess was taxable.

After 26 March 1984

18.04 Benefits taken after 26 March 1984 from any disponer are aggregated. Once the combined value of benefits taken exceeds the threshold, the excess is taxable. The appropriate threshold is the highest "revised class threshold" which is computed separately for each gift or inheritance included in the aggregate. Each revised class threshold is the lesser of:

(*a*)   the appropriate class threshold (£150,000/£20,000/£10,000 as indexed),

(*b*)   the total of the taxable values of all taxable gifts/inheritances within that class threshold included in the aggregate.

Rates of tax

18.05 Taxable inheritances are taxed at the following rates:

	On or after 30 January 1991	26 March 1984 to 29 January 1991
Threshold amount	Nil	Nil
Next £10,000	20%	20%
Next £40,000	30%	30%
Next £50,000	35%	35%
Next £50,000		40%
Next £50,000		45%
Balance	40%	55%

Gift tax is 75% of the calculated inheritance tax.

References
CATA 1976 Sch 2.

Computation of tax

Format of computation

18.06 The general format of a capital acquisitions tax computation is:

	£	£
Market value[1] (or agricultural value)[2] of benefit		
Less liabilities, costs, expenses[3] (or proportion as appropriate)	_____	
Incumbrance-free value		
Less consideration[4] given (or proportion as appropriate)	_____	
Taxable value (absolute interest)		
Limited interest factor[5] (where applicable)_____	_____	
Less annual small gift allowance[6] (gifts only)		_____
Net		
Tax at appropriate rates		
Tax relief[7] (if any)		_____
Net tax		

Notes

1. Market value is the price the property would fetch if sold in the open market on the valuation date, assuming a willing buyer (CATA 1976 s 15(1)).

2. Agricultural value. As regards gifts or inheritances taken on or after 30 January 1991 this is the gross (unencumbered) market value of agricultural property (farmland, woodland, farm buildings etc) reduced by 55% (previously 50%) of that value or £200,000 whichever is the lesser.

As regards *gifts* taken on or after 17 June 1993, agricultural value is the market value of agricultural property reduced by 75% or £250,000 whichever is the lesser.

An individual must be a "farmer" (domiciled and resident in the State, at least 80% of the market of whose property consists of agricultural property - including livestock, machinery) to qualify for the lower agricultural value (CATA 1976 s 19).

3. Any liabilities, costs or expenses "payable out of" a taxable gift or inheritance are deductible in calculating the incumbrance-free value (CATA 1976 s 18(1)). Only one deduction is allowed for the same liability, where, for example, several benefits are taken from the same disponer (CATA 1976 s 18(7)(*a*)). No deduction is allowed for contingent payments (CATA 1976 s 20), reimbursable expenses, interest on tax or costs relating to exempt property (CATA 1976 s 18(5)). If agricultural relief is claimed, only a proportionate deduction of the liabilities, costs etc is given (CATA 1976 s 19(2)).

4. The full amount of any bona fide consideration in money (or money's worth) is deductible from the incumbrance-free value in calculating the taxable value of a gift or inheritance, except where a reduced "agricultural value" (see above) has been substituted for the market value. In such instances, only a proportionate deduction is allowable (CATA 1976 ss 18(2), 19(2)).

5. A limited interest is an interest (other than a leasehold interest) for the duration of a life (or for a period certain) or any interest which is not an absolute interest.

An absolute interest includes the interest of a person who has a general power of appointment over property. As the term is not further clarified, it takes its ordinary non-technical meaning: an interest which is complete and unconditional and which can be sustained, to the extent of the interest involved against allcomers. A general power of appointment is one where there is no restriction on the power of the holder to appoint property (CATA 1976 s 2(1)).

In keeping with this definition, the holder of a general power of appointment is to be regarded as the disponer, in respect of any benefit passing from the exercise, the failure to exercise, or the release of the power (CATA 1976 s 27(1)).

A special power of appointment is a power which is not a general power. The disponer of a settlement which created a special power of appointment is also to be regarded as the disponer in respect of any benefits taken in possession from the exercise of such a power (CATA 1976 s 27(2)).

The value of a limited interest is calculated using percentage factors contained in CATA 1976 Sch 1.

6. The first £500 of the taxable value of all taxable gifts taken from any one disponer is any 12 month period (ending after 31 December 1978) is exempt (CATA 1976 s 53(1)).

7. As regards gifts or inheritances taken on or after 2 June 1982, the same property, if chargeable to either gift tax or inheritance tax more than once on the same event, is not to be included more than once on one person for capital acquisitions tax charging purposes. This relief would apply for example on the release by a life tenant of his or her interest in favour of the remainderman under the original governing disposition (FA 1985 s 61).

If tax is paid more than once on the same event (for example, where a benefit in expectancy has been transferred at a earlier time before it came into possession) the net tax arising which is earlier in priority is not to be *deducted* in arriving at the taxable value of the later gift or inheritance but is to be allowed as a *credit* against any liability arising on the later benefit (CATA 1976 s 34(*a*) as inserted by FA 1985 s 62).

Where after 29 January 1985, a capital acquisitions tax charge and a capital gains tax charge arise on the same event in relation to the same property, no deduction is given for the capital gains tax liability in computing the taxable value of the gift or inheritance. The liability is allowed by way of credit against the capital acquisitions tax due. For events happening on or after 6 April 1988 the relief is confined to the lesser of the capital gains tax charge and the inheritance tax charge (FA 1988 s 66).

Example

A, by will, gave his widow B a life interest in farm property with remainder over absolutely to C, a child of a brother of A. In 1991 B gave up her life interest in favour of C. The value of the farm property at that time was £40,000, B was aged 60 and C qualified as a farmer within CATA 1976 s 19(1).

C in 1988 had taken a gift of £5,000 from his father.

Liability of C	£
1988:	
Taxable value of gift (5,000 - 500)	4,500
Threshold amount	150,000
1991:	
Inheritance taken from A	
Market value	40,000
Agricultural value (moiety)	20,000
Agreeable gift	4,500
Class threshold	20,000
Threshold amount (FA 1990 s 128)	21,520
Inheritance tax (24,500 - 21,520)	2,980
£2,980 @ 20%	596
Inheritance taken from B	25,900
(Tables in CATA 1976 Sch I, Pt II)	
40,000 x 0.6475	
Agricultural value (moiety)	12,950
Agreeable gift	4,500
Class threshold	10,000
Threshold amount (FA 1990 s 128)	10,760
Inheritance tax (17,450 - 10,760)	
£6,690 @ 20%	1,338

Future interests

18.07 The creation of a future interest does not involve any capital acquisitions tax charge as there is no interest in possession taken at that time. When the interest "falls in" at a later date and is then taken in possession by the expectant donee or successor, tax is chargeable on the value of the property passing at that time.

Problems occur where the future interest never comes into possession because it has been disposed of before the termination of the earlier interest in possession. Anti-avoidance rules provide that any disposal of a future interest by the holder of that interest before it comes into possession is ignored for capital acquisitions tax purposes. The future interest holder is deemed to take an inheritance on the death of the original disponer. [1] The disposition made by the future interest holder creating a further interest gives rise to a separate charge.[2]

Example

B, a widow, had a life interest in the estate of her late husband which was to be taken in remainder by C. C, during the lifetime of B, disposes of his interest in favour of D. The inter vivos settlement made between C and D does not give rise to any immediate interest in possession as there is no gift tax charge applicable on the transfer of the future interest concerned. When B dies the following inheritances are taken:

A (disponer) to C, and
C (disponer) to D.[3]

If D had made a further disposal of his expectant interest to E an additional inheritance tax charge with D as the disponer (D to E) would have arisen on the death of B.

References
1   Resettlements of future interests made by a disponer in favour of himself are also covered: CATA 1976 s 25(1).
2   CATA 1976 ss 23 and 59.
3   This is an inheritance as it arises on a death: CATA 1976 s 31(1).

18.08 Any money or money's worth paid as consideration on the creation of a future interest is deductible in calculating the taxable value when the gift or inheritance comes into possession.[1]

The deduction is to be the proportion which the amount of the consideration bore to the market value of the future interest when the payment was made.[2]

The limited interest tables in CATA 1976 Sch 1 set out detailed rules for ascertaining the value of benefits of donees or successor but there is no official method for valuing a future interest which is disposed of at the time of its disposal. The figure ascertained by calculating the amount of unexpired limited interest under the tables would give a good value for the benefit arising but because there is no method provided by the legislation, it seems that an actuarial valuation would be required.

References
1   CATA 1976 s 18(2) and (4)(*b*).
2   CATA 1976 s 18(10).

18.09 The person who actually takes in possession a future interest which had been disposed of earlier is the person primarily responsible for the payment of any tax due in respect of that interest. Thus that person is liable for the inheritance tax on the deemed inheritance by the original future interest holder from the disponer. He is also liable for the inheritance tax on the interest which he receives from the original future interest holder. Under the original legislation a *deduction* was given for the first liability against the second liability.[1] In 1985, however, an amending provision was introduced, backdated to 1976, which allows a more beneficial tax credit.[2]

Example

A, by his will, bequeathed his farm property in successive life interests to his brothers B and C with remainder over to D, a son of C. C gave up his future life interest during the life of B. On the death of B in 1991 when C was still living the inheritance tax benefits taken were as follows:

(a) A to C. A life interest determined by reference to the age of C, in accordance with the tables in CATA 1976 Sch I Pt II.

Any entitlement to claim the reduced agricultural value [3] is determined by reference to the qualifying status of D who is also the person primarily liable for the payment of the tax.

(b) A to D. The full market value of the property is chargeable with deductions for:

(i)   liabilities, costs and expenses incurred by D;

(ii) any consideration paid by D to C;

(iii) agricultural property if D is a qualified farmer; and

(iv) a tax credit for the tax at (a) when paid is also due from the direct charge on D.

Any disclaimer of a benefit under a will, intestacy or an entitlement to an interest in settled property which has not been taken into possession is disregarded for capital acquisitions tax purposes.[4]

The exercise of a disclaimer to an entitlement to property is not the same as the disposal of a future interest. The latter is itself a disposition.

References
1   CATA 1976 s 18(1).
2   CATA 1976 s 34(*a*) as inserted by FA 1985 s 62.
3   CATA 1976 s 19(1).
4   CATA 1976 s 13.

Release of limited interest in possession

18.10 The market value for capital acquisitions tax purposes of a limited interest, whether for a life or a period certain is determined from the official tables.[1]

Where a limited interest in possession is disposed of prematurely "by any means whatever" before the end of the limitation period no review is made of the earlier liability arising on that interest but it is provided that gift or inheritance tax, as appropriate, is to be levied as if the provisions of the disposition originally creating the limited interest were effective immediately after the early cesser of that limited interest.[2]

This deemed disposal creates a double charge on the property on the same day that the limited interest is disposed of except where the premature release was made by the disponer who created the limited interest in the first instance.

Example

A, by an inter vivos disposition, settles property on B for life with remainder over to C.
B disposes, also by an inter vivos disposition, of his interest to C.
Capital acquisitions tax charges arise:

(*a*) At the date of the original disposition.
    A to B. The value of the gift chargeable is determined by the rules for limited interest benefits taken in possession as set out in CATA 1976 Sch I Pt II. (If the gift had been taken within two years of the date of death of A it would become an inheritance.[3])

(*b*) At the date of the second disposition.
    (i)   A to C. Inheritance tax is chargeable on the full market value;[4]
    (ii) B to C. Inheritance tax is chargeable on the market value of B's unexpired life interest determined under the rules in CATA 1976 Sch I Pt II.[5]

Example

A, by an inter-vivos disposition, created a life interest in property in favour of himself with remainder over absolutely to B. At a later date A gave up his limited interest. In these circumstances there is only one charge to inheritance tax arising on the full market value of the property taken by B on the date of the second disposition.[6]

References
1   CATA 1976 Sch I Pts II, III.
2   CATA 1976 s 24(3).
3   CATA 1976 s 3(1)(*c*).
4   CATA 1976 s 24(1).
5   CATA 1976 ss 24(2) and 26(1).
6   CATA 1976 s 24(3).

Discretionary trusts

Once-off 3% charge

18.11 A once-off 3% charge applies to the chargeable value of discretionary trusts (including accumulation trusts) in existence (or coming into existence) on or after 25 January 1984. Exempt are:[1]

(*a*) Trusts where any of the principal objects of the trust (spouse of disponer, child of disponer, or child of a deceased child of the disponer) are under 21 years of age. A 25 year age limit applies to trusts created before 30 January 1993. A liability arises once this condition ceases to be satisfied.

(*b*)   Trusts created for public or charitable purposes in the State or Northern Ireland.

(*c*)   Revenue approved pension scheme trusts. Pension schemes (within ITA 1967 s 235(9)) that include arrangements unrelated to the employment are *not* exempt.[2]

(*d*)   Trusts operative for the purposes of a units scheme within the meaning of the Unit Trust Act 1972.

(*e*)   Trusts which came into existence to assist one or more incapacitated individuals.

(*f*)   Trusts where the proceeds are used for the upkeep of an approved stately home or garden.[3]

(*g*)   Property comprised in a gift or inheritance taken by the State.

(*h*)   An inheritance taken by a discretionary trust that represents free use of property or a non-interest bearing loan.[4]

The discretion of trustees under a discretionary trust to appoint the trust funds to beneficiaries is absolute: *In the matter of the Trustee Act 1893 s 36 and others*, HC, 24 July 1991.

References
1   FA 1984 s 108.
2   FA 1990 s 129.
3   FA 1978 s 39.
4   FA 1985 s 65.

18.12 A benefit taken in possession under a discretionary trust is to be treated as a gift or inheritance, as appropriate, with the provider of the trust property as the disponer.[1] Any relevant vesting will arise from the exercise of a special power of appointment by the trustees.

References
1   CATA 1976 s 22.

1% annual charge

18.13 A 1% annual charge applies to the value of property held under discretionary trusts in existence on or after 25 January 1984 (discretionary trusts that are subject to the 3% once-off charge introduced by FA 1984 Pt V (ss 104-109)). The valuation date for the charge is 5 April each year. Discretionary trusts that are exempt[1] from the 3% once-off charge are also exempt from the 1% annual charge.

The once-off 3% charge and the 1% annual charge cannot both be imposed in the same 12 month period.[2]

The trustees are primarily accountable for the tax[3] and they must lodge returns and pay the tax on a self-assessment basis within three months of the valuation date.

Real property and certain unquoted shares, may, by agreement with the Revenue Commissioners, retain the same valuation for a three year period.

References
1   FA 1984 s 108.
2   FA 1984 s 103(4).
3   FA 1984 s 104(*c*).

Payment

18.14 The trustees of a discretionary trust are the persons primarily liable to pay any inheritance tax due and are also seized with the obligation to furnish a return of chargeable property within three months of the valuation date.[1]

The general self-assessment procedures introduced for capital acquisitions tax with effect from 1 September 1989, also apply to the inheritance tax charges on discretionary trusts.[2]

References
1   FA 1984 s 107(*c*) and (*e*).
2   FA 1989 Pt V; CATA 1976 s 36(2) and (4) as substituted.

Part 8

Local taxation

Chapter 19

Local taxation: exemption from rating

Introduction

UK rating law

19.01 Rates were first levied by the English Parliament in 1597.[1] Since 1601, property for public purposes was exempt from rates. In 1865 "public purposes" was clarified as pertaining property of the Crown, and the immediate servants of the Crown.[2]

The beneficial occupier of the property is the person liable to pay the rates. A property is beneficially occupied if it is capable of yielding, whether or not so used, a clear rent after meeting outgoings.

If the legal owner, because the public is occupying his property, is prevented from beneficially occupying his property, he will generally be exempt from rates.

The general and unrestricted use by the public of property in which the legal owners have been deprived of the possibility of beneficial occupation has been accepted by the English courts as constituting a ground for exemption from a rating charge in that the occupying public is not a chargeable person.[3]

References
1 Poor Rate Act 1597. A national charge was imposed by the Poor Rate Act 1601 which remained in force until it was repealed by the Poor Rate Act 1967 s 117(1).
2 *Mersey Docks and Harbour Board Trustees v Cameron* [1865] 11 HLC 443.
3 *Hare v Overseers of Putney* [1881] 7 QB D 223 (a bridge). *Lambeth Overseers v London County Council* [1897] AC 625 (a public park).

Irish rating law

19.02 No rating legislation was passed in Ireland until 1838.[1]

References
1 Poor Relief (Ireland) Act 1838 s 63.

19.03 The Irish legislation applies to land, buildings and mines together with rights and profits arising out of land, fishery and navigation rights, rights of way and tolls levied on rights or easements.[1] However

> no church, chapel or other building exclusively dedicated to religious worship, or exclusively used for the education of the poor, nor any infirmary, hospital, charity school or other building used exclusively for charitable purposes shall be rateable except where private profit or use shall be directly derived therefrom, in which case the person deriving such profit shall be liable to be rated according to the annual value of such profit or use.

References
1   The value of machinery is to be excluded: Valuation (Ireland) Act 1860 s 7. The meaning of machinery was examined by Costello J in *Commissioner of Valuation v Pfizer Chemical Corporation*, Unreported, HC, 9 May 1989, Case 1988/706SS.

Rateable valuations

Commissioners of Valuation

19.04 The Commissioners of Valuation are responsible for compiling the lists used to calculate the rateable valuation for each property.[1] In doing so, they must

> distinguish all the hereditaments and tenements, or portions of the same, of a public nature, or used for charitable purposes, or for purposes of science, literature and the fine arts[2]

and

> all such hereditaments or tenements, or portions or same, so distinguished shall, so long as they continue to be of a public nature, and occupied for public service, or used for the purposes aforesaid, be deemed exempt from all assessments

for poor rates.

No hereditaments or tenements etc are deemed to be of a public nature, or used for such charitable or scientific purposes, unless they are

> altogether of a public nature or used exclusively for such charitable, scientific or other purposes aforesaid.[3]

References
1   Valuation (Ireland) Act 1854 s 2 which replaced the Valuation (Ireland) Act 1852 s 15. The same class of hereditaments ("of a public nature and occupied for public service") were exempted by the Poor Relief (Ireland) Act 1838 s 63.
2   Scientific Societies Act 1843.
3   Valuation (Ireland) Act 1852 s 16.

Rate charges

Power to levy rates

19.05 The law governing the charging of rates was consolidated in 1946. A county rate is leviable by a council of a county to supply any deficiency in a county fund (the poor rate).[1] This power includes a right of recourse to urban areas within the county. A similar general right was given to municipal authorities.[2]

References

1   Local Government Act 1946 ss 11-12.
2   Local Government Act 1946 s 18.

Homes, schools, community halls

19.06 A rating charge is not to be levied on "the specified valuation" of domestic homes (including a proportion where the property is also used for purposes other than a dwelling), a secondary school, a community hall or a farm building.[1]

A secondary school is defined as a property that is not exempt from rating and consists wholly or partly of premises used as, or as part of, secondary school recognised by the Department of Education.[2] The qualifying specified valuation for such a school is limited to the actual school premises but includes any land attached thereto up to a rateable valuation of £40.

A community hall is defined as a building (not exempt from rating, not a club premises,[3] not used mainly for profit or gain) which is used for recreational or social purposes by the local population. The fact that a hall is used for one or more particular sports debars it from a rates exemption.[4] On the other hand, a restriction of use by reference to a particular age grouping or the membership of a religious denomination will not prevent a hall being eligible for exemption.[5]

References

1   Local Government (Financial Provisions) Act 1978 ss 2-3.
2   Local Government (Financial Provisions) Act 1978 s 1.
3   Registered under the Registration of Clubs Act 1904.
4   Local Government (Financial Provisions) Act 1978 s 1(4)(*a*).
5   Local Government (Financial Provisions) Act 1978 s 1(4)(*b*).

Appeals against valuations

19.07 Appeals against rateable valuations made by the Commissioner of Valuations are heard by the Valuations Tribunal.

If the Valuation Tribunal's decision is unsatisfactory, the appellant may make a further appeal by way of case stated to the Circuit Court.[1]

References
1   Valuation Act 1988 ss 2, 3, 5.

Exemption from rates

Introduction

19.08 The property exempted from poor rates may, accordingly, be classified under three headings:

(*a*)   those altogether of a public nature and occupied for public service;

(*b*)   those used exclusively for charitable purposes (see Chapter 7); and

(*c*)   those used exclusively for the purposes of science, literature and the fine arts.

19.09 Although property that is of a public nature (or used for charitable purposes, or for the purposes of science, literature or the fine arts) is exempt from poor rates, such property may be liable to other rates.[1]

References
1   In *Moylan v Dublin Port and Docks Board* IR 6 CLR 299; IR 9 CLR 457, it was held that rates in Dublin known as the policy rate, improvement rate, district sewer rate, domestic water rate, bridge tax and vestry cess abolition rate did not come within the exemption available for poor rates

19.10 Although property that is of a public nature (or used for charitable purposes, or for the purposes of science, literature or the fine arts) is exempt from poor rates, a landlord receiving rent from such a premises (beneficially occupied for such purposes) could not avail of the exemption. Such rent was charged to the poor rate at a half of the general poundage on such rents.[1]

References
1   Poor Relief (Ireland) Act 1849 s 10. This charge was repealed by the Local Government (Rateability of Rents) (Abolition) Act 1971.

19.11 Since 1838, when local rates were first introduced, many decisions have been made by the courts as to what property qualifies as being of a public nature (or of use for charitable purposes or for the purposes of science, literature or the fine arts) and is therefore exempt from poor rates.

Many of the decisions appear contradictory.[1]

References
1   *Second Report of the Inter-departmental Committee on Local Finance and Taxation (Exemptions from and Remissions of Rates)* 1967, see Appendix IV.

Public purposes

Meaning of "public purposes"

19.12 While the English courts have held that property for "public purposes" means, strictly, property of the Crown (or the immediate servants of the Crown)[1] the Irish courts have not given such a restrictive meaning to the words.

Thus, where a Board of Commissioners who built a bridge over the River Foyle had power to use the surplus from tolls (after maintenance etc costs) to repay a loan incurred for the construction cost (with the object of making the bridge toll-free) the court, by a four to three majority, reversed the decision of the lower court and accepted that the bridge was exempt from rates as being for a public purpose.

> The Statute to which it refers is not the Irish Statute, but the English Statute, the 43 Eliz c 2 [The Poor Rate Act 1601]. Statutes largely different in their origin, in their operation, and quod the question for our decision, altogether different in their terms. The judgment determines liability under the English, and not the Irish Statute, and the foundation of it really rests on the omission in the former of clear words inserted in the latter. The case is conclusive, so far as it applies, but I do not think it is applicable here.

> The judgment of the learned Lords appear to me to make the distinction palpable. The Lord Chancellor states the question for the House to be "what is the occupation of real property which is liable to be rated under the first section of the Act of the 43 Eliz c 2. That is not the question before us. We are to consider "what is the occupation of property liable to be rated under the 63rd section of the Act 1 and 2 Vict 56 [The Poor Relief (Ireland) Act 1838]. These are wholly different questions; and the decision on the one in no way involves the decision on the other.[2]

References
1   *Mersey Docks and Harbour Board Trustees v Cameron* [1865] 11 HLC 443.
2   O'Hagan J in *Guardians of the Londonderry Union v Londonderry Bridge Commissioners* [1868] IR 2 CLR 577.

Public utilities

19.13 Following the decision handed down in the Londonderry Bridge case, that the property of Sligo Harbour Commissioners was held exclusively for public purposes and, accordingly, qualified for a poor rates exemption.[1]

However, public bodies were not entitled to an exemption from rates on all their activities. The Mayor of Limerick had claimed that a gas works which had been acquired by the Corporation of Limerick and in respect of which the surplus profits were to be applied in reducing the town improvement rate in accordance with a special Act should be exempted from a poor rate charge. The claim was disallowed as it was held that any profit arising was not one from which every member of the community would benefit, but only the ratepayers of Limerick.[2]

The meaning of the phrase "public purposes", as used in the Valuation Code, therefore covers purposes in which all members of the community are interested, but excludes purposes in which the benefit is conferred on a particular class, or on the inhabitants of a particular locality. Hereditaments used for municipal purposes are, accordingly, not within the exemption.

References
1   *Commissioner of Valuation v Sligo Harbour Commissioners* [1899] 2 IR 214.
2   *Commissioner of Valuation v Mayor of Limerick* IR 6 CLR 420.

Baths and washhouses

19.14 In a further case, the local Corporation had looked for an exemption from poor rates on baths and washhouses erected under the provisions of the Baths and Washhouses Act 1846. The claim was refused as there was no right by members of the *public* to use the facilities.

In considering the meaning of the word "public", the judge remarked:

> In its most restricted sense it may be used as applying to Crown property, and as only exempting from liability to taxation property actually vested in the Crown. It has frequently been pointed out that such an interpretation would render the exemption unnecessary, inasmuch as Crown property is, as such, exempt from taxation unless it is specifically named as being liable by the statute imposing the tax. Accordingly, in the Londonderry Bridge Case (IR 2 CL 577) it was held to bear a broader meaning and to apply to a bridge across which there was a public right of way open to all subjects of the Crown without exception, though the structure of the bridge was not vested in the Crown, but in local Commissioners. To come within the exemption established by that case, however, not only must the public purposes be such as to exclude all private profit, but the advantages conferred must be for the benefit of the public at large - the whole community.[1]

References
1   Cherry, L C J in *Commissioner of Valuation v Corporation of Cork* [1916] 2 IR 77 at p 119.

County council premises

19.15 The Supreme Court judgment has held that the administrative offices of a County Council did not qualify as exempt from a rating charge as being held altogether for public purposes and used for such purposes.[1]

References
1   *Commissioner of Valuation v Kerry County Council* [1934] IR 527.

Property occupied by semi State bodies

19.16 Aer Rianta CPT, while established by Statute in 1936, is subject to the provisions of the Companies Acts 1963 to 1990 and produces annual financial accounts in the usual format. However, all leasing of property is effected by the Minister for Tourism, Transport and Communications and revenue collected by Aer Rianta is held on behalf of and accounted for to the Minister who demands and is paid from time to time sums which are not related to or restricted by the level of profitability arising.

The High Court has recently held that the company's Dublin Airport activities are carried out as agent for the State.

The judge also stated that while he was necessarily restricted to determining the ownership status of the Dublin Airport property on the specific questions posed by the District Court Justice in the case stated coming before him a much wider problem was involved:

> This is not really the determining issue between the Complainant and the Defendant. The real issue is whether or not the rateable hereditaments should be distinguished as being for public purposes. And on that issue it is immaterial whether Aer Rianta or the Minister is listed as rateable occupier. It is unfortunate therefore that issue which is presently being litigated should not have been taken to a conclusion instead of the present proceedings.[1]

In view of the financial implications involved the relevant question of determining whether the Dublin Airport property qualifies for exclusion from the rating lists by the Commissioner of Valuation [2] is likely to reach the Supreme Court for a final decision.

References
1   Barron, J in *County Council of the County of Dublin v Aer Rianta CPT*, Unreported, HC, 15 May 1992.
2   Poor Relief (Ireland) Act 1838 s 63 (2nd proviso)

Charitable purposes

Introduction

19.17 As discussed in Chapter 7, for income tax purposes there are four main categories of "charitable purposes":

(*a*)   the relief of poverty,

(*b*)   the advancement of education,

(*c*)   the advancement of religion,

(*d*)   the benefit of the general public.

These categories were clearly defined in 1891.[1] Before that, since 1838, property of a public nature, or used for "charitable purposes" or for purposes of science, literature and the fine arts was exempt from poor rates.[2]

After 1891, the income tax categories of "charitable purposes" were generally applied by the courts in considering exemption from poor rates.[3]

References
1   Lord MacNaghten in *Special Commissioners of Income Tax v Pemsel* [1891] AC 531; 7 TLR 657.
2   Poor Relief (Ireland) Act 1838 s 2.
3   *Guardians of Waterford Union v Barton* [1896] 2 IR 538; *Commissioner of Valuation v Clancy and Others* [1911] 2 IR 173. A number of the judges concerned in these cases subsequently decided that exemption from poor rates for charitable bodies was more restricted on the wording of the Poor Relief (Ireland) Act 1838 s 63 (see 19.24).

Educational purposes

Introduction

19.18 While a number of educational establishments have been exempted from a poor rate charge on the grounds that they were carried on exclusively for a public purpose not all such establishments have been allowed relief. As previously discussed, public purposes relate to circumstances where all the public is in a position to benefit.

Buildings used for educational purposes will only be exempt from poor rates if the building is "exclusively used for education of the poor".[1]

References
1   Poor Relief (Ireland) Act 1838 s 63 (2nd proviso).

Schools

19.19 Thus, because the Ballsbridge Technical School was open to allcomers, without limitation of class or locality, and there was no compulsory payment of any fees it was held that it was used for public purposes and therefore qualified for exemption from poor rates.[1]

References
1   *Commissioner of Valuation v Pembroke Council* [1904] 2 IR 429.

19.20 On the other hand, a college founded and endowed for the education of young men for the ministry of the Presbyterian Church was refused exemption as it did not meet the entry limitations, even though the trustees received no payment from the students because the students paid fees directly to the professors.[1]

References
1   *Commissioner of Valuation v Trustees of Magee College, Londonderry* [1871] IR 4 CLR 438.

19.21 Similarly, a college premises in Waterford built by the De la Salle community to train national school teachers was held not to be exempt from rates because some the pupils were fee paying.[1]

References
1   *Commissioner of Valuation v Guardians of Waterford Union* [1896] 2 IR 538.

19.22 Exemption from rates was also refused to the owners of a residential hotel for Catholic university students, and to the governing body of a Protestant second level college, on the basis that the activities of the establishments were not confined to education of the poor.[1]

References
1   *Commissioner of Valuation v O'Neill* and *Commissioner of Valuation v Council of Alexandra College and School* [1914] 2 IR 447. Both cases were heard together. These decisions were subsequently criticised by the House of Lords in *Commissioner of Valuation in Northern Ireland v Governors of Campbell College, Belfast* [1964] 2 All ER 705 (HL).
   Up to that time, the English courts had held (following the decision in *Mersey Docks and Harbour Board Trustees v Cameron* [1865] 11 HLC 443) that property "for public purposes" meant strictly, property of the Crown (or the immediate servants of the Crown). The Irish courts (following the decision in *Guardians of the Londonderry Union v Bridge Commissioners* [1868] IR 2 CL 577) held that public purposes meant for the use of the public, because the statute under consideration was the Poor Relief (Ireland) Act 1838, not the (English) Poor Rate Act 1601.
   Although the Valuation (Ireland) Act 1854 (under which appeals are held) refers to the same class of hereditaments ("of a public nature and occupied for public service") as the Poor Relief (Ireland) Act 1838 s 63, and the Irish courts had read both provisions in conjunction, the House held that the Valuation Act 1854 s 2 was to be separately construed. The current position in Northern Ireland is that, effectively,the income tax meaning for "charitable purposes" (see 19.20) is applied when examining the scope of a charge to poor rates (Local Government (Financial Provisions) Act 1978 s 2).

Seminary

19.23 In 1934 the Supreme Court rejected a claim that a vow of religious poverty taken by members of a religious order consequently qualified a seminary run by the Order for the education of students for the priesthood for exemption from a rating charge.[1]

Exemption from rates was also denied to Maynooth College, because, although established for public purposes, entry was restricted to Catholic male students who had received Episcopal approval and were studying for the priesthood.[2]

References

1   Murnaghan J in *Commissioner of Valuation v McGahan & Ryan* [1934] IR 736.
2   *Commissioner of Valuation v Maynooth College* [1958] IR 189.

Agricultural college

19.24 An agricultural college founded by the Catholic Diocese of Clogher where the premises continued to be vested in diocesan trustees but the general running expenditure was effectively subsidised, under formal and informal arrangements, by the State which also directly paid the teachers' salaries was refused exemption from a rates charge as having been carried on for a public purpose.[1]

References

1   *Commissioner of Valuation v St Macartan's Diocesan Trust (In the matter of St Patrick's Agricultural College, Co Monaghan* [1990] IR 508). Gannon, J, in the High Court, noted that a claim for exemption on charitable grounds did not arise as "the use made of hereditaments, although being for education, is not for the education of the poor".

Convent building

19.25 The High Court has also held that a convent building attached to a primary and secondary school for the education of poor girls, while used extensively for educational purposes, remained the residence of the nuns and, accordingly, the building was not used exclusively for such purposes. The claim for rating exemption was refused.[1]

References

1   *Commissioner of Valuation v Rev Mother Mary Brendan* [1969] IR 202.

Industrial school

19.26 An industrial school (a detention centre for young offenders) in respect of which maintenance grants were paid by the State was to be exempt from rating. A temporary home for "wayward women" also qualified for relief under the same decision, but not the convent premises and a laundry managed by the nuns.[1]

References

1   *Commissioner of Valuation v Good Shepherd Nuns* [1930] 1 IR 646.

University buildings

19.27 The buildings of University College Cork, being altogether of a public nature and used exclusively for such purposes, were held to be exempt from a poor rate charge. The evidence tendered showed that the College, one of the constituent colleges of the National University, provided the highest class of education and instruction, and was open to all classes for education and instruction. The buildings were vested in the Board of Works and the professors were paid by the State. All the students were charged fees which were paid into the general funds of the College. The College was bound to present annual accounts to the Comptroller and Auditor General, and the accounts, together with the report of the Comptroller and Auditor General were laid before Parliament.[1]

The Queen's College Belfast was given a similar exemption.[2]

On the other hand, Trinity College Dublin did not qualify for any relief because the College, the Provost House and the botanical gardens at Ballsbridge were not altogether "of a public nature or used exclusively for public purposes".[3] While the benefits of the College when established in 1591 were originally confined to members of the Church of Ireland the college was subsequently open to persons of all religious denominations. The judicial distinction made with the case of University College, Cork was that Trinity was free from all external control as regards both teaching and finance.

References

1   *Commissioner of Valuation v University College Cork* [1911] 2 IR 598; [1912] 2 IR 328.
2   *Commissioner of Valuation v Queen's College Belfast* [1911] 45 ILTR 96.
3   *Commissioner of Valuation v Trinity College Dublin* [1919] 2 IR 493.

Religious purposes

Parish priest residence

19.28 A house built by parishioners for, and used by, a parish priest as a residence (and which was also used for parochial purposes) was held not to be used exclusively for charitable purposes, and therefore did not qualify for exemption from rates.

A room in such a residence occupied solely by the cleric does not qualify either. This also applies to a room used for keeping parish registers and other articles for the ministrations of the office of a parish priest unless it is exclusively so used.

There is no doubt that a valid charitable trust was imposed upon the house and premises in question ... but to be so exempt they must be "used" and "used exclusively" for charitable purposes. Any use of such premises by a person who is not an object of the charity is, to my mind, a private profit or use ... directly derived therefrom within 1 and 2 Vict c 63 [Poor Relief (Ireland) Act 1838] and such profit or use, if it exists, prevents the premises from being used "exclusively" for charitable purposes. ... Now the charity in the present case is the advancement of religion; and it is not only settled by authority, but it is involved in the character which the law deems necessary to a charity (viz. that it be in the nature of a public use) that the trust is charitable because it provides a benefit, not to the clergyman as such, but to the Roman Catholic parishioners of the parish, to whom his ministrations are a benefit. But he is not the object of the charity. [1]

References

1   Pallas, L J in *Commissioner of Valuation v O'Connell* [1906] 2 IR 479. At the time of the judgment, Baron Pallas believed that "charitable purposes" for rating exemption had the same meaning as it had for income tax purposes (ie the advancement of education, the advancement or religion, the relief of poverty and other public purposes, as decided by Lord MacNaghten in *Special Commissioners of Income Tax v Pemsel* [1891] AC 531; 7 TLR 657). Baron Pallas subsequently changed his mind on the issue in *Commissioner of Valuation v Council of Alexandra College and School* [1914] 2 IR 447. This mental change does not affect the validity of the conclusions which led the Baron to refuse exemption in the earlier case.

Residence used as classroom

19.29 The Commissioner of Valuation was successful in resisting a claim by members of the Christian Brothers in Co. Carlow that a residential premises which was also used as a classroom should be exempted from a poor rate charge.[1]

References

1   *Commissioner of Valuation v McKenna* 49 ILTR 103.

Franciscan Friary

19.30 The Franciscan Friary, Ennis was occupied as a residence by the members of the Franciscan Community, which was bound by religious vows of poverty. The Community was engaged solely in charitable work among the sick and poor of the district. The King's Bench Division held that the premises were not used exclusively for charitable purposes so as to be exempt from poor rates.[1]

References

1   *Commissioner of Valuation v Dore* 50 ILTR 105, following the precedent in *Commissioner of Valuation v O'Connell* [1906] 2 IR 479.

Catholic seminary

19.31 While the decision to refuse relief in respect of a catholic seminary[1] was directly concerned with a failure to establish the required qualification on educational grounds, the principle was established that exemption from rates should be refused for hereditaments used for the advancement of religion.

A Methodist hall adjoining a church, which was used occasionally on social occasions, while it might be considered as used for the advancement of religion, was held in the High Court not to qualify for poor rate exemption.[2]

One of the claims made for an exemption from poor rates on behalf of Maynooth College in 1958 was that the College was being used for charitable purposes as having being established for the advancement of religion. The President of the High Court in the course of his judgment rejected this proposition:

> In view of the decision in McGahon's case, as interpreted, I believe, correctly, in Elliott's case it is not now open to this Court to hold that the advancement of religion is a charitable purpose within the meaning of the proviso to s 63 of the Poor Relief Act 1838.[3]

References
1 *Commissioner of Valuation v McGahon and Ryan* [1934] IR 736.
2 *Commissioner of Valuation v Elliott* [1935] IR 607.
3 *Commissioner of Valuation v Maynooth College* [1958] IR 189 at p 210.

Convent

19.32 A poor rates exemption was also refused to the Convent of Mercy, Castlerea, Co Roscommon, on the grounds that the advancement of religion was not a charitable purpose (for exemption from rates).[1]

References
1 *Commissioner of Valuation v Rev Mother Mary Brendan* [1969] IR 202.

Northern Ireland

19.33 In Northern Ireland, since 1964[1] the advancement of religion is a charitable purpose which will allow a property to be exempt from rates provided it is "used exclusively for charitable purposes".[2]

A generous interpretation of the relief was taken by the Northern Ireland Court of Appeal which held in 1971, admittedly by a majority decision, that a monastery of the Redemptorist Fathers at Clonard, Belfast and the residence used by the Christian Brothers at Newry, Co Down both qualified for exemptions from poor rates.

In the High Court Henchy, J has declared,[3] that even if he had followed the House of Lords decision in the Campbell College case he would still have held that the convent buildings were chargeable to rates because, to qualify for exemption[4] they were required to have been used exclusively for charitable purposes and he was not satisfied that this condition had been met.

References
1   *Commissioner of Valuation in Northern Ireland v Governors of Campbell College* [1964] 2 All ER 705 (HL).
2   Valuation (Ireland) Act 1852 s 16, as applied by Valuation (Ireland) Act 1854 s 6.
3   *Commissioner of Valuation v Rev Mother Mary Brendan* [1969] IR 202.
4   In accordance with the Valuation (Ireland) Act 1852 s 16 as applied by the Valuation (Ireland) Act 1854 s 6.

Miscellaneous purposes

Temperance hall

19.34 Although a temperance hall, which was used occasionally for social purposes, was held to be exempt from a poor rating charge,[1] the decision must, in the light of subsequent decisions,[2] be regarded as an aberration.

References
1   *Commissioner of Valuation v Clancy & Others* [1911] 2 IR 173.
2   *Commissioner of Valuation v O'Neill* [1914] 2 IR 447.

Cemetery

19.35 Despite the specific reference to burial grounds in the legislation,[1] the Trustees of Glasnevin Cemetery were refused exemption from poor rates in 1897 as they were free to apply surplus funds at their discretion.[2]

References
1   Poor Relief (Ireland) Act 1838 s 63 (2nd proviso).
2   *Commissioner of Valuation v Dublin Cemeteries Committee* [1897] 2 IR 157. The Cemeteries Committee, under a private Act passed by the Oireachtas in 1970, have been restricted to applying surplus funds for purely charitable purposes, which enables them to obtain an exemption from a poor rates charge.

Hospital

19.36 Barrington's Hospital, Limerick, founded in 1830 was exempt from rates up to 1950, but was rated in 1951 and appealed that decision. Rates were imposed because a limited number of fee paying private patients were treated in the hospital and the Commissioner of Valuation claimed that this precluded an entitlement to exemption.[1]

Kingsmill-Moore, J considered the meaning of "charitable purposes" for rate exemption purposes to be less extensive that the meaning applicable for income tax purposes[2] but kept open the nature of the limitations which required to be operated. He also declared that the exemption from rates was not confined to purposes which are exclusively charitable but related to those which are exclusively for charitable purposes.[3]

Ultimately, the Judge, with whom the Chief Justice concurred, agreed that the presence of fee paying patients did not debar the hospital's claim.

A separate written judgment was given in favour of the hospital by O'Dálaigh, J who held:

> in my opinion the proviso to section 63 of the Act of 1838 does not confer exemption on the hospital nominatum. The word "hospital" is found associated with four other substantives, the last of which is followed by the clause "used exclusively for charitable purposes". The context, to my mind, makes it clear that the qualifying clause governs, not only the last but also the three other substantives.

Judge O'Dálaigh also accepted that Barrington's Hospital was charitable on the basis that it constituted a public benefit, ie a

> trust beneficial to the community not fully within any of the other more specific categories and it was exclusively so established.

While Barrington's Hospital had its claim allowed, the Supreme Court decisions handed down appear to confuse further rather than clarify the meaning of "charitable purposes" for exemption from rates. O'Dálaigh, J appears to concur with the broader 1964 House of Lords interpretation,[4] but this view receives no support from Kingsmill-Moore.

References

1 *Commissioner of Valuation v Barrington's Hospital and City of Limerick Infirmary* [1959] IR 299.
2 The advancement of education, the advancement of religion, the relief of poverty, the benefit of the general public. MacNaghten, J in *Commissioners for Special Commissioners of Income Tax v Pemsel* [1891] AC 531; 3 TC 53.
3 Poor Relief (Ireland) Act 1838 s 63 (2nd proviso). "The word "exclusively" in no way alters or modifies the meaning of "charitable purposes"."
4 *Commissioner of Valuation in Northern Ireland v Governors of Campbell College* [1964] 2 All ER 705 (HL).

Staff accommodation

19.37 While the decision in the Barrington's Hospital case has ensured that hospitals open to the general public with facilities for private patients are exempt from poor rates, the question remained open as to whether buildings provided for nursing or medical staff were also exempt.

In 1958, the Supreme Court held that nurses' accommodation in the hospital qualified for poor rates exemption.[1]

In contrast, the President of the High Court, when refusing a claim for rates exemption in respect of a convent attached to a school run by the Mercy Order,[2] distinguished that decision on the grounds that the nuns resided in the Convent, which was separated from the school premises, primarily as members of the Order and not by virtue of their teaching activities.

References

1   *Commissioner of Valuation v Clonmel Mental Hospital* [1958] IR 381.
2   *Commissioner of Valuation v Rev Mother Mary Brendan* [1960] IR 202.

Scientific or literary societies

Introduction

19.38 Exemption from "County Borough, Parochial and other Rates" for "Land and Buildings occupied by Scientific or Literary Societies" was introduced in 1843.[1] The exemption does not extend to charges levied by reference to the poor rate valuation for specific purposes. The Act applied to the entire United Kingdom at that time, including Ireland. The provisions were repealed by the United Kingdom Parliament in 1961[2] but still have the force of law in this country.

The Act applies to "any society instituted for the purposes of science, literature or the fine arts exclusively" in respect of houses or buildings occupied for the transaction of its business either as tenant or owner. A qualifying society must be supported in whole or in part by annual voluntary contributions and no dividends, gifts or money loans may be made to members. These conditions must be certified as having been satisfied by the Registrar of Friendly Societies.

References

1   Poor Relief (Ireland) Act 1843.
2   Rating and Valuation Act 1961 s 11. In subs (4) a discretionary power was given to local authorities to reduce or remit the consequent charges arising. This discretion was withdrawn for England and Wales by the General Rate Act 1967. The 1967 Inter-Departmental Committee on Local Finance and Taxation in its second report (see Appendix IV) recommended that the legislation should be repealed in the State as anomalous, but up to the present time no action has been taken.

19.39 A "society" is not defined. Exemption can therefore theoretically apply to any body of persons which is recognised as a separate entity under the law.

Fine arts

19.40 The interpretation of the phrase "fine arts" can be subjective and may lead to arbitrary decisions as to whether a society is exempt from poor rates.[1]

References
1   The English Court of Appeal refused exemption in *O'Sullivan (Valuation Officer) v English Folk Dance and Song Society* [1955] 2 All ER 845.

Voluntary contribution

19.41 The meaning of a "voluntary contribution" for the purpose of the Act has also been considered. Where a subscriber obtains benefits equivalent at least to the amount contributed there is no voluntary element involved.[1]

References
1   *Savoy Overseers v Art Union of London* [1896] HC 296; 7 LT 497.

Subsequent review

19.42 An exemption granted to a society may be reviewed at a later time. The Limerick Protestant Young Men's Association had in 1908 been allowed exemption from poor rates as scientific, literary or fine arts society. In 1935 the Commissioner of Valuation rated the premises of the Association and the matter was appealed. The High Court reviewed the position on the basis of the current activities being carried on by the Association and found that the use of the premises for social purposes precluded a continuance of the exemption enjoyed earlier.[1]

References
1   *F J Cleeve & Others v The City Manager & Town Clerk of Limerick & the Commissioner of Valuation* [1942] IR 77.

Appendix I

Trustee Act 1893 (as amended)

(56 and 57 Victoria, Chapter 53)
An Act to consolidate enactments relating to trustees (22 September 1893).

Part 1

1 Investments

[1. A trustee may, unless expressly forbidden by the instrument (if any) creating the trust, invest any trust funds in his hands, whether at the time in a state of investment or not, in manner following, that is to say:

(*a*)   in securities of the Government (including Savings Certificates);

(*b*)   in securities guaranteed as to capital and interest by the Minister for Finance;

(*c*)   in the stock of the Bank of Ireland;

(*d*)   in securities of the Electricity Supply Board;

(*e*)   in securities of the Agricultural Credit Corporation Limited;

(*f*)   in securities of Bord na Móna;

(*g*)   on real securities in the State;

(*h*)   in securities or mortgages of any of the following authorities in the State:

(i)   the council of a county,

(ii)   the corporation of a county borough,

(iii)   the corporation of Dun Laoghaire

(iv)   the Dublin Port and Docks Board,

(v)   the Cork Harbour Commissioners,

(vi)   the Limerick Harbour Commissioners,

(vii)   the Waterford Harbour Commissioners;

(*i*)   in debentures or debenture stock, quoted on a Stock Exchange, of any industrial or commercial company registered in the State, provided that the total of the debentures, debenture stock or debentures and debenture stock of the company does not exceed the paid-up share capital (including payments in respect of share premiums) and that a dividend of not less than 5% has been paid on the ordinary shares of the company in each of the five years last past before the date of investment;

(*j*)   in an interest bearing deposit account with any of the following banks:

(i)   Bank of Ireland,

(ii)   Guinness & Mahon,

(iii)   Hibernian Bank Ltd,

(iv)   Munster & Leinster Bank Ltd,

[(v)   National Bank of Ireland],[1]

(vi)   National City Bank Ltd,

(vii)   Northern Bank Ltd,

(viii)   Provincial Bank of Ireland Ltd,

(ix)   Royal Bank of Ireland Ltd,

(x)   Ulster Bank Ltd,

(xi)   the Post Office Savings Bank,

(xii)   a Trustee Savings Bank in the State,

[(xiii)   Barclays Bank International Ltd,

(xiv)   Irish Bank of Commerce Ltd,

(xv)   Standard Chartered Bank Ireland Ltd],[2]

[(xvi)   Barclays Bank Ireland Ltd];[3]

(*k*)   in British Government securities inscribed or registered in the State,

and may also from time to time vary any such investment.][1]

Amendments

1   Section 1(*j*)(v) substituted by National Bank Transfer Act 1966 s 8.
2   Section 1(*j*)(xiii)-(xv) inserted by Trustee (Authorised Investments) Order 1983 (SI 58/1983).
3   Section 1(*j*)(xvi) inserted by Trustee (Authorised Investments) Order 1985 (SI 224/1985).
4   Section 1 substituted by Trustee (Authorised Investments) Act 1958 s 1.

Notes

This section may be varied by Ministerial Order: Trustee (Authorised Investments) Act 1958 s 2(1). The following ministerial orders have been made:
Trustee (Authorised Investments) Order SI 285/1967;
Trustee (Authorised Investments) Order SI 241/1969;
Trustee (Authorised Investments) Order SI 377/1974;
Trustee (Authorised Investments) Order SI 41/1977;
Trustee (Authorised Investments) (No 2) Order SI 344/1977;
Trustee (Authorised Investments) Order SI 407/1979;
Trustee (Authorised Investments) Order SI 58/1983;
Trustee (Authorised Investments) Order SI 366/1983;
Trustee (Authorised Investments) Order SI 244/1985;
Trustee (Authorised Investments) Order SI 372/1986.
A trustee shall not be liable for breach of trust by reason only of his continuing to hold an investment which has ceased to be an investment authorised by the instrument of trust or by the general law: Trustee Act 1893, Amendment Act 1894 s 4.

2 Purchase at a premium of redeemable stocks

(1) A trustee may under the powers of this Act invest in any of the securities mentioned or referred to in section one of this Act, notwithstanding that the same may be redeemable, and that the price exceeds the redemption value.
(2) ...[1]
(3) A trustee may retain until redemption any redeemable stock fund, or security which may have been purchased in accordance with the powers of this Act.

Amendments
1   Subs (2) repealed by Trustee (Authorised Investments) Act 1958 s 6 and Sch.

---

3 Discretion of trustees

Every power conferred by the preceding sections shall be exercised according to the discretion of the trustee, but subject to any consent required by the instrument (if any) creating the trust with respect to the investment of the trust funds.

4 Application of preceding sections

The preceding sections shall apply as well to trusts created before as to trusts created after the passing of this Act, and the powers thereby conferred shall be in addition to the powers conferred by the instrument (if any) creating the trust.

5 Enlargement of express powers of investment

(1) A trustee having power to invest in real securities, unless expressly forbidden by the instrument creating the trust, may invest and shall be deemed to have always had power to invest:-

   (*a*)   on mortgage of property held for an expired term of not less than two hundred years, and not subject to a reservation of rent greater than a shilling a year, or to any right of redemption or to any condition for re-entry, except for non payment of rent; and

   (*b*)   on any charge, or upon mortgage of any charge, made under the Improvement of Land Act 1864.

(2) A trustee having power to invest in the mortgages or bonds of any railway company or of any other description of company may, unless the contrary is expressed in the instrument authorising the investment, invest in the debenture stock of a railway company or such other company as aforesaid.
(3) A trustee having power to invest money in the debentures or debenture stock of any railway or other company may, unless the contrary is expressed in the instrument authorising the investment, invest in any nominal debentures or nominal debenture stock issued under the Local Loans Act 1875.

(4) A trustee having power to invest money in securities in the Isle of Man, or in securities of the government of a colony, may, unless the contrary is expressed in the instrument authorising the investment, invest in any securities of the Government of the Isle of Man, under the Isle of Man Loans Act 1880.

(5) A trustee having a general power to invest trust moneys in or upon the security of shares, stock, mortgages, bonds or debentures of companies incorporated by or acting under the authority of an Act of Parliament, may invest in or upon the security of mortgage debentures duly issued under and in accordance with the provisions of the Mortgage Debenture Act 1865.

6 Power to invest notwithstanding drainage charges

A trustee having power to invest in the purchase of land or on mortgage of land may invest in the purchase, or on mortgage of any land, notwithstanding the same is charged with a rent under the powers of the Public Money Drainage Acts 1846 to 1856, or the Landed Property Improvement (Ireland) Act 1847, or by an absolute order made under the Improvement of Land Act 1864, unless the terms of the trust expressly provide that the land to be purchased or taken in mortgage shall not be subject to any such prior charge.

7 Trustees not to convert inscribed stock into certificates to bearer

(1) A trustee, unless authorised by the terms of his trust, shall not apply for or hold any certificate to bearer issued under the authority of any of the following Acts; that is to say:

- (*a*)   The India Stock Certificate Act, 1863;
- (*b*)   The National Debt Act, 1870;
- (*c*)   The Local Loans Act, 1875;
- (*d*)   The Colonial Stock Act, 1877.

(2) Nothing in this section shall impose on the Bank of England or of Ireland, or on any person authorised to issue any such certificates, any obligation to inquire whether a person applying for such a certificate is or is not a trustee, or subject them to any liability in the event of their granting any such certificate to a trustee, nor invalidate any such certificate if granted.

8 Loans and investments by trustees not chargeable as breaches of trust

(1) A trustee lending money on the security of any property on which he can lawfully lend shall not be chargeable with breach of trust by reason only of the proportion borne by the amount of the loan to the value of the property at the time when the loan was made, provided that it appears to the Court that in making the loan the trustee was acting upon a report as to the value of the property made by a person whom he reasonably believed to be an able practical

surveyor or valuer instructed and employed independently of any owner of the property, whether such surveyor or valuer carried on business in the locality where the property is situate or elsewhere, and that the amount of the loan does not exceed two equal third parts of the value of the property as stated in the report, and that the loan was made under the advice of the surveyor or valuer expressed in the report.

(2) A trustee lending money on the security of any leasehold property shall not be chargeable with breach of trust only upon the ground that in making such loan he dispensed either wholly or partly with the production or investigation of the lessors title.

(3) A trustee shall not be chargeable with breach of trust only upon the ground that in effecting the purchase of or in lending money upon the security of any property he has accepted a shorter title than the title which a purchaser is, in the absence of a special contract, entitled to require, if, in the opinion of the Court, the title accepted be such as a person acting with prudence and caution would have accepted.

(4) This section applies to transfers of existing securities as well as to new securities, and to investments made as well before as after the commencement of this Act, except where an action or other proceeding was pending with reference thereto on the Twenty-fourth day of December, One thousand eight hundred and eighty-eight.

9 Liability for loss by reason of improper investments

(1) Where a trustee improperly advances trust money on a mortgage security which would at the time of the investment be a proper investment in all respects for a smaller sum than is actually advanced thereon, the security shall be deemed an authorised investment for the smaller sum, and the trustee shall only be liable to make good the sum advanced in excess thereof with interest.

(2) This section applies to investments made as well before as after the commencement of this Act except where an action or other proceeding was pending with reference thereto on the Twenty-fourth day of December, One thousand eight hundred and eighty-eight.

Part 2

Various powers and duties of trustees

Appointment of new trustees

10 Power of appointing new trustees

(1) Where a trustee, either original or substituted, and whether appointed by a Court or otherwise, is dead, or remains out of the United Kingdom for more than twelve months, or desires to be discharged from all or any of the trusts or powers reposed in or conferred on him, or refuses or is unfit to act therein, or is incapable of acting therein, then the person or persons nominated for the purpose of appointing new trustees by the instrument (if any) creating the trust, or if there is no such person, or no such person able and willing to act, then the surviving or continuing trustees or trustee for the time being, or the personal representatives of the last surviving or continuing trustee, may, by writing, appoint another person or other persons to be a trustee or trustees in the place of the trustee dead, remaining out of the United Kingdom, desiring to be discharged, refusing, or being unfit or being incapable as aforesaid.

(2) On the appointment of a new trustee for the whole or any part of trust property:

- (*a*)   the number of trustees may be increased; and

- (*b*)   a separate set of trustees may be appointed for any part of the trust property held on trusts distinct from those relating to any other part or parts of the trust property, notwithstanding that no new trustees or trustee are or is to be appointed for other parts of the trust property, and any existing trustee may be appointed or remain one of such separate set of trustees; or, if only one trustee was originally appointed, then one separate trustee may be so appointed for the first-mentioned part; and

- (*c*)   it shall not be obligatory to appoint more than one new trustee where only one trustee was originally appointed, or to fill up the original number of trustees where more than two trustees were originally appointed; but, except where only one trustee was originally appointed, a trustee shall not be discharged under this section from his trust unless there will be at least two trustees to perform the trust; and

- (*d*)   any assurance or thing requisite for vesting the trust property, or any part thereof, jointly in the persons who are the trustees, shall be executed or done.

(3) Every new trustee so appointed, as well before as after all the trust property becomes by law, or by assurance, or otherwise, vested in him, shall

have the same powers, authorities and discretions, and may in all respects act, as if he had been originally appointed a trustee by the instrument (if any) creating the trust.

(4) The provisions of this section relative to a trustee who is dead include the case of a person nominated trustee in a will but dying before the testator, and those relative to a continuing trustee include a refusing or retiring trustee, if willing to act in the execution of the provisions of this section.

(5) This section applies only if and as far as a contrary intention is not expressed in the instrument (if any) creating the trust, and shall have effect subject to the terms of that instrument and to any provisions therein contained.

(6) This section applies to trusts created either before or after the commencement of this Act.

11 Retirement of trustee

(1) Where there are more than two trustees, if one of them by deed declares that he is desirous of being discharged from the trust, and if his co-trustees and such other person (if any) as is empowered to appoint trustees, by deed consent to the discharge of the trustee, and to the vesting in the co-trustees alone of the trust property, then the trustee desirous of being discharged shall be deemed to have retired from the trust, and shall, by the deed, be discharged therefrom under this Act, without any new trustee being appointed in his place.

(2) Any assurance or thing requisite for vesting the trust property in the continuing trustees alone shall be executed or done.

(3) This section applies only if and as far as a contrary intention is not expressed in the instrument (if any) creating the trust, and shall have effect subject to the terms of that instrument and to any provisions therein contained.

(4) This section applies to trusts created either before or after the commencement of this Act.

12 Vesting of trust property in new or continuing trustees

(1) Where a deed by which a new trustee is appointed to perform any trust contains a declaration by the appointor to the effect that any estate or interest in any land subject to the trust, or in any chattel so subject, or the right to recover and receive any debt or other thing in action so subject, shall vest in the persons who by virtue of the deed become and are the trustees for performing the trust, that declaration shall, without any conveyance or assignment, operate to vest in those persons, as joint tenants, and for the purposes of the trust, that estate, interest, or right.

(2) Where a deed by which a retiring trustee is discharged under this Act contains such a declaration as is in this section mentioned by the retiring and continuing trustees, and by the other person (if any) empowered to appoint

trustees, that declaration shall, without any conveyance or assignment, operate to vest in the continuing trustees alone, as joint tenants, and for the purposes of the trust, the estate, interest, or right to which the declaration relates.

(3) This section does not extend to any legal estate or interest in copyhold or customary land, or to land conveyed by way of mortgage for securing money subject to the trust, or to any such share, stock, annuity, or property as is only transferable in books kept by a company or other body, or in manner directed by or under Act of Parliament.

(4) For purposes of registration of the deed in any registry, the person or persons making the declaration shall be deemed the conveying party or parties, and the conveyance shall be deemed to be made by him or them under a power conferred by this Act.

(5) This section applies only to deeds executed after the Thirty-first of December, One thousand eight hundred and eighty-one.

Purchase and sale

13 Power of trustee for sale to sell by auction etc

(1) Where a trust for sale or a power of sale of property is vested in a trustee, he may sell or concur with any other person in selling all or any part of the property, either subject to prior charges or not, and either together or in lots, by public auction or by private contract, subject to any such conditions respecting title or evidence of title or other matter as the trustee thinks fit, with power to vary any contract for sale and to buy in at any auction, or to rescind any contract for sale and to re-sell, without being answerable for any loss.

(2) This section applies only if and as far as a contrary intention is not expressed in the instrument creating the trust or power, and shall have effect subject to the terms of that instrument and to the provisions therein contained.

(3) This section applies only to a trust or power created by an instrument coming into operation after the Thirty-first of December, One thousand eight hundred and eighty-one.

14 Power to sell subject to deprecatory conditions

(1) No sale made by a trustee shall be impeached by any beneficiary upon the ground that any of the conditions subject to which the sale was made may have been unnecessarily depreciatory, unless it also appears that the consideration for the sale was thereby rendered inadequate.

(2) No sale made by a trustee shall, after the execution of the conveyance, be impeached as against the purchaser upon the ground that any of the conditions subject to which the sale was made may have been unnecessarily depreciatory,

unless it appears that the purchaser was acting in collusion with the trustee at the time when the contract for sale was made.

(3) No purchaser, upon any sale made by a trustee, shall be at liberty to make any objection against the title upon the ground aforesaid.

(4) This section applies only to sales made after the Twenty-fourth day of December, One thousand eight hundred and eighty-eight.

15 Power to sell under 37 and 38 Vict c 78

A trustee who is either a vendor or a purchaser may sell or buy without excluding the application of Section two of the Vendor and Purchaser Act 1874.

16 ...

Amendments
Section 16 repealed by Married Women's Status Act 1957 s 19 and Sch.

Various powers and liabilities

17 Power to authorise receipt of money by banker or solicitor 44 and 45 Vict c 41

(1) A trustee may appoint a solicitor to be his agent to receive and give a discharge for any money or valuable consideration or property receivable by the trustee under the trust, by permitting the solicitor to have the custody or, and to produce, a deed containing any such receipt as is referred to in Section Fifty-six of the Conveyancing and Law of Property Act, 1881; and a trustee shall not be chargeable with breach of trust by reason only of his having made or concurred in making any such appointment; and the producing of any such deed by the solicitor shall have the same validity and effect under the said section as if the person appointing the solicitor had not been a trustee.

(2) A trustee may appoint a banker or solicitor to be his agent to receive and give a discharge for any money payable to the trustee under or by virtue of a policy of assurance, by permitting the banker or solicitor to have the custody of and to produce the policy of assurance with a receipt signed by the trustee, and a trustee shall not be chargeable with a breach of trust by reason only of his having made or concurred in making any such appointment.

(3) Nothing in this section shall exempt a trustee from any liability which he would have incurred if this Act had not been passed, in case he permits any such money, valuable consideration or property to remain in the hands or under the control of the banker or solicitor for a period longer than is reasonably necessary to enable the banker or solicitor (as the case may be) to pay or transfer the same to the trustee.

(4) This section applies only where the money or valuable consideration or property is received after the Twenty-fourth day of December, One thousand eight hundred and eighty-eight.

(5) Nothing in this section shall authorise a trustee to do anything which he is in express terms forbidden to do, or to omit anything which he is in express terms direct to do, by the instrument creating the trust.

18 Power to insure buildings

(1) A trustee may insure against loss or damage by fire any building or other insurable property to any amount (including the amount of any insurance already on foot) not exceeding three equal fourth parts of the full value of such building or property, and pay the premiums for such insurance out of the income thereof or out of the income of any other property subject to the same trusts, without obtaining the consent of any person who may be entitled wholly or partly to such income.

(2) This section does not apply to any building or property which a trustee is bound forthwith to convey absolutely to any beneficiary upon being requested to do so.

(3) This section applies to trusts created either before or after the commencement of this Act, but nothing in this section shall authorise any trustee to do anything which he is in express terms forbidden to do, or to omit to do anything which he is in express terms directed to do, by the instrument creating the trust.

19 Power of trustees of renewable leaseholds to renew and raise money for the purpose

(1) A trustee of any leaseholds for lives or years which are renewable from time to time, either under any covenant or contract or by custom or usual practice, may, if he thinks fit, and shall, if thereto required by any person having any beneficial interest, present or future or contingent, in the leaseholds, use his best endeavours to obtain from time to time a renewed lease of the same hereditaments on the accustomed and reasonable terms, and for that purpose may from time to time make or concur in making a surrender of the lease for the time being subsisting, and do all such other acts as are requisite: Provided that, where by the terms of the settlement or will the person in possession for his life or other limited interest is entitled to enjoy the same without any obligation to renew or to contribute to the expense of renewal, this section shall not apply unless the consent in writing of that person is obtained to the renewal on the part of the trustee.

(2) If money is required to pay for the renewal, the trustee effecting the renewal may pay the same out of any money then in his hands in trust for the persons beneficially interested in the lands to be comprised in the renewed lease, and if he has not in his hands sufficient money for the

purpose, he may raise the money required by mortgage of the hereditaments to be comprised in the renewed lease, or of any other hereditaments for the time being subject to the uses or trusts to which those hereditaments are subject, and no person advancing money upon a mortgage purporting to be under this power shall be bound to see that the money is wanted, or that no more is raised than is wanted for the purpose.

(3) This section applies to trusts created either before or after the commencement of this Act, but nothing in this section shall authorise any trustee to do anything which he is in express terms forbidden to do, or to omit to do anything which he is in express terms directed to do, by the instrument creating the trust.

20 Power of trustee to give receipts

(1) The receipt in writing of any trustee for any money, securities, or other personal property or effects payable, transferable, or deliverable to him under any trust or power shall be a sufficient discharge for the same, and shall effectually exonerate the person paying, transferring, or delivering the same from seeing to the application or being answerable for any loss or misapplication thereof.

(2) This section applies to trusts created either before or after the commencement of this Act.

21 Power for executors and trustees to compound etc

(1) ...

(2) ... two or more trustees, acting together, or a sole acting trustee where by the instrument (if any) creating the trust a sole trustee is authorised to execute the trusts and powers thereof, may, if and as he or they may think fit, accept any composition or any security, real or personal, for any debt or for any property, real or personal, claimed, and may allow any time for payment for any debt, and may compromise, compound, abandon, submit to arbitration, or otherwise settle any debt, account, claim or thing whatever relating to the testators or intestates estate or to the trust, and for any of those purposes may enter into, give, execute, and do such agreements, instruments of composition or arrangement, releases and other things as to him or them seem expedient, without being responsible for any loss occasioned by any act or thing so done by him or them in good faith.

(3) This section applies only if and as far as a contrary intention is not expressed in the instrument (if any) creating the trust, and shall have effect subject to the terms of that instrument, and to the provisions therein contained.

(4) This section applies to ... trusts constituted or created either before or after the commencement of this Act.

22 Powers of two or more trustees

(1) Where a power or trust is given to or vested in two or more trustees jointly, then, unless the contrary is expressed in the instrument, (if any) creating the power or trust, the same may be exercised or performed by the survivor or survivors of them for the time being.

(2) This section applies only to trusts constituted after or created by instruments coming into operation after the Thirty-first day of December, One thousand eight hundred and eighty one.

23 Exoneration of trustees in respect of certain powers of attorney

A trustee acting or paying money in good faith under or in pursuance of any power of attorney shall not be liable for any such act or payment by reason of the fact that at the time of the payment or act the person who gave the power of attorney was dead or had done some act to avoid the power, if this fact was not known to the trustee at the time of his so acting or paying.

Provided that nothing in this section shall affect the right of any person entitled to the money against the person to whom the payment is made, and that the person so entitled shall have the same remedy against the person to whom the payment is made as he would have had against the trustee.

24 Implied indemnity of trustees

A trustee shall, without prejudice to the provisions of the instrument (if any) creating the trust, be chargeable only for money and securities actually received by him notwithstanding his signing any receipt for the sake of conformity, and shall be answerable and accountable only for his own acts, receipts, neglects, or defaults, and not for those of any other trustee, nor for any banker, broker, or other person with whom any trust moneys, or securities may be deposited, nor for the insufficiency or deficiency of any securities, nor for any other loss, unless the same happens through his own wilful default; and may reimburse himself, or pay or discharge out of the trust premises, all expenses incurred in or about the execution of his trusts or powers.

Part 3

Powers of the court

Appointment of new trustees and vesting orders

25 Power of the court to appoint new trustees

(1) The High Court may, whenever it is expedient to appoint a new trustee or new trustees, and it is found inexpedient, difficult, or impracticable so to do without the assistance of the Court, make an order for the appointment of a new trustee or new trustees either in substitution for or in addition to any existing trustee or trustees, or although there is no existing trustee. In particular and without prejudice to the generality of the foregoing provision, the Court may make an order for the appointment of a new trustee in substitution for a trustee who is convicted of felony, or is a bankrupt.

(2) An order under this section, and any consequential vesting order or conveyance, shall not operate further or otherwise as a discharge to any former or continuing trustee than an appointment of new trustees under any power for that purpose contained in any instrument would have operated.

(3) Nothing in this section shall give power to appoint an executor or administrator.

Notes
Power of court extended: Trustee Act 1931 ss 3, 4.

26 Vesting orders as to land

In any of the following cases: namely:
- (*a*)   Where the High Court appoints or has appointed a new trustee; and
- (*b*)   Where a trustee entitled to or possessed of any land, or entitled to a contingent right therein, either solely or jointly with any other person:
    - (i)   is an infant, or
    - (ii)   is out of the jurisdiction of the High Court, or
    - (iii)   cannot be found; and
- (*c*)   Where it is uncertain who was the survivor of two or more trustees jointly entitled to or possessed of any land; and
- (*d*)   Where, as to the last trustee known to have been entitled to or possessed of any land, it is uncertain whether he is living or dead; and
- (*e*)   Where there is no heir or personal representative to a trustee who was entitled to or possessed of land and has died intestate as to that

land, or where it is uncertain who is the heir or personal representative or devisee of a trustee who was entitled to or possessed of land
and is dead; and

(*f*)   Where a trustee jointly or solely entitled to or possessed of any land,
or entitled to a contingent right therein, has been required, by or on
behalf of a person entitled to require a conveyance of the land or a
release of the right, to convey the land or to release the right, and
has wilfully refused or neglected to convey the land or release the
right for twenty-eight days after the date of the requirement;

the High Court may make an order (in this Act called a vesting order) vesting
the land in any such person in any such manner and for any such estate as the
Court may direct, or releasing or disposing of the contingent right to such
person as the Court may direct.

Provided that:

(*a*)   Where the order is consequential on the appointment of a new trustee the land shall be vested for such estate as the Court may direct in
the persons who on the appointment are the trustees; and

(*b*)   Where the order relates to a trustee entitled jointly with another
person, and such trustee is out of the jurisdiction of the High Court
or cannot be found, the land or right shall be vested in such other
person, either alone or with some other person.

27 Orders as to contingent rights of unborn persons

Where any land is subject to a contingent right in an unborn person or class of
unborn persons who, on coming into existence would, in respect thereof,
become entitled to or possessed of the land on any trust, the High Court may
make an order releasing the land from the contingent right, or may make an
order vesting in any person the estate to or of which the unborn person or class
of unborn persons would, on coming into existence, be entitled or possessed in
the land.

28 Vesting order in place of conveyance by infant mortgagee

Where any person entitled to or possessed of land, or entitled to a contingent
right in land, by way of security for money, is an infant, the High Court may
make an order vesting or releasing or disposing of the land or right in like
manner as in the case of an infant trustee.

29 Vesting order in place of conveyance by heir or devisee of heir etc, or personal representative of mortgagee

Where a mortgagee of land has died without having entered into the possession
or into the receipt of the rents and profits thereof, and the money due in respect

of the mortgage has been paid to a person entitled to receive the same, or that last-mentioned person consents to any order for the reconveyance of the land, then the High Court may make an order vesting the land in such person or persons in such manner and for such estate as the Court may direct in any of the following cases, namely:

(*a*)   Where an heir or personal representative or devisee of the mortgagee is out of the jurisdiction of the High Court and cannot be found; and

(*b*)   Where an heir or personal representative or devisee of the mortgagee on demand made by or on behalf of a person entitled to require a conveyance of the land has stated in writing that he will not convey the same, or does not convey the same for the space of twenty-eight days next after a proper deed for conveying the land has been tendered to him by or on behalf of the person so entitled; and

(*c*)   Where it is uncertain which of the several devisees of the mortgagee was the survivor; and

(*d*)   Where it is uncertain as to the survivor of several devisees of the mortgagee or as to the heir or personal representative of the mortgagee whether he is living or dead; and

(*e*)   Where there is no heir or personal representative to a mortgagee who has died intestate as to the land, or where the mortgagee has died and it is uncertain who is his heir or personal representative or devisee.

30 Vesting order consequential on judgment for sale or mortgage of land

Where any Court gives a judgment or makes an order directing the sale or mortgage of any land, every person who is entitled to or possessed of the land, or entitled to a contingent right therein ...[1] and is a party to the action or proceeding in which the judgment or order is given or made, or is otherwise bound by the judgment or order, shall be deemed to be so entitled or possessed as the case may be, as a trustee within the meaning of this Act; and the High Court may, if it thinks expedient, make an order vesting the land or any part thereof for such estate as that Court thinks fit in the purchaser or mortgagee or in any other person.

Amendments

1   Words "as heir, or under the will of a deceased person, for payment of whose debts the judgment was given or order made" repealed by Trustee Act 1893, Amendment Act 1894 s 1.

---

31 Vesting order consequential on judgment for specific performance, etc

Where a judgment is given for the specific performance of a contract concerning any land, or for the partition, or sale in lieu of partition, or exchange, of any land, or generally where any judgment is given for the conveyance of any land either in cases arising out of the doctrine of election or otherwise, the High Court may declare that any of the parties to the action are trustees of the land or any part thereof within the meaning of this Act, or may declare that the interests of unborn persons who might claim under any party to the action, or under the will or voluntary settlement of any person deceased who was during his lifetime a party to the contract or transactions concerning which the judgment is given, are the interests of persons who, on coming into existence, would be trustees within the meaning of this Act, and thereupon the High Court may make a vesting order relating to the rights of those persons, born and unborn, as if they had been trustees.

32 Effect of vesting order

A vesting order under any of the foregoing provisions shall in the case of a vesting order consequential on the appointment of a new trustee have the same effect as if the persons who before the appointment were the trustees (if any) had duly executed all proper conveyances of the land for such estate as the High Court directs, or if there is no such person, or no such person of full capacity, then as if such person had existed and been of full capacity and had duly executed all proper conveyances of the land for such estate as the Court directs, and shall in every other case have the same effect as if the trustee or other person or description of class of persons to whose rights or supposed rights the said provisions respectively relate had been an ascertained and existing person of full capacity, and had executed a conveyance release to the effect intended by the order.

33 Power to appoint person to convey

In all cases where a vesting order can be made under any of the foregoing provisions, the High Court may, if it is more convenient, appoint a person to convey the land or release the contingent right, and a conveyance or release by that person in conformity with the order shall have the same effect as an order under the appropriate provision.

34 Effect of vesting order as to copyhold

(1) Where an order vesting copyhold land in any person is made under this Act with the consent of the lord or lady of the manor, the land shall vest accordingly without surrender or admittance.

(2) Where an order is made under this Act appointing any person to convey any copyhold land, that person shall execute and do all assurances and things for completing the assurance of the land; and the lord and lady of the manor and every other person shall, subject to the customs of the manor and the

usual payments, be bound to make admittance to the land, and to do all other acts for completing the assurance thereof, as if the persons in whose place an appointment is made were free from disability and had executed and done those assurances and things.

35 Vesting order as to stock and choses in action

(1) In any of the following cases, namely:

(*a*)   Where the High Court appoints or has appointed a new trustee; and

(*b*)   Where a trustee entitled alone or jointly with another person to stock or to a chose in action:

(i)   is an infant, or

(ii)   is out of the jurisdiction of the High Court, or

(iii)   cannot be found, or

(iv)   neglects or refuses to transfer stock or receive the dividends or income thereof, or to sue for or recover a chose in action, according to the direction of the person absolutely entitled thereto for twenty-eight days next after a request in writing has been made to him by the person so entitled, or

(v)   neglects or refuses to transfer stock or receive the dividends or income thereof, or to sue for or recover a chose in action for twenty-eight days next after an order of the High Court for that purpose has been served on him; or

(*c*)   Where it is uncertain whether a trustee entitled alone or jointly with another person to stock or to a chose in action is alive or dead,

the High Court may make an order vesting the right to transfer or call for a transfer of stock, or to receive the dividends or income thereof, or to sue for or recover a chose in action, in any such person as the Court may appoint:

Provided that:

(*a*)   Where the order is consequential on the appointment by the Court of a new trustee, the right shall be vested in the persons who, on the appointment, are the trustees; and

(*b*)   Where the person whose right is dealt with by the order was entitled jointly with another person, the right shall be vested in that last-mentioned person either alone or jointly with any other person whom the Court may appoint.

(2) In all cases where a vesting order can be made under this section, the Court may, if it is more convenient, appoint some proper person to make or join in making the transfer.

(3) The person in whom the right the transfer or call for the transfer of any stock is vested by an order of the Court under this Act, may transfer the

stock to himself or any other person, according to the order, and the Banks of England and Ireland and all other companies shall obey every order under this section according to its tenor.

(4) After notice in writing of an order under this section it shall not be lawful for the Bank of England or of Ireland or any other company to transfer any stock to which the order relates or to pay any dividends thereon except in accordance with the order.

(5) The High Court may make declarations and give directions concerning the manner in which the right to any stock or chose in action vested under the provisions of this Act is to be exercised.

(6) The provisions of this Act as to vesting orders shall apply to shares in ships registered under the Acts relating to merchant shipping as if they were stock.

36 Persons entitled to apply for orders

(1) An order under this Act for the appointment of a new trustee or concerning any land, stock or chose in action subject to a trust, may be made on the application of any person beneficially interested in the land, stock, or chose in action, whether under disability or not, or on the application of any person duly appointed trustee thereof.

(2) An order under this Act concerning any land, stock, or chose in action subject to a mortgage may be made on the application of any person beneficially interested in the equity of redemption, whether under disability or not, or of any person interested in the money secured by the mortgage.

37 Powers of new trustee appointed by court

Every trustee appointed by a court of competent jurisdiction shall, as well before as after the trust property becomes by law, or by assurance, or otherwise, vested in him, have the same powers, authorities, and discretions, and may in all respects act as if he had been originally appointed a trustee by the instrument (if any) creating the trust.

38 Power to charge costs on trust estate

The High Court may order the costs and expenses of and incident to any application for an order appointing a new trustee, or for a vesting order, or of and incident to any such order, or any conveyance or transfer in pursuance thereof, to be paid or raised out of the land or personal estate in respect whereof the same is made, or out of the income thereof, or to be borne and paid in such manner and by such persons as to the Court may seem just.

39 Trustees of charities

The powers conferred by this Act as to vesting orders may be exercised for vesting any land, stock, or chose in action in any trustee of a charity or society over which the High Court would have jurisdiction upon action duly instituted, whether the appointment of the trustee was made by instrument under a power or by the High Court under its general or statutory jurisdiction.

40 Orders made upon certain allegations to be conclusive evidence
53 and 54 Vict c 5

Where a vesting order is made as to any land under this Act or under the Lunacy Act, 1890, or under any Act relating to lunacy in Ireland, founded on an allegation of the personal incapacity of a trustee or mortgagee, or on an allegation that a trustee or the heir or personal representative or devisee of a mortgagee is out of the jurisdiction of the High Court, or cannot be found, or that it is uncertain which of several trustees or which of several devisees of a mortgagee was the survivor, or whether the last trustee or the heir or personal representative or last surviving devisee of a mortgagee is living or dead, or on an allegation that any trustee or mortgagee has died intestate without an heir, or has died and it is not known who is his heir or personal representative or devisee, the fact that the order has been so made shall be conclusive evidence of the matter so alleged in any Court upon any question as to the validity of the order; but this section shall not prevent the High Court from directing a reconveyance or the payment of costs occasioned by any such order if improperly obtained.

41 Application of vesting orders to land out of England

The powers of the High Court in England to make vesting orders under this Act shall extend to all land and personal estate in Her Majestys dominions, except Scotland.

Notes
These powers may also be exercised by the High Court in Ireland: Trustee Act 1893, Amendment Act 1894 s 2.

42 Payment into court by trustees

(1) Trustees, or the majority of trustees, having in their hands or under their control money or securities belonging to a trust, may pay the same into the High Court; and the same shall, subject to rules of Court, be dealt with according to the orders of the High Court.
(2) The receipt or certificate of the proper officer shall be a sufficient discharge to trustees for the money or securities so paid into Court.
(3) Where any moneys or securities are vested in any persons as trustees, and the majority are desirous of paying the same into Court, but the concurrence

of the other or others cannot be obtained, the High Court may order the payment into court to be made by the majority without the concurrence of the other or others; and where any such moneys or securities are deposited with any banker, broker, or other depositary, the Court may order payment or delivery of the moneys or securities to the majority of the trustees for the purpose of payment into court, and every transfer payment and delivery made in pursuance of any such order shall be valid and take effect as if the same had been made on the authority or by the act of all the persons entitled to the moneys and securities so transferred, paid, or delivered.

Notes

Section 42 applied: Dublin and Blessington Steam Tramway Act 1932 s 15.

Miscellaneous

43 Power to give judgment in absence of a trustee

Where in any action the High Court is satisfied that diligent search has been made for any person who, in the character of trustee, is made a defendant in any action, to serve him with a process of the Court, and that he cannot be found, the Court may hear and determine the action and give judgment therein against that person in his character of a trustee, as if he had been duly served, or had entered an appearance in the action, and had also appeared by his counsel and solicitor at the hearing, but without prejudice to any interest he may have in the matters in question in the action in any other character.

44 Power to sanction sale of land or minerals separately

(1) Where a trustee [or other person][1] is for the time being authorised to dispose of land by way of sale, exchange, partition, or enfranchisement, the High Court may sanction his so disposing of the land with an exception or reservation of any minerals, and with or without rights and powers of or incidental, to the working, getting, or carrying away of the minerals, or so disposing of the minerals, with or without the said rights or powers, separately from the residue of the land.

(2) Any such trustee [or other person][1] with the said sanction previously obtained, may, unless forbidden by the instrument creating the trust or direction, from time to time, without any further application to the Court, so dispose of any such land or minerals.

(3) Nothing in this section shall derogate from any power which a trustee may have under the Settled Land Acts 1882 to 1890, or otherwise.

Appendix I

Amendments
Inserted by Trustee Act 1893, Amendment Act 1894 s 3.

45 Power to make beneficiary indemnity for breach of trust

(1) Where a trustee commits a breach of trust at the instigation or request or with the consent in writing of a beneficiary, the High Court may, if it thinks fit, [and notwithstanding that the beneficiary may be a married woman entitled for her separate use and restrained from anticipation][1] make such order as to the Court seems just, for impounding all or any part of the interest of the beneficiary in the trust estate by way of indemnity to the trustee or person claiming through him.

(2) This section shall apply to breaches of trust committed as well before as after the passing of this Act, but shall not apply so as to prejudice any question in an action or other proceeding which was pending on the Twenty-fourth day of December, One thousand eight hundred and eighty-eight, and is pending at the commencement of this Act.

Amendments
1   Words "and notwithstanding ... anticipation" repealed by Married Women's Status Act 1957 s 19 and Sch.

46 Jurisdiction of palatine and county courts

The provisions of this Act with respect to the High Court shall, in their application to cases within the jurisdiction of a palatine court or county court, include that court, and the procedure under this Act in palatine courts and county courts shall be in accordance with the Acts and rules regulating the procedure of those courts.

Part 4

Miscellaneous and supplemental

47 Application to trustees under Settled Land Acts of provisions as to appointment of trustees 44 and 45 Vict c 41

(1) All the powers and provisions contained in this Act with reference to the appointment of new trustees, and the discharge and retirement of trustees, are to apply to and include trustees for the purposes of the Settled Land Acts 1882 to 1890, whether appointed by the Court or by the settlement, or under provisions contained in the settlement.

(2) This section applies and is to have effect with respect to an appointment or a discharge and retirement of trustees taking place before as well as after the commencement of this Act.

(3) This section is not to render invalid or prejudice any appointment or any discharge and retirement of trustees effected before the passing of this Act, otherwise than under the provisions of The Conveyancing and Law of Property Act 1881.

48 Trust estates not affected by trustee becoming a convict 33 and 34 Vict c 23

Property vested in any person on any trust or by way of mortgage shall not, in the case of that person becoming a convict within the meaning of the Forfeiture Act 1870, vest in any such administrator as may be appointed under that Act, but shall remain in the trustee or mortgagee, or survive to his co-trustee or descend to his representative as if he had not become a convict; provided that this enactment shall not affect the title to the property so far as relates to any beneficial interest therein of any such trustee or mortgagee.

49 Indemnity

This Act, and every order purporting to be made under this Act, shall be a complete indemnity to the Banks of England and Ireland, and to all persons for any acts done pursuant thereto; and it shall not be necessary for the bank or for any person to inquire concerning the propriety of the order, or whether the Court by which it was made had jurisdiction to make the same.

50 Definitions

In this Act, unless the context otherwise requires:

The expression bankrupt includes, in Ireland, insolvent:

The expression contingent right, as applied to land, includes a contingent or executory interest, a possibility coupled with an interest, whether the object of the gift or limitation of the interest, or possibility is or is not ascertained, also a right of entry, whether immediate or future, and whether vested or contingent:

The expressions convey and conveyance applied to any person include the execution by that person of every necessary or suitable assurance for conveying, assigning, appointing, surrendering, or otherwise transferring or disposing of land whereof he is seised or possessed, or wherein he is entitled to a contingent right, either for his whole estate or for any less estate, together with the performance of all formalities required by law to the validity of the conveyance, including the acts to be performed by married women and tenants in tail in accordance with the provisions of the Acts for abolition of fines and recoveries in England and Ireland respectively, and also including surrenders and other acts which a tenant of customary or copyhold lands can himself perform preparatory to or in aid of a complete assurance of the customary or copyhold land:

The expression devisee includes the heir of a devisee and the devisee of an heir, and any person who may claim right by devolution of title of a similar description:

The expression instrument: includes Act of Parliament:

The expression land includes manors and lordships, and reputed manors and lordships, and incorporeal as well as corporeal hereditaments, and any interest therein, and also an undivided share of land:

The expressions mortgage and mortgagee include and relate to every estate and interest regarded in equity as merely a security for money, and every person deriving title under the original mortgagee:

The expressions pay and payment, as applied in relation to stocks and securities, and in connexion with the expression into Court include the deposit or transfer of the same in or into Court:

The expression possessed applies to receipt of income of, and to any vested estate less than a life estate, legal or equitable, in possession or in expectancy, in any land:

The expression property includes real and personal property, and any estate and interest in any property, real or personal, and any debt, and any thing in action, and other right or interest, whether in possession or not:

The expression rights includes estates and interests:

The expression securities includes stocks, funds, and shares; and so far as relates to payments into Court has the same meaning as in the Court of Chancery (Funds) Act, 1872:

The expression stock includes fully paid up shares; and, so far as relates to vesting orders made by the Court under this Act, includes any fund, annuity, or security transferable in books kept by any company or society, or by instrument of transfer either alone or accompanied by other formalities, and any share or interest therein:

The expression transfer, in relation to stock, includes the performance and execution of every deed, power of attorney, act, and thing on the part of the transferor to effect and complete the title in the transferee:

The expression trust does not include the duties incident to an estate conveyed by way of mortgage; but with this exception, the expressions trust and trustee include implied and constructive trusts, and cases where the trustee has a beneficial interest in the trust property, and the duties incident to the office of personal representative of a deceased person.

51 Repeal

The Acts mentioned in the Schedule to this Act are hereby repealed, except as to Scotland, to the extent mentioned in the third column of that Schedule.

References
Wording of Schedule not included in present print.

52 Extent of Act

This Act does not extend to Scotland.

53 Short title

This Act may be cited as the Trustee Act 1893.

54 Commencement

This Act shall come into operation on the First day of January, One thousand eight hundred and ninety four.

Appendix II

Charities Act 1961

49 Construction of gifts for mixed purposes

(1) Where any of the purposes of a gift includes or could be deemed to include both charitable and non-charitable objects, its terms shall be so construed and given effect to as to exclude non-charitable objects and the purpose shall, accordingly, be treated as charitable.

(2) Subsection (1) shall not apply where:

    (*a*)   the gift takes effect before the 1st day of January 1960, or

    (*b*) (i)   the terms of the gift make, or provide for the making of, an apportionment between the charitable and the non-charitable objects, and

        (ii)   the non-charitable objects are identifiable from an express or implied description.

3 This section shall not, by its operation on any gift as respects the period from the 1st day of January 1960, to the 24th day of September 1960, entitle any person to reclaim any tax or duty paid or borne during that period, nor (save as respects tax or duty) require the objects declared by the gift to be treated as having been charitable so as to invalidate anything done or any determination given during that period.

Appendix III

1990 Report of the Committee on Fundraising Activities for Charitable and Other Purposes

Reliefs from tax on income and property of charities (prepared by the Office of the Revenue Commissioners)

Introduction

1.1 The tax code provides for certain exemptions from tax on income and property of charities. For tax purposes a charity is a body of person or trust established for charitable purposes only. This means that for an institution or trust to be regarded as charitable for tax purposes, its objects and powers must be so framed that every object to which its income or property can be applied is charitable and it must be bound as to its objects and the application of its income and property by a binding trust.

1.2 The Revenue Commissioners are responsible for the administration of the various exemptions and for this purpose determine whether a body of persons or trust claiming the benefit of any exemption is established for charitable purposes only. Exemptions are available with respect to income tax, capital gains tax, corporation tax (in the case of companies), capital acquisitions tax and stamp duty on a transfer of land. There is no exemption in respect of value added tax and employees of a charity are liable to income tax under the PAYE system.

Meaning of charitable purposes

2.1 Charitable purposes are not defined in the Tax Acts, but have been broadly defined by the Courts* as follows:

- (*a*)   the relief of poverty,
- (*b*)   the advancement of education,
- (*c*)   the advancement of religion, and
- (*d*)   other purposes (of a charitable nature) beneficial to the community, not falling within any other heading.

* *Income Tax Special Purposes Commissioners v Pemsel* 3TC 53, page 96.

2.2 The fourth category covers the widest group of charities. It covers:

Illness and disability

(*a*) The relief and prevention of sickness and disability, both physical and mental by, for example, the provision and staffing of hospitals, nursing and convalescent homes and clinics; the promotion of medical research; the provision of medical advice, treatment or comfort; the establishment of homes, workshops or other centres for the disabled or the mentally or physically handicapped; or the provision of housing for the sick or disabled.

(*b*) The relief of suffering, distress or disability caused by old age including the provision of homes or community centres for the care and maintenance of the old.

(*c*) The provision of care and welfare services for those in need, for example, the aged, the sick and the disabled.

Welfare services

(*a*) The welfare and development of children.

(*b*) The welfare of disadvantaged sections of the community, for example, one parent families, battered spouses, travellers, emigrants or immigrants.

(*c*) The provision of rehabilitation and resettlement services for victims of crime, drug abuse, alcoholism.

(*d*) The prevention of cruelty to children and animals.

(*e*) The relief of distress caused by natural disasters and sudden catastrophes.

(*f*) The provision of housing to the needy.

Advancement of knowledge

(*a*) The promotion of research into any serious field of study whereby the common stock of knowledge may be increased and made available to the public.

(*b*) The advancement of science and the maintenance of institutions therefor, including support and maintenance of learned societies.

(*c*) The promotion of the arts, music, literature, painting, sculpture, dance, film and fine craftsmanship.

(*d*) The promotion of Irish culture and language.

(*e*) The provision and maintenance of museums, art galleries and concert halls.

Public utility

(*a*)   The provision of public works for the benefit of the community and protection of the lives and property of the community.

(*b*)   The maintenance of graveyards.

(*c*)   The advancement and improvement of the standards of efficiency of industry, commerce and agriculture.

(*d*)   The protection of the environment and the national heritage.

Sport and recreation

In the United Kingdom the promotion of sport and recreation within the meaning of the Recreational Charities Act 1958 is charitable whereas in Ireland it is not unless sport and recreation are necessary to the well being of the sick, disabled or mentally or physically handicapped or are to be used as an aid to recovery.

There is, however, a separate exemption from tax given under Section 349 of the Income Tax Act 1967 to bodies established for the promotion of amateur or athletic games or sports. This gives exemption to sports clubs in respect of income tax on income received or profits made from club activities.

Exemptions and relevant statutory provisions

4.1 Section 333 of the Income Tax Act 1967 provides that exemption from income tax shall be granted in respect of rents and profits from property belonging to any hospital, public school or almshouse, or vested in trustees for charitable purposes, so far as they are applied to charitable purposes only. It goes on to exempt any interest, annuities, dividends and shares of annuities; also any yearly or annual payment forming part of the income of any body of persons or trust established for charitable purposes only and which is applicable to charitable purposes only according to the rules or regulations established by statute, charter, decree, deed or trust or will.

4.2 Section 334 of the same Act provides exemption from income tax for the profits of a trade carried on by a charity provided that trade is exercised in the carrying out of a primary purpose of the charity and or the work in connection with the trade is mainly carried on by beneficiaries of the charity.

4.3 Section 22 of the Capital Gains Tax Act 1975 provides exemption from capital gains tax in respect of gains accruing to a charity.

4.4 The above categories of income and gains when received by a company which has charitable status are exempt from corporation tax by virtue of Sections 11(6) and 13(2) of the Corporation Tax Act 1976.

4.5 Section 54 of the Capital Acquisitions Act 1976 provides exemption from capital acquisitions tax on a gift or an inheritance received by a charity and Section 50 of the Finance Act 1979 exempts from stamp duty any conveyance or transfer of land to a charity.

Limits to exemption

5.1 The income, profits, gains, gift or inheritance must actually be applied for the specified charitable purposes to qualify for exemption. If it is not so applied it remains taxable notwithstanding the charitable status of the recipient.

5.2 The income of a charity must be applied within the year of its receipt. However, carry over of income from one tax year to another is allowed in practice provided the income is then expended. If income is accumulated and forms into capital this is taxable unless the charity has a particular reason for the accumulation and this is notified to the Revenue Commissioners. The purchase of a property is a common reason.

Failure to get exemption

6.1 There are various reasons why exemption may be refused. Chief among these is that the objects of the charity are not exclusively for charitable purposes. That is, they contain amongst them objects which are not charitable.

6.2 Other reasons for refusal can be that the charity distributes benefits or profits among its members, or if it trades in a way unrelated to its objects. The charity must be law abiding and must not be political in its activity.

6.3 Exemption is refused where the documentation does not demonstrate that the charity is the subject of a binding trust. Where inadequate documentation is received it is the practice of the Revenue Commissioners to indicate the type of documentation that would be considered acceptable.

Types of application and statistics

7.1 Bodies who apply for exemption must be the subject of a binding trust for charitable purposes only and this is usually achieved in the following ways:

- (*a*)   by articles and memorandum of association,
- (*b*)   by constitution,
- (*c*)   by deed or trust,
- (*d*)   by will trust,
- (*e*)   by rules,
- (*f*)   by statute.

7.2 The applications breakdown in percentage terms:

- (*a*)   22%
- (*b*)   14%
- (*c*)   8%

(*d*) 2%

(*e*) 4%

(*f*) 15%

The remaining 35% apply in letter form unsupported by documentation. While some of these are accepted following correspondence a very high proportion of these are rejected. It is estimated that currently exemption has been granted to:

1,496 bodies whose annual income is under £10,000

679 bodies whose annual income is between £10,000 and £20,000

784 bodies whose annual income is between £20,000 and £50,000

834 bodies whose annual income is over £50,000.

Appendix IV

1967 Report by an Interdepartmental Committee on Local Finance and Taxation

Extract from report

Rating exemptions under the Poor Relief and the Valuation Acts

7. Section 63 of the Poor Relief (Ireland) Act 1838 exempts from rating, any church, chapel or other building exclusively dedicated to religious worship or exclusively used for the education of the poor, any burial ground or cemetery, any infirmary, hospital, charity school or other building used exclusively for charitable purposes, and any building, land or hereditament dedicated to or used for public purposes. These exemptions are, generally, subject to the proviso that no private profit or use is directly derived from the property concerned.

8. Under section 2 of the Valuation (Ireland) Act 1854 the Commissioner of Valuation must distinguish in the valuation lists premises of a public nature or used for charitable purposes or for the purposes of science, literature and the fine arts. Hereditaments so distinguished are to be exempt from rating as long as they continue to be used for the purposes mentioned.

9. These statutory exemptions and the great body of judicial decisions relating to them have brought about many rating anomalies. The position in this regard can be illustrated by some examples of current rating concessions in Dublin City many of which are based directly or consequentially on the 1838 and 1854 Acts. The Dogs and Cats Home at Grand Canal Quay is exempt from rates. The premises of the Royal National Lifeboat Institution are rated. The Institute for Industrial Research and Standards is exempt but the Institute for Advanced Studies is rated. The Civics Institute is rated but Conradh na Gaeilge premises are not. An Comhairle Leabharlanna is exempt from rating but the Hospitals Library Council pays rates. The Royal Society of Antiquaries of Ireland is exempt and the Chester Beatty Library is rated. In the case of higher education, the Apothecaries Hall is rated on full valuation. Kings Inn on 60% valuation, the College of Surgeons on 56% valuation, Trinity College on 34% valuation and University College, Dublin on 14% valuation. Other exempted properties in Dublin City include public and voluntary hospitals, homes for the aged and afflicted, land and premises occupied by such bodies as the Royal Irish Academy, Royal Dublin Society, Royal Hibernian Academy, Royal Irish

Academy of Music, Royal Zoological Society, National Council for the Blind, National Society for the Prevention of Cruelty to Children, Infantile Paralysis Fellowship of Ireland, etc. On the other hand, rates are levied, for example, on premises occupied by Bord Fáilte Éireann, Coras Trachtála, Bord na gCon, the Racing Board, Pharmaceutical Society of Ireland, Medical Research Council of Ireland, Agricultural Credit Corporation, Bord Iascaigh Mhara, Irish Agricultural Organisation Society, Radio Telefís Éireann, Mater Training School for Nurses, Hospitals Commission, Society for Prevention of Cruelty to Animals, St. Lukes Cancer Hospital.

Table of cases

Table of statutes

Index

358

Principal private residence
Capital gains tax relief, 15.12, 16.02

Private trusts

Prize bond winnings
Capital gains tax, non-chargeable gain, 16.02

Professional agents
General, 4.07

Professional trust companies
General, 4.04, 4.06

Profit sharing schemes
Allocation of shares, 11.31
Approval by Revenue, 11.28
Deduction for employee, 11.29
Deduction to company supplying funds, 11.30
Formation and management, 9.43
Income on shares held by trustees, 11.31, 11.33
Income tax provisions, 9.43, 9.61
Repeal, 11.28
Shares, 11.31

Property
Capital acquisitions tax,
    Defined, 17.02
    Free use of, 17.14
    Unpaid, a charge, 17.19
Returns, income tax provisions, 9.45
Right of trustee to sell, 4.04
Vesting of, duty of trustee, 4.04

Public benefit (gifts for)
Amateur societies, 7.37
Animals, 7.33
Charitable object, 6.10
Charity, meaning, 6.04
Local areas, gifts for, 7.30
Non-charitable gifts, 7.32
Political gifts, 7.35
Sport, 7.36, 12.09
State, Gifts to, 12.10
Vegetarian society, 7.34

Public purpose
Local taxation,
    Baths and washhouses, 19.14
    County council premises, 19.15
    Meaning of, 19.12
    Public utilities, 19.13
    Semi State bodies, 19.16

Purpose trusts
Chapter 7.

Q
Qualifying activities, business expansion scheme, 11.52

R
Rates
See LOCAL TAXATION

Rates of tax
Capital gains tax, 15.03, 16.26

Real property
Capital acquisitions tax, defined, 17.02

Receipts
Trustee's power to issue, 4.04

Relief for investment in corporate trades
See BUSINESS EXPANSION SCHEME

Religion, Advancement of
Clergymen and preachers, gifts to, 7.24
English legal precedents, 7.18
Limitations on religious gifts, 7.28
Maintenance of churches, 7.25
Maintenance of churchyards, 7.26
Male religious communities, 7.17
Masses, gifts for, 7.27
Non-Christian religions, 7.19
Pious purposes, meaning, 7.21
Promotion of religion , 7.20
Religious purposes, meaning, 7.21

Religious bodies
Whether charitable, 6.11

Religious community
Carrying on a trade, 12.17

Religious purposes
Advancement of religion, 7.16-7.28
Charitable object, 6.11
Income arising before vesting, 5.18
Local taxation,
    Catholic Seminary, 19.31
    Convent, 19.32
    Franciscan Friary, 19.30
    Northern Ireland law, 19.33
    Parish priest residence, 19.28
    Residence used as classroom, 19.29
Meaning, 7.21
Rights against life tenant, 5.17, 5.20-5.21

Remuneration
Trustee not entitled to, 4.03

Residence of a trust
Capital gains tax provisions, 16.12
Income tax provisions, 10.06
Ireland-UK Double Taxation Agreement, 10.07
Residence of trustees , 10.08

Resident persons
Capital gains tax, defined, 16.04
Non resident persons, 16.05

Resulting trust
Application, 3.08-3.12
Meaning, 3.01